The Gamification of Higher Education

The Gamification of Higher Education

Developing a Game-Based Business Strategy in a Disrupted Marketplace

Neil B. Niman

palgrave
macmillan

First published in 2014 by
PALGRAVE MACMILLAN®
in the United States—a division of St. Martin's Press LLC,
175 Fifth Avenue, New York, NY 10010.

Where this book is distributed in the UK, Europe and the rest of the world, this is by Palgrave Macmillan, a division of Macmillan Publishers Limited, registered in England, company number 785998, of Houndmills, Basingstoke, Hampshire RG21 6XS.

Palgrave Macmillan is the global academic imprint of the above companies and has companies and representatives throughout the world.

Palgrave® and Macmillan® are registered trademarks in the United States, the United Kingdom, Europe and other countries.

ISBN: 978–1–137–33873–0

Library of Congress Cataloging-in-Publication Data

Niman, Neil B., 1956–

    The gamification of higher education : developing a game-based business strategy in a disrupted marketplace / Neil B. Niman.
      pages cm
    Includes bibliographical references and index.
    ISBN 978–1–137–33873–0 (hardback : alk. paper)
      1. Education, Higher—Economic aspects. 2. Universities and colleges—Business management. 3. Educational planning. 4. Strategic planning. 5. Games—Psychological aspects. 6. ame theory. 7. Distance education—Economic aspects. 8. Educational innovations. I. Title.

LC67.6.N56 2014
338.43378—dc23   2014001404

A catalogue record of the book is available from the British Library.

Design by Newgen Knowledge Works (P) Ltd., Chennai, India.

First edition: July 2014

10 9 8 7 6 5 4 3 2 1

Contents

Preface

It would be natural to think that years of playing games would have given birth to a book about Gamification. However, that would be far from the truth. At the risk of destroying my credibility before you even begin reading the first chapter, the reality is that I don't play games. Sure, I might have tried to be a good father and played some games when my two sons were younger, but the video game era passed me by and anything involving a controller is for me, just an exercise in futility. Thus it might seem strange that someone who doesn't play games has chosen to write a book about how game design can transform higher education.

My interest in games emerged as part of a series of conversations that I had with my son Joshua as part of my recovery from surgery. My doctor assured me that things would heal a lot faster if I walked every day and Joshua became my companion. At the time, Josh was an aspiring video game designer and hence we spent a great deal of time talking about the structure of games and the unique characteristics of virtual worlds. It is interesting how concerns about death leads one to look at life from a new perspective.

All of this led me to relive my interest in social theory that was first kindled as an undergraduate at the University of California, Santa Cruz, where I majored in Modern Society and Social Thought. Given my more current interest in Behavioral Economics, it seemed an interesting way to bring together the past and the present and I began to think about the inner workings of synthetic societies.

Gamification as a business strategy emerged from a different series of conversations that I had over lunch with President Mark Huddleston at our favorite Chinese restaurant (or should I say the only Chinese restaurant in the Town of Durham). Mark has been concerned about the future of bricks and mortar universities as costs have skyrocketed while real incomes have remained stagnant. As we tried to solve the problems of higher education over lunch, it slowly dawned on me that Gamification could form the basis for shifting the value proposition offered by colleges and universities in a way that would embrace changing technologies and reflect the new economic realities that are forcing changes to current financial models.

Any meaningful changes in higher education will have a large impact on the student experience. Fortunately, Sami Virga let me probe her psyche and shared with me a large number of insights into the behavior of today's college student. Economists like to employ representative agents and for the purposes of this book, Sami was my representative student.

Thus it should come as no surprise that the book consists of three parts; each reflecting a different conversation that together have become *The Gamification of Higher Education*. Fortunately, writing the book has just been the starting point of my own journey to rethink how we teach economics and view the broader student experience. This led to the creation of the EconJourney project that you can learn more about at: http://econjourney.com. EconJourney began with a paper I presented at the American Economic Association's Third Annual Conference in Teaching Economics, became operational after my wife, Debbie Hodge, shared with me her Story Coach idea developed for her online scrapbooking business, and has now grown into a much larger enterprise located at: http://higheredgames.com.

A number of current and past students have helped with the project and I would be remiss if I didn't take this opportunity to thank them for their assistance. They include: Elizabeth Assaf, Kyle Berge, David Ellis, Abby Hahr, Nick Mignanelli, Gregory Traquair, Jennifer Trudeau, Sami Virga, Kate Ward, Mason White, and Tyler Will. My wife Debbie Hodge assisted with the line art, my son Joshua Niman with a number of game references, Sandy Peart helped get the project started, and of course, Mark Huddleston for prompting me to think more about higher education as an industry.

Introduction

Many young people today think nothing about spending hours upon hours killing trolls in a role-playing game, freeing Angry Birds on their smartphone, or making social connections via Words with Friends. However, when it comes to studying for their classes (where the costs and future rewards are very real), it is the last thing many find themselves doing. We are failing our students. Some think it is because the material we teach is not very relevant for today's economy. Others think it is because something fundamental has shifted and as a result, learning styles are no longer in step with the way higher education is delivered. I think it is because we have not engaged students in a way that has made their educational experience a personal one with demonstrable benefits and a clear rationale for how it is going to make them more successful.

The goal of *The Gamification of Higher Education* is not to trivialize the learning process by making it more gamelike in the sense of a marketer who introduces game mechanics in order to sell a product. Rather, it asks the question: is there anything we can learn from game design that would enable us to make higher education more engaging, relevant, and exciting so that the average student would want to spend their time studying or take part in activities that help them grow and develop as a real rather than virtual being?

Instead of thinking about education in terms of mastering a body of knowledge, we should conceive of it as a process that draws out the best in individuals and prepares them for happy, productive, and successful lives. If we can design an educational experience where learning is a part of personal growth and development, it becomes possible to create empowered individuals who would be better positioned to make a contribution upon their entry into the "real world."

One potential model for change can be found in massively multi-player online games. These games seemingly are able to accomplish something that universities are finding more and more elusive; how to engage a population of distracted students who seem less and less interested in learning. Learning is something that comes naturally to many gamers who must develop entirely new skill sets if they are to advance to a higher level, slay the dragon, or save the world from some natural catastrophe.

Both the development of games and the delivery of higher education are at their very core enterprises that try to provide a transformative experience for the participant. Yet it seems as if successful game companies are able to more effectively accomplish this goal than colleges and universities. This raises the question: *Can insights from the game industry form the foundation of an effective business strategy for use by traditional bricks and mortar universities in order to overcome the challenges created by an increasingly competitive market and growing financial constraints?* Such a strategy would be designed to not only maintain the relevancy of a university education but also provide a means for traditional bricks and mortar institutions to effectively compete in a changing environment where market entry and new technologies have significantly altered the landscape.

To see the need for change, we need to look no farther than the recent rise of the MOOC (Massively Open Online Course). While it is an opportunity that is still looking for a profitable business model, it poses perhaps the most serious threat to any research-based university.

Many universities rely on large introductory courses as one of its most important revenue streams. Able to spread the cost of a professor or lecturer over a large number of students, enormous introductory courses are the cash cows for any department. Large lecture courses not only fund general operations, but they also mitigate the relatively high cost of providing lower enrollment specialized ones at the upper division level.

By offering a low cost alternative featuring a superstar faculty members from a prestigious institutions, MOOCs threaten to topple this precarious financial structure. That being said, the threat to the university is not necessarily the MOOC but rather anything that will take away the cash cow and leave the high cost/low revenue courses without an adequate funding stream. MOOCs are just a symptom of a much larger problem. From this perspective, community colleges are just as big a threat as students looking to reduce the cost of education search for affordable substitutes in order to complete their general education courses.

What has held back this trend in the past has been a series of artificial barriers designed to lock-in students and keep rivals at bay by restricting the transfer of credits from one institution to another. However, it is just a matter of time before we see a new type of institution emerge that merely cobbles together a collection of MOOC courses and confers a degree. If enough quality courses are offered from some of the best institutions then it will be difficult to challenge the excellence of instruction that is provided.

With few costs, these new institutions will be able to significantly undercut the price of higher education while still retaining a large portion of the revenues needed to engage in a vast and expensive marketing campaign. With the right marketing, such an institution will be able to both attract students and find jobs for its graduates.

The appropriate response to this coming competitive threat is not by engaging low cost providers on their own field of battle. Fortunately (depending on your perspective), a successful learning experience requires more than just sitting passively in front of a computer and viewing a series of video lectures. There needs to be an entire supporting structure that transforms what could be a passive experience into an active one.

Because of this, institutions with a substantial legacy investment in physical infrastructure may still have a higher cost structure, but at the same time, possesses a unique opportunity to leverage its physical plant to create added value. However, to unlock additional value, what is needed is a different approach that seeks to integrate what happens inside *and* outside the classroom into a coherent whole. The creation of a value proposition capable of generating something in excess of what can be created by cobbling together a series of courses from random institutions.

The solution resides in the power of games. There are very good reasons why both the young and old spend hour after hour playing games each week. What has become a popular form of recreation, can become the basis for a strategy that seeks to fend off competitive challenges by adding value where it matters most: improving learning outcomes.

To make the case for Gamification as an effective business strategy, the nine chapters have been divided into three parts.

Part I: The Business of Higher Education uses the disruptive changes occurring in other industries to illustrate how a similar set of dynamics will force higher education to adapt in order to survive. It discusses how insights from the game industry can help form the foundation for an effective business strategy by traditional residential institutions to overcome the threat posed by for-profit institutions and massively open online courses.

Part II: Gaming Fundamentals discusses why individuals find games so compelling and explores the design elements and mechanics that are used that make them so effective. By understanding the structure of games, we can begin to articulate the steps colleges and universities need to take in order to create a cohesive student experience that is focused on creating empowered learners.

Part III: Transformation through Gamification focuses on how game design can be used to create learning communities that take advantage of the bricks and mortar found in traditional institutions. The future survival of colleges and universities is not found in the transformation of students into customers who must be enticed to purchase their product in an increasingly competitive market. Rather, it is to conceive of students as individuals who, with a little guidance, will become better learners and as a result, become a more productive, vibrant, and happy members of society.

All of this leads to the conclusion that if traditional bricks and mortar universities do not produce a cohesive learning experience that focuses on creating lifelong learners, then the growing trend toward e-learning and the increasing growth of for-profit universities will make it difficult for existing institutions with substantial physical infrastructures to compete. It is about implementing a strategy that is capable of generating greater value from past investments that now, no longer appear to be relevant.

By redefining the student experience, new life can be breathed into past investments enabling them to assume a fresh and important role in the educational process. In order for that to occur, we need to shift away from the model where all of the learning takes place on a single campus organized around mastering a body of knowledge. Instead, we need to think of students as empowered members of a learning community that knows no boundaries. One that will better position them to acquire the skills they need over an entire lifetime in order to remain relevant in an ever changing world.

PART I

The Business of Higher Education

CHAPTER 1

The Coming "Perfect Storm" in Higher Education

Depending on one's penchant for risk, change is either a breath of fresh air or a horrible nightmare. The hard part to managing change is when it comes time to evaluate whether it represents a short-term fad that may shake things up for a brief period and then go away, or if it represents something more fundamental that represents a true game changer. Many firms are no longer with us because they either thought a permanent change was only a temporary flirtation with a bad idea, or could not respond to a major shift in the marketplace. Realizing that the future is not going to follow the patterns of the past is only the first step that must be taken in response to change. Adapting your organization to meet the challenges of a new reality is something entirely different.

Many like to think (especially those in academia) that their institution of higher learning is immune to the vagaries of the world in which we live. They are in essence an "oasis" that breathes life into the surrounding desert. However, universities are no more immune to the laws of economics, the whims of politicians, or changing demographics than any other large organizations that are a part of modern society. It is perhaps easy to sit back and gaze upon those ivy halls that have been an essential part of university life for in some cases, hundreds of years, and think that those changes taking place today are no different from previous ones. To believe that those sturdy walls have seen it all and will be around long after the current changes have come and gone.

However, as technology continues to redefine the meaning of space and time from an educational perspective, it is not clear that institutions of higher education will be able to ignore the fundamental changes that are taking place. After all, the path to the future has been paved with the wreckage from many industries that were thought to be immune to the changes that were taking place around them. More importantly, those forces that are trying to change higher education can be found in a number of different industries who have encountered many of the same challenges. Hence it is rather naive to think that higher education is insulated from the problems facing other industries. In fact, there is much to be learned from the recent experiences that have transformed much of the economy as we know it.

The Higher Education Bubble

What does going to college and owning your own home have in common? For many, they are necessary stepping stones for reaching the American Dream.[1] While it may make more sense in today's economy to rent rather than own, there is something special about becoming a person of property. The freedom to do what you want, when you want, and where you want often trumps whatever savings you might achieve as the result of renting.

In the same way, going to college opens doors that would otherwise remain closed.[2] At the most basic level, we see that the unemployment rate for college graduates is substantially lower than for those with just a high school education.[3] But it is more than whether you have a job or not, it is the quality of work and the ability to have a career as opposed to just a job that makes the decision to go to college much more than a simple economic choice that balances the costs against tangible economic benefits.[4]

With so much to be gained, it should come as no surprise that our elective representatives who populate the halls of government (either at the federal or state level) would want to do their best to make the dream come true. If the government can open the door to home ownership or a lifelong career, what is wrong with that? Well, as we are about to see, it can have adverse consequences that, in the long run, does more harm than good.

Let's begin by exploring the recent housing crisis that played a major role in throwing the world into a global recession. It is not a new policy on the part of the federal government to try and make home ownership economically viable for as many as possible. One can just look at the mortgage home deduction available to those who file US tax returns. It is perhaps the most visible sign of support for home ownership. What is less obvious are the set of forces that tried to make home ownership possible for those segments of the population who previously were denied the ability to borrow the funds needed to purchase a home.

The seeds of the crisis lay in a fundamental transformation that occurred in the market for mortgages. What had previously been a local affair became in the course of 20 some odd years a national and then an international market. With the rise to prominence of two quasi-government firms (Fannie Mae and Freddie Mac), a national market emerged where bundles of mortgages could be traded just like any other financial instrument.[5] The creation of a national market enabled capital to flow where it could enjoy the highest rate of return and with improvements in the flow of capital, home ownership became possible for an ever expanding pool of buyers,

Of course, having worked at the national level, there was no reason to believe that it couldn't be successful on an international scale. By bundling these mortgages together into what has become known as collateralized debt obligations, securities could be created that might be attractive to international investors. Using a process known as securitization, it became possible to open a door to an even bigger pool of funds that could finance home mortgages and hence made the dream come alive for even more Americans.[6]

Under increased government pressure to make loans to previously underserved segments of the population in combination with a pool of new potential purchasers of these securities, mortgage originators began to experiment with new products that could eliminate some of the traditional barriers that prevented some individuals from obtaining a mortgage.[7] The creation of no income verification loans, interest only loans, mortgages that artificially lowered interest rates for the first few years of the loan, or loans that could be obtained with no money down are all examples of products that were designed to make home ownership affordable to entirely new segments of the population.

All of this was done with the best of intentions in order to enable as many as possible to obtain the American Dream. And it worked beautifully as long as interest rates remained low and housing prices continued to rise. The easy availability of cheap money drove up housing prices to the benefit of everyone. Whether you worked in the construction industry, the financial industry, or were a homeowner who could sit back and watch their investment appreciate on a monthly basis, the benefits spread throughout the entire economy. All was well and good until the supply of cheap money dried up seemingly overnight and the industry collapsed. The aftermath was a dramatic fall in housing prices, the collapse of many financial institutions, and the decimation of an entire industry (construction).[8]

By this time you are probably wondering what this has to do with higher education. After all, housing is not education and since they are unrelated, why should what happened in one industry be relevant for the other? While the two may be unrelated in many respects, they are similar in the sense that they have both been targeted by the federal government for support in an effort to make their product accessible to as many as possible.[9] As a result, the question that comes (at least to my mind) is that if government policies based on the best of intentions created a bubble in the housing market, could similar policies be generating a nearly identical bubble in the market for higher education?

Before going any further, it is important to note that the decisions that ultimately create bubbles leading to one crisis or another defy the rational choices that well-trained economists believe that individuals make.[10] For example, there was no reason to think that mortgage loans were being made to less than credit worthy borrowers. Furthermore, there would be no reason to assume that all of the smart individuals that were making lending decisions and purchased mortgage-backed securities did not know that at some point, the Fed would raise interest rates and borrowers would need to have the financial wherewithal to be able to continue to make their monthly payment at a higher interest rate.

Based on the best information that was publicly available, the smart decision was to purchase real estate. Of course, after the fact we realized that many of the loans were not very good and could not absorb higher interest rates.[11] Therefore as the Fed raised rates, many could no longer afford their adjustable rate loans and what had been an imbalance created by too much demand and too little supply, reversed itself seemingly overnight. Hence it did not matter how well you considered your options with the information that was available, for many purchasers of mortgage-backed securities and investment properties, the decision that they ultimately made was the wrong one.

Thus, despite the best research by noted economists who write that students are not overburdened by debt, that the wage premium associated with a college degree is as strong as ever, and that college will enable you to start a career rather than just a job is still true, all of that may go out the window.[12] If there is the perception that a college education prepares you for nothing more than living at home with mom and dad as you can't find anything more financially rewarding than driving a taxicab while the bills pile up because you are mired in student loan debt, then why go to college?

The Anatomy of a Crisis

In drawing parallels between the financial crisis of 2008 and a potential one in higher education, we need to start with the two primary drivers that have changed the competitive landscape. The first can be found in the general support at both the state and the federal level for higher education.[13] There has been strong recognition on the part of elected leaders that education can not only be a powerful driver for economic growth, but can also improve the quality of the society in which we all live.[14] The impact has been to increase access to higher education by lessening the impact of rising tuition. However, just like any other industry chased by too many dollars, net revenues (profits) rise and with that, an incentive for others to enter the industry so that they can obtain their share of a growing market.[15]

The other driver stems from the new technologies that offer the potential to redefine the way that courses are delivered. Whether under the heading of distance learning, e-learning, massively open online courses (MOOCs), or something else, technology is lowering some of the barriers that have kept institutions of higher learning well protected from much if any competition.[16] While students still exhibit a strong preference to attend schools that are located in relatively close proximity to where they grew up, there is little certainty (if any) that those preferences will not change especially if competitive offerings emerge at substantially lower prices.[17]

Let's now work through the anatomy of a crisis.

1. The potential for greater net revenues (profits) along with easier entry resulting from changes in technology encourages new institutions to enter the industry.
2. As more institutions enter the market, it creates an increase in the supply of available seats that need to be filled by students.[18]
3. The excess capacity in the industry provides incentive for some institutions to lower their admissions standards in order to boost their head count.[19]
4. Increased numbers of students are recruited based on the relaxation of current admissions standards (lower SAT scores or the equivalent), less motivated individuals (reaching into the pool for those who are not really interested in advancing their education), or by making promises in terms of career or other opportunities that will never come true.[20]
5. Admitting students who otherwise would not enroll will reduce graduation rates (as long as academic standards are maintained).[21]
6. A decline in graduation rates will reduce the return on investment for those who are borrowing money to finance an education. It will also buttress stories about whether or not college is worth the price.[22]
7. As the number of stories increases calling into question the value of higher education, enrollment declines; thereby creating a crisis for many institutions.

Unlike the financial crisis, no massive debt defaults are required (though it would definitely exacerbate the problem).[23] The important point is that it is not just one demand driver, but rather the totality, that could potentially lead to a serious problem. The list might include

- A structural change that alters the way that government subsidies are distributed in the form of student aid. This affords the potential of greatly reducing revenues for underperforming institutions.[24]
- A growing perception that the return on the investment in higher education no longer makes sound financial sense either

in terms of the ability to get a job or the type of job that a recent graduate actually wants.[25]

- A growing gap between the ability to pay and what it costs to earn a degree. While the growth of financial aid seems to have kept pace with increases in tuition on a percentage basis, in dollar terms it has not.[26]
- A shift in governmental priorities. As the demand for government support grows in multiple areas, will state and local governments be able to continue to support higher education at current or expanded levels?[27]
- A failure to perform. As more students fail to graduate or take longer to graduate and employer complaints about the quality of graduates rise, the value associated with a degree becomes less clear.[28]
- As more and more education moves online and the residential experience is lost, the nonacademic benefits associated with higher education disappear as well.[29]

All that is needed is a spark to trigger the bust. It can come from a decrease in the ability to pay, but it may come from a realization that it is no longer worth it. One need look no further than the current hysteria over STEMs graduates to see a sign of things to come.[30] The fear that we are not producing the "right" graduates as we continue to face new competitive challenges associated with being part of a global economy may be all it takes to disassemble centuries of tradition.[31]

The Attack of the Zombies

The unraveling of higher education could come with a debt crisis similar to the recession of 2008, or stem from the creation of zombie institutions similar to the S&L crisis in the 1980s. In the old days when savings and loans populated the financial landscape, they served as the primary source for local mortgage origination. They were built on the principle of taking in local savings in the form of deposits and turning around and lending those savings to borrowers who wanted to purchase local real estate. Notice my emphasis on the word local. In the old days, mortgages and the corresponding buying and selling of homes were primarily a community driven affair.

However, with the financial deregulation that occurred as the result of the Monetary Decontrol Act of 1980, by the end of the decade many S&Ls ceased to exist.[32]

The demise of savings and loans leading to their eventual extinction can be an important lesson for institutions of higher education. With the high inflation of the 1970s, many S&Ls were seriously underwater as they held portfolios consisting of mortgage loans written at interest rates that were substantially lower than the rate of inflation.[33] If that was not a serious problem in and of itself, the emergence of what at the time were called nonbank banks, made things dramatically worse. Nonbank banks were institutions that fell outside government regulations and therefore were able to offer new types of accounts that paid substantially higher rates. Without the shackles of government regulations that limited what products traditional financial institutions could offer and what rates they could charge, this new class of financial institution found itself free to compete by offering new and improved services while paying higher rates on customer deposits. This led to a large exodus of funds from the regulated banking sector into the expanded deregulated one. Following a process known as disintermediation, banks were finding it increasingly difficult to attract and retain deposits. In response, the federal government decided to unshackle the banks and allow them to compete with the new entrants to the market.[34]

Gone were those protections that had prevented entry and exit into what had previously been geographically separated markets. In addition, a plethora of new products appeared as rates became deregulated. While banks discovered that they were able to take advantage of new opportunities for putting their capital to work, they also saw a dramatic rise in costs.

In the abstract, the policy at the time probably made a great of deal of sense. However, in reality it turned a bunch of financial institutions who were all but dead into zombies. It freed managers of S&Ls to raise the rates it paid to depositors in an effort to generate reserves that could then be turned into loans. However, as the cost of deposits increased, S&Ls could no longer make a profit by turning around and investing in low cost mortgages. Instead, they were forced to make new and different types of loans in order to try and preserve the spread between the cost of deposits and the return on their loans.

Rather than a solution to a serious problem, deregulation just made a bad situation worse. Institutions that had financial problems to begin with were now making riskier loans in an area where they had no experience or idea of what they were doing. As these new loans went bad, they were forced to try and attract larger and larger amounts of deposits until finally the whole process could no longer be sustained. Forced to buy bad assets for pennies on the dollar, the Fed initiated a number of forced marriages in order to preserve confidence in the financial system as a whole.

The more serious problem was that institutions that should have been allowed to fail were propped up in an effort to support the system as a whole. The effect however was to create a number of zombie institutions that were in effect nothing more than something akin to the walking dead. As these zombie institutions raised rates on deposits in an effort to attract new reserves, they in effect forced other institutions to raise their rates in order to stay competitive. This in turn led other institutions to make riskier loans in order to preserve the spread between the higher cost of capital and the rates they charged on loans. The unintended consequence was that ultimately they were also turned into zombies. Thus a policy that sounded good in the abstract turns into a crisis that ultimately costs upwards of $50 billion dollars and led to the disappearance of what had been a local fixture for decades.

Turning to higher education, traditional institutions are now finding themselves in a similar position of having to compete against the rise of for-profit institutions who have entered the industry in an effort of capturing their share of the premium being generated in part from government subsidies. At the same time, all institutions will potentially lose tuition dollars with the rise of MOOCs and other online efforts based on an entirely different and potentially lower cost model. When combined with a decrease in graduation rates and if nothing more, a rise in the stories of graduates who either fail to find employment or are underemployed, a serious enrollment problem may be looming on the horizon.

With a decline in the number of students looking for a traditional residential experience, established institutions will find it harder to attract qualified students. One strategy would be to artificially lower the cost by increasing the amount of financial aid.[35] Another may take the form of creating new academic programs that sound attractive in a desperate attempt to take a stodgy curriculum and try to make it relevant. In either case, costs will rise and thus net revenues (profits) will fall. This will fuel the need for even more students. To attract additional students, institutions may be forced to take the more aggressive stance of lower prices, particularly in light of the large number of information sharing services that have recently cropped up on the Internet to make it easier to compare prices. In response, every institution (except for a select few at the top) may find that they need to lower their price; thereby creating a slow death spiral culminating in a massive shake out in the industry.

The Threat of Becoming Irrelevant

Music has been synonymous with human culture for centuries. It was always a special day when an artist came to town to perform live for a local audience. However, in 1877 with the invention of the phonograph by Thomas Edison, the world of music underwent a fundamental transformation. By decoupling the creation of music from the act of performing live in front of an audience, anyone who was able to purchase the technology could enjoy listening to music any time they wanted in their own home. Thus an industry was born. One artist, could now reach thousands and eventually millions who could listen to their recordings; first in their home, then in their car, and finally in portable devices anywhere and anytime.

Growth in scale and scope led to the creation of an industry where talent was nurtured and recordings were manufactured and distributed within a tightly controlled supply chain. The industry was blessed in the sense that it controlled not only the content but also the means by which its product was manufactured and distributed. Through vertical integration, the music labels were able to extract huge profits from willing consumers who had a large appetite for a growing supply of music.

However, the business model that for decades had been the source of its success became an albatross around its neck as a new technological revolution occurred with the development of a digital compression technology (MP3), the development of new electronic devices (iPod) and the means for easily and seamlessly placing those digital files into the memory of those electronic devices (iTunes). As a result, recording companies are looking more and more like dinosaurs whose time has come and gone.

It was not the development of a music compression technology (MP3) and the creation of new devices capable of playing back digital files that has led to the disassembly of an entire industry. Rather, it was the unwillingness of the major record labels to rethink how they might continue to earn huge profits when they no longer controlled the manufacturing and distribution of their products.[36]

The recording industry had been dependent on controlling each facet of the process from the development of talent to the distribution of physical media to retail outlets that would then sell the product to consumers. Whether it was in nurturing a truly talented artist, or in their marketing efforts designed to shape the tastes and preferences of an entire generation of consumers, the record labels were in control of a desirable commodity that could not be easily replicated by competitors. We might have a lively debate whether or not the Beatles were the greatest rock band of all times, but what everyone can agree on is that there was only one group that called themselves the Beatles and many of the others paled in comparison.[37]

At the same time, control over the manufacturing and distribution of these recordings also gave the record labels a large amount of market power. Since music from different artists was not considered to be a perfect substitute and recordings could only be obtained on media manufactured by those same companies that controlled the artists, the record labels were able to obtain market power at the other end of the supply chain. An example of this market power was the invention of the record album. Rather than allowing the consumer to purchase a single "hit" song, the record album bundled several songs together in a single package. In order to buy the "hit," the consumer was forced to spend more and buy the entire package.[38]

These two sources of market power were self-reinforcing. The profits earned from manufacturing and selling songs were used to develop new sources of talent or invent entire new genres of music. At the same time, control over certain artists enabled the record labels to then use those name brand artists to extract higher prices from consumers. Each end of the economic transaction reinforced the other.

With the elimination of physical media as a means for controlling the distribution of their product, the record labels have lost their traditional means for extracting monopoly profits from consumers.[39] Without those profits, they have found it increasingly difficult to develop new talent using those tried and true methods of the past. More importantly, the elimination of physical media as a prerequisite for distributing music and the rise of alternate channels has further eroded the position of the recording companies.[40] This has threatened their very survival by making them irrelevant.

It is not difficult to draw the requisite parallels between the music and higher education industries. The mission of a research university is very similar to that of a major recording label. Professors are recruited to create knowledge through their research activities. Knowledge is bundled into courses that are distributed through a university curriculum. To access specific knowledge, students matriculate through a particular curriculum by enrolling in various courses. Bundled together, these courses represent a certain level of knowledge that is capable of becoming a product that is purchased by the student (consumer).[41]

Just as the record label amasses a stable of artists and distributes their efforts through a controlled medium and method of distribution, the university does the same. Hence it becomes easy to understand the threat posed by MOOCs. They open the door to knowledge that had been previously locked behind the closed doors of an institution for higher learning. Moreover, it represents a challenge to existing distribution channels by making it possible to bypass the physical classroom and hence makes these courses available to anyone with an Internet connection.[42] Thus, just as the recording labels have lost the source of their market power, the concern is that many universities will share the same fate.

The Dysfunctional Collegiate Organization

Businesses that have been around for a while generally like to make reference to their date of origin in whatever marketing literature they distribute. Being around for a long time often eases the mind of consumers who may wonder about the quality of a product or whether a company will be around long enough to support their purchase. Time creates a sense of stability and implicitly connotes a form of success. After all, if the product was so bad or the service so horrible, the company would have been forced to exit the market a long time ago.

While conferring certain advantages, being around for a long time has its drawbacks. Companies with a history tend to form processes and procedures that persist if for no other reason than that is the way things have always been done. People get set in their ways and it becomes difficult to respond to changes in the market. This becomes particularly challenging when it is unclear where the market is headed or ultimately where it will be five or ten years down the road. Hence what may confer one of the firm's best advantages can now become a serious liability when it comes time to transform an organization or a product in response to a radical change in the direction market.[43]

One of the best examples we can draw from today comes from the area of information technology. Take, for example, a company like Microsoft. Microsoft rose to a dominant position by almost single handedly creating a market for package software. One of the first companies to see the potential of the personal computer, Microsoft created packaged solutions that unlocked the potential of the new technology. Instead of providing customized solutions that met all of a customer's needs, Microsoft could instead take advantage of the economies of scale and scope associated providing packages that met the most important, and many of the other needs of its customers.[44] Thus, only relatively short period of time passed before the company came to dominate an entire industry.

All would be well and good if technology was not subject to change, but rather stayed in place ad infinitum. Unfortunately for Microsoft, its business model is being challenged on two fronts. The first can be seen in the rising dominance of mobile computing. The other challenge is emerging from what has become known as the cloud. In a cloud environment, data, applications, and many of the functions traditionally managed by the operating system, now resides outside the control of the local device. Hence we see the emergence of the mobile device and the cloud as the twin hammers that are threatening to tear down Microsoft's package business.

The change in landscape has forced Microsoft to respond and their strategy is perhaps best seen with the release of Windows 8. Windows 8 tries to be everything to everybody. Want to continue working with a personal computer? Windows 8 has the answer. Want to include a touchscreen on the computer to create more of a tablet feel? Windows 8 can do that. Want to abandon your personal computer for a tablet? No problem, Windows 8 can handle that as well. Do you find that most of your needs are satisfied by your smart phone? No problem, Windows 8 can satisfy your needs. Windows 8 provides one experience regardless of device or computing needs. It is truly designed as a one size fits all solution.

Compare this strategy with two of Microsoft's largest competitors: Apple and Google. Apple can be viewed as the prime force behind what we might refer to as Device Computing. Whether it is an iPhone, iPad, iTouch, or any number of other devices that will emerge down the road, Apple has pioneered entirely new devices and hence created new markets for its technology. However, in contrast to Microsoft, Apple did not try and extend its core computing technologies to these personal devices. Instead of using a streamlined version of its personal computer operating system, it created an entirely new system (IOS) in an effort to better meet the needs of device computing and the technical requirements associated with low power microprocessors, small storage capabilities, and less raw computing power. By developing an operating system that could bring out the best that these devices could offer, Apple has steadily been creating products that have reduced the need for a traditional personal computer.

Google on the other hand is implementing a strategy based on a much different view of where technology will be five or ten years out. As the network grows in scale, scope and power, there is little reason to process or store information on a local level. As a result, even more innovative devices can be created (e.g., Google Glass) that serve as mere conduits to a rich online environment. Hence Google has also undertaken its own development of an operating system that is called Chrome OS. Chrome OS contains the bare minimum of what is required to get someone access to all of the information that resides in the cloud. Applications that reside in the cloud can be used to manipulate data, stream content, or engage in a multiplayer game. With all of the intelligence residing in the brain of the user and the technology that resides in the cloud, low cost devices are used as a conduit and nothing more.

While the cloud may be the future of computing, there is still a ways to go before it becomes the established method of doing things. In the interim, Microsoft still controls the personal computer and Apple enjoys a dominant share of the device market.[45] Both represent a threat to the development and ultimate transition to the cloud model. To ensure that a pathway exists as the cloud becomes more fully realized, Google created an operating system called Android. Android serves several purposes for Google. It ensures that access to its current sources of revenue are not shut off by other companies that control through their operating systems how consumers interface with the Internet. More importantly, it serves as a set of "training wheels" that will help educate consumers to the power of the cloud and provide a mechanism for helping them transition to the cloud model once the infrastructure has been fully built out and is waiting for their arrival.

Thus, what we essentially have seen emerge are three different approaches. Apple, with no vested interest in the cloud and a modest share of the market for personal computers has reinvented itself as a device manufacturer. Google's future is the cloud and hence it has entered the mobile market in order to bring the cloud to everyone. Microsoft is trying to hold on to the past by being everything to everybody. However, when you try to be everything, you run the risk of being nothing.

Drawing parallels to higher education is a relatively easy task. Those institutions that have chosen to narrow their focus and concentrate on doing one thing very well can be thought of as the equivalent of device makers. Engineering schools, arts schools, liberal arts colleges are all examples of institutions that do not try to be everything to everybody, but instead target a particular niche in the marketplace. At the other end, it is easy to characterize the emergence of for-profit universities and their focus on online education as characteristic of the cloud strategy being played out in the technology sector. That leaves large universities with their diversified curriculum and their multifaceted missions as the equivalent of the Microsoft who tries to be everything to everybody. However, just as Microsoft has discovered that it is challenging to provide general solutions in a world where it has become relatively easy to cobble together focused efforts that create a comprehensive solution meeting the needs of a changing environment, generalist universities find themselves in a similar predicament.

At the risk of offering a dated solution that is no longer relevant to the needs of individuals and a society that has undergone a fundamental shift, it is simple to just say that every institution in the middle needs to run as fast as it can to one extreme or the other.[46] Calls to shed unessential functions and activities or to jump on the new technology bandwagon are easy to make. The difficulty, as experienced by Microsoft, is found when it comes time to take an organization where individual careers have been built on a way of doing business that no longer appears relevant and transform it into a dynamic and flexible one that meet the needs of a changing market.

If a company like Microsoft is finding it difficult to accept the new reality, is it reasonable to assume that a university would be any better? The modern university is built on the principles of shared governance where the faculty member plays the preeminent role in establishing curriculum, requisite requirements, instruction, and finally certification that a body of knowledge has been mastered.[47] Financial responsibility and accountability are the least of the faculty member's concerns. However, in a changing market where increased competition, new technologies, and declining public sector support are making it difficult to balance budgets, the concept of sharing governance between faculty members and administrators is being stretched to the breaking point. Faculty see no reason to change time-honored traditions while the new economic reality is already dictating that many cherished ways of doing things are no longer affordable.

Can universities rise to the challenge when those who run them (the faculty) have little incentive to change? This becomes even more difficult if such changes make faculty predominately worse off. It is difficult for an organization to succeed when everyone does not have a vested interest in change. Without a realignment of incentives, it is difficult to see how today's universities will be able to rise to the challenge.[48]

It is easy to blame tenure as the main source of the problem. What began as a means for protecting academic freedom morphed into an economic bargain.[49] Upon demonstrating in the sixth year of employment a certain level of competency, the candidate was rewarded with lifetime employment. Conferring tenure on a professor, however, became both a blessing and a curse. The blessing took on the form of a job for life; a measure of security that is rarely found in other professions. The curse is that once tenure is earned, it is difficult for all but the very best researchers in a field to move to another institution with tenure.[50]

Thus it should come as no surprise that in such an environment, faculty have little if any incentive to change. It is not that professors are a lazy bunch of malingers. Rather the problem lies in the structure of incentives. The only way that a faculty member can move and along with that, earn a significant higher salary is by making themselves more attractive in a very limited job market. Institutions are only interested in higher senior faculty members with tenure if they can significantly raise the reputation of the institution or generate millions of dollars in the form of grant-funded research into the university's coffers.[51]

Thus the tenure system creates organizational problems not because it promotes laziness, but rather because it promotes behavior that encourages the faculty member to place their own self-interest ahead of the more basic needs of the institution.[52] The interest of the institution is to fashion a creative strategy designed to handle a changing marketplace while the efforts of the individual faculty contribute little if anything to either the formation or the execution of such a strategy. As far as the development of new curricula, outreach programs, methods for delivering knowledge or student programs, they become of consequence to only a small minority of faculty who eventually find their way into administration.

The Fragmented Student Experience

Do you Yahoo? Or, more importantly, why does anyone still Yahoo? Yahoo! was one of the pioneers of the Age of the Internet and created the whole category of Internet Search Engines. The company was a testament to the concept of First Mover Advantages. Having created an entirely new category, the company was able to not only develop a strong brand identity but also capture a coveted slot in the list of bookmarks found in a person's browser. Even better would be to become the default home page for a user.

People are nothing, if not creatures of habit. Despite the fact that the World Wide Web encompasses millions of websites, they only visit a small number on a regular basis. Thus becoming a favorite site carries with it a lot more influence than may appear at first blush. Thus despite losing its preeminent position in search to Google, Yahoo! is still the fourth most visited site on the Internet.[53]

Why you might ask when Google has captured over three quarters of all search activity that takes place.[54] Early on, Yahoo! realized they needed to expand their value proposition beyond search. It would be difficult and very expensive to erect barriers sufficiently high to prevent other companies from entering the search space. To maintain its advantage, the company decided to leverage its early lead in search by developing the concept of a web portal. They wanted Yahoo! to not only be the first place one goes when they a looking to find something on the Internet but also become the preeminent provider of content.

It is all about eyeballs and getting someone to spend as much time as possible on your website. Only by keeping a user at your site does it become possible to convert those eyeballs into revenue. As a result, Yahoo! grew or acquired a number of different content providers and technology companies in an effort to create as many reasons as possible for users to come to the Yahoo! portal and stay for hours on end.

Losing its lead in search and other areas, Yahoo! has still remained a dominant force not because they are necessarily the leader in any particular content or technology area, but because they have assembled a stable of offerings where the whole is greater than the sum of the parts. It does not have to lead as long as it is able to create a wide array of offerings that in total offer more value than any other website that attempts to serve the same function as a web portal.[55]

However, relying on the fact that people are creatures of habit and having a wide array of content that is at best second or third in its particular areas does not make a compelling recipe for success. A problem that has grown worse as the concept of a website has been declining in importance. With the ascension of mobile computing, having a popular website is no longer a valuable asset. The name of the game is now apps that can be combined using widgets to create a more compelling value proposition for the person who accesses the Web using a smartphone or tablet. This shift is growing in importance as tablets by 2014 will almost rival personal computers in terms of the number of devices shipped.[56] Thus while Yahoo! may continue to have the fourth most visited website, if the number of visitors for the industry as a whole is declining, pretty soon it no longer matters.

So now we are back to the essential question: Is Yahoo! a collection of individual services or is it a whole that is greater than the sum of its parts? This question is fundamental to setting the strategic direction of the company. Yahoo! as a company succeeds based on whether it can turn its individual services from being also-rans to segment leaders, or if it somehow can turn the tide against the invasion of mobile devices and their apps and widgets that make a portal less important.

The choices facing Yahoo! are not all that different from the ones staring universities directly in the face. One can think of a university as a collection of different fields that when combined, provide a broad education for the individual student. However, just as Yahoo! must decide if the source of greatest value is in terms of the strength of its individual services, or in the portal experience, universities must grapple with the same issue. Is their strength in the individual disciplines and the ability of the faculty in those disciplines to create and disseminate knowledge, or does their strength exist in the melding of disciplines to create a complete educational experience?

While each university has general education requirements, many students do not understand the value added. For that matter, some majors along with their requirements appear to make little sense. Coupled with a social experience that seems at odds with the academic environment; today's student is inundated by a similar abundance of mix messages, fuzzy goals, and inconsistent rewards and expectations.

In a growing economy where the creation of new jobs is outpacing growth in the labor force and competition is leading firms to create new higher paying jobs that require advanced skills, a lack of focus in the delivery of the academic experience could perhaps be easily ignored. Is the change in the economy something akin to the mobile revolution being faced by Yahoo!? If the modern university is something akin to a web portal, will the growing use of apps be the equivalent of the beginning of the end for today's university?

What Does It All Mean?

What should become clear by this point is that the problems facing higher education are not something unique. They can be found in many different industries. The conclusion one will hopefully draw is that higher education therefore is not exempt from those fundamental forces that have been shaping a wide range of industries. Moreover, just as solutions are available for solving the problems that are spread throughout the economy, some of them may be appropriate for higher education.

However, searching for an answer can become a journey without end if you don't know where to look. Perhaps the greatest problem facing higher education today is one that no one seems to want to discuss. For many students, rather than understanding that what happens during college will, to a large extent, shape the rest of their lives, they instead squander the opportunity. Missing classes, waiting to the last minute to complete assignments, cramming a semester's worth of material into the last moments before an exam, is for many the norm rather than the exception.

Just as an entire industry may defy the rational tenets that we like to believe shape the choices that are made, there is no reason to assume that students are more impervious to those same forces. It is not that the student of today is any less rational than the student of 50 years ago. Rather, what made sense 50 years ago is no longer relevant for today.[57] Hence if we are to understand how bricks and mortar universities are best equipped to compete in a changing market, we need to make sure we understand how traditional students have adapted to changes in their environment.

CHAPTER 2

Insights from the Game Industry

Industries can be insular places where leaders get so caught up in using their own jargon and following past practice that it becomes difficult to rise to the challenge when crisis hits. It becomes hard to break out of habitual modes of thought and look at the problem from a different perspective. This becomes particularly challenging when something like technological innovation has disrupted current practices to the point where doing the same old thing no longer makes any sense.

To gain some perspective on just how much everything has changed, it might make sense to leave the challenges facing higher education and look in a different direction. A suitable candidate would be something that has been around for centuries and yet has embraced all that modernity has to offer. An excellent example would be the game of chess.

The components used to play the game can be purchased or constructed by the players. The rules are readily available in the public domain. A player must have a person or a thing (computer) to play against. Play may be enhanced when multiple players are involved. The game can be played without much understanding or experience. However, greater proficiency and success can be attained through instruction and repeated play.

New technologies however have led to some important changes in the game of chess. While this may pain traditionalists, technological innovation has created new variants of the game. Whether enabling game play without a physical board and pieces, the creation of multidimensional versions of the game, or eliminating the need for another human being in order to play, technology has created many new options. Additionally, technology has increased the potential pool of opponents by decoupling play from physical time and space by allowing an individual to challenge someone located somewhere else around the globe.

True, while many individuals who might otherwise play chess have been seduced by other game offerings, many have become players because they can now easily find opponents to play against. For others, the appeal rises because the cost of play (board, pieces, instruction) has decreased to the point of being close to zero. The challenge from a business perspective is how to monetize the game of chess in a way that is capable of producing a revenue stream that creates a positive economic profit.

When thinking about chess as a potential business opportunity, it is important to remember why a person plays the game in the first place and then keeps playing it again and again. An economist might say that once an individual has taken the time to create the human capital needed to learn the game, they are looking to earn a return on that investment by playing it time after time. A gamer on the other hand would look at it differently. Two equally matched opponents with a certain level of competency can create a challenging, exciting, and exuberant experience that has the potential of being recreated over and over again. The thrill associated with winning, or the rewards in terms of nontangible things like the approval of peers or the feeling of empowerment that comes with doing something well is what keeps someone playing game after game.

Here we see perhaps the greatest source of contrast between games and enterprise. In the context of a game, the benefits emerge as part of the process of play. It is the contest itself and not the rules, pieces, or stage (environment) that is the principle source of value. A game is nothing more than a mechanism designed to enable play. The value of that mechanism is totally contingent on the quality of the experience. The most ornate chess set or the most visually striking virtual world is limited in terms of the value that it creates. How often the set is used or the world is visited depends almost entirely on what occurs after the pieces are set up.

If the game industry is to offer insights that will help institutions of higher learning cope with the coming crisis, it will need to come to grips with this very important distinction. While it may be difficult to have a distinguished institution of higher learning without the ivy covered walls, the walls themselves are merely the starting point for a potentially life changing experience.

Competitive Challenges

According to the Entertainment Software Association, revenues generated from the sale of video games in 2012 were approximately $20.77 billion dollars.[1] That pales in comparison to the revenues generated by a different kind of game: sports. According to Plunkett Research, the entire size of the U.S. Sports Industry was somewhere around $470 billion dollars in 2013. In 2012, the combined revenues from the major professional sports that include Major League Baseball ($6.8B), the National Football League ($8.8B), the National Basketball Association ($3.7B), and the National Hockey League ($3.4B) was estimated to be $22.7 billion; just about the same size as the entire entertainment software industry.[2]

Professional sports serve as an excellent example of the tension that exists in any game involving more than one person. On the one hand, contestants want to win. In a test of strength, agility, competence, or intelligence, it is satisfying to come out on top; to become the winner. However, while it is important to win, contestants also like to be challenged. Not only do they want to be victorious, but they also want to be pushed in a way that brings out their best efforts. Winning against a strong and talented opponent is much more satisfying than winning against someone who is clearly out matched. This dynamic is illustrated in Figure 2.1.

This same tension exists in professional sports as a business. The owner of a professional sports team wants a winner. In part because the success of a team's players reflects positively on the abilities and judgment of the owner, but also in part because winning teams are worth more than losing ones. Moreover, a winning team stands a better chance of earning a profit. Teams at the top of the standings

Figure 2.1

are able to garner stronger fan support leading to higher ticket and concession sales, a higher demand for licensed merchandise, and greater public support when it comes time to build a new stadium.

The desire to win and the gains associated with fielding a winner leads many owners to engage in the equivalent of an "arms race."[3] Winning teams often have the best players, the most experienced coaches, and the finest facilities. A dramatic increase in spending on the part of one team owner often generates a similar response on the part of the other owners in the league who must either match that level of spending or find themselves fielding a perennial loser. It is no different than any other oligopolistic industry where the decision of one firm can affect the outcome reached by the other firms in the industry. Hence an aggressive move to steal market share must elicit a response or a firm might soon find itself without any customers.

It is commonly believed that what differentiates professional sports like baseball from other industries is that they have an exemption from US antitrust laws and therefore can legally collude. This collusion often takes the form of agreements designed to keep the aggressive spending that could lead to the financial ruin of the entire league in check through various devices such as player spending caps and revenue sharing between teams. Collusive league agreements can prevent one team from dominating the sport or from driving less successful teams out of the league because they cannot financially compete with teams in larger markets.[4]

However, there is another reason why professional leagues have an interest in ensuring that one team does not dominate all others.[5] While each fan likes to see their team win, they might soon grow bored with the sport if the same team wins each and every contest (particularly if that team is not their own). It is much more exciting to watch a contest that is decided with only ten seconds left on the clock and it is the final shot, kick, or play that leads one team to victory over another. If the same teams won lopsided contests over and over time after time, fans might abandon the sport for another one that generates more exciting contests. Hence fan interest is not just a function of which team wins, but whether the game is sufficiently interesting to keep them locked to the television screen or willing to buy tickets for the next regularly scheduled contest. Everyone loves a winner, but to keep fans engaged, a team needs to win in style. Often that means winning in the most dramatic way possible.

Professional sports are not the only industry where we see this tension. A similar tension exists in higher education. Landing in the top 20, a university can use its ranking to attract better students and faculty, find itself in a stronger position to compete for research grants, and generate much greater levels of private and public support for its endeavors.[6] Expanding the number of administrators, upgrading facilities, paying for star faculty, developing additional programming, and the proliferation of commissions and special interest groups, have all been part of a concerted effort to gain a competitive advantage relative to a select number of comparator schools.[7]

Moving up in the rankings is the equivalent of winning a league championship and has all of the benefits associated with it. However, those efforts designed to enhance the reputation of an institution do not necessarily lead to the ideal student experience. If we think of students as comparable to sports fans, their engagement and enjoyment are not solely dependent on the outcome of the contest.

A university that can attract the best professors does not mean that the typical undergraduate will ever take a class with that person. On the other hand, who wouldn't want their meals prepared by a world class chef before retiring to a private room with its own bath in a climate controlled environment just after working out in the new upgraded fitness facilities?[8] While everyone benefits when the reputation of an institution improves, those benefits have limited value to a student who has not learned very much. Spending what are becoming increasingly limited resources in the equivalent of an "arms race" to gain a superior competitive position may lead to a very hollow victory if students are not engaged in learning.[9]

Yet the problem is exacerbated when it is easier to compare dorm amenities than it is to evaluate the quality of what goes on in the classroom. As a result, many administrators believe that they have no other choice than participate in an infrastructure race that no one can win. In the game industry it is the equivalent of being driven by the next greatest graphics system or gaming console. Education becomes a complementary good that lives or dies with factors that have nothing to do with the education experience itself.

The Value Proposition

In an industry where the ability to deliver education is being decoupled from the physical infrastructure that has traditionally been required (e.g., classrooms), continuing to invest millions of dollars in improvements that no one may ever use does not seem to make a great deal of sense. Rather, the smarter move is to rethink what makes an education valuable and to develop a strategy designed to create a value proposition that reflects current competitive conditions rather than past historical patterns. The focus needs to shift from the ancillary components that have traditionally formed the foundation of an education to one that more intensively looks at building a better educational experience. One that goes beyond look and feel or various amenities and is designed to make a meaningful difference in a young person's life.

One of the best examples where experience triumphs over sizzle and flash can be found in a game called Minecraft. Developed independently by Swedish programmer Markus Persson, Minecraft is a game comprised of 3D blocks that are used to create various objects. It does not rely on the latest technological wizardry, nor did Minecraft have a million dollar marketing budget or the backing of a major publisher. Yet despite all of that, the game received five awards at the 2011 Game Developers Conference. In 2012, Minecraft XBLA was awarded a Golden Joystick Award and also received a TIGA games Industry Award. By September 2013, the game had sold over 12 million copies on the PC and 33 million across all platforms.[10]

Minecraft is an open world game where players are essentially left on their own to build whatever they would like with 3D blocks. The game was designed with a great deal of flexibility. It is subject only to the limits of the player's own imagination, or can follow a predefined pattern. Play can be in response to the needs of a particular storyline, or can emerge as part of a creative process; just as one can buy a Lego model, a Lego set that is part of a storyline, or a building set comprised of generic bricks.

The game has spawned an active developer community that has provided a growing number of mods for the game. It has also developed a number of merchandise tie-ins. The most prominent one is with Lego.

Successful gaming models like the one utilized by Minecraft focus on process rather than outcome. Players move closer to achieving a goal, but final resolution remains elusive in order to prolong play (and hence revenues per player). Success is not defined in terms of some stated outcome, but rather results from engaging in play.[11]

Figure 2.2

Players express their autonomy by choosing what they do, become powerful as they master different challenges, and build esteem as their online identities grow, develop, and experience success. There exists very concrete symbols that serve as measures for success and each time they log in, these symbols serve to reinforce a positive self-image. This dynamic is shown in Figure 2.2.

One of the most difficult challenges in developing a successful game environment is to create enough structure that players can have an interesting or unique experience, but not too much structure that it seriously limits individual autonomy and the freedom to assist in the development of the game experience. Drawing a fine line between offering direction and encouraging players to innovate in ways that are beyond the vision of the game developers is a challenging task. However, what successful game designers are able to accomplish is the creation of a coherent and integrated experience. The general rules of the game are easily understood, standard constructs form the basis for achievements, requirements exist for reaching higher levels, and the overall look and feel create a singular experience.[12]

This stands in stark contrast to the university experience where outcomes triumph over process. Most college courses are outcomes based. Students are assigned a certain amount of knowledge to be learned and are rewarded based on how well they master that knowledge. Coursework serves as the major activity and therefore source of earning achievements. However, in an environment where each professor can create their own set of standards and assessment mechanisms and there is little integration across courses, then the student experience becomes highly fragmented. The problem this creates is that when the reward structure is haphazard and not well integrated, it becomes difficult to motivate behavior—let alone sustain a high level of performance.

Thus while students might become more proficient in solving problems, interpreting readings, or analyzing situations, a connection is missing between their greater understanding of a particular subject and what it means in terms of who they are or how they stack up relative to their peers. Students feel only marginally more powerful and in many cases, are just as confused about who they are or what they are capable of doing.

In such a fragmented environment, it is difficult to gain momentum or assess how well one is doing over time. There is no single assessment measure or objective standard for evaluating performance other than a grade which becomes a noisy rather than a clear signal of performance. As a result, it is difficult for the student to internalize success in a meaningful way. Coupled with the challenge involved in making relevant comparisons with others, it becomes very difficult for students to build self-esteem. Rather than one success building on another to develop a more knowledgeable and confident student, environmental factors instead have the exact opposite effect.

Compare this to a well-designed game environment where accomplishment reinforces identity and changes in identity reinforce a feeling of self-worth. The game builds self-esteem and as players feel better about themselves, they devote more time and energy to game play in order to achieve an even stronger image of their self.[13] At college however, educational outcomes are in many cases, divorced from individual identity. While positive outcomes are recognized, they often do little to improve feelings of self-worth.

Thus for universities to become more effective in generating educational outcomes, they need to find ways to create process achievements that are tied directly to the development of the individual.

Moreover, through the adoption of game design principles, faculty, and administrators can create a more coherent and integrated student experience. Fashioning a more tightly coupled system of rewards that supports an overarching framework can infuse a sense of purpose. A greater sense of purpose can elevate ordinary activities capable of bringing out the best in students and generating a higher level of student satisfaction. As a result, greater engagement through gamification can create graduates who will be better able to succeed later in life because they have learned more, have a better sense of self, and a higher level of self-esteem.

User Experience

Underlying any game is a platform that serves as the foundation for play. In a board game like chess, that platform is a flat surface consisting of 64 equally sized squares that alternate in color. It could be nothing more than two vertical and two horizontal lines drawn with a stick in a patch of dirt for playing a game as simple as tic-tac-toe. Alternatively, it could be an elaborate virtual world created using a gaming engine such as Source or Unreal that simplifies the development process. In each case, a platform of some sort or another serves as the foundation for the construction of a game, and ultimately, an entire experience.

At first glance, this doesn't appear to be any different than the role that platforms play in other industries. Take, for example, the personal computer industry. Twenty years ago we would be debating the superiority of Wintel (Windows/Intel) over Apple or Apple over Wintel.[14] Today, the same debate rages, but it is now between Android and IOS as smartphones and tablets have grown in importance. Of course the debate is not just about the superiority of one operating system over another, it is a disagreement over development philosophy.

Apple has always been about the user experience. As such, Apple looked to keep tight control over every facet of its products. Whether through the development of proprietary technology, the use of cutting edge industrial design, or the number of painstaking hours spent ensuring the look and feel were just right, Apple has tried to provide a comprehensive and complete solution. As far back as the original design of the Macintosh computer, it was about defining the future and bringing the consumer to a place they had no idea existed.

What is perhaps the most notable difference between the Apple today and the one from 30 years ago is recognition of the value of a product ecosystem. No single company can conceive, finance, or implement every possible product extension that may have the effect of making its own products more valuable. Whether we are talking about an iPod, and iPhone, or an iPad, the success of each product category can in part be attributed to the revolutionary nature of Apple's products, but as importantly, because of the thousands of products that use an Apple product as the core for accepting an add-on product that expands the functionality of the original Apple product. Just as operating systems for personal devices are rated in terms of the number and quality of available apps, the same holds true for hardware platforms. The availability of docking stations, protective cases, chargers, and the list can go on and on enhances the value of the foundational product.

One can think of the value created as being the result of what we might call family effects. Family effects are the additional gains that are created when compatible devices or software programs enhance the value of the original product by creating a whole that is greater than the sum of the parts. These platform externalities are similar in concept to the more widely referenced network externalities. However, the value of these external benefits is not tied to the number of users, but instead, the number of devices that comprise the total "family" of products that when combined, expand and enhance the user experience.[15]

This stands in stark contrast to the philosophy that stood behind the dominant Wintel Platform when it came to personal computers and now is driving the acceptance of Google's Android operating system for personal devices. The contrast in development philosophy cannot be any more striking. Rather than focusing on the user experience, this other philosophy is, for the most part, about price and performance. Utilizing the concept of the division of labor to its fullest extent, these platforms begin with the recognition that no single company has a monopoly on good ideas, can amass the capital necessary to finance each and every new innovation, and have the singular focus that is sometimes needed to become the best at some small facet of a larger effort. Hence by dividing product development between hardware, software, peripherals, applications, and other categories, a greater degree of specialization affords the possibility that the individual parts will see continuous leaps in performance that will eventually lead to a dramatic fall in prices.

What differentiates the dominance of the Windows/Intel platform from the current implementation of Android is not that there has been a shift in the underlying philosophy that preaches substantial gains from those specialized efforts that become possible by adherence to a set of technical specifications, but instead, it springs forth from the opportunities that arise with the emergence of a powerful set of personal devices. For companies like Amazon, smartphones and tablets are nothing more than digital gateways to purchasing the myriad of products that it sells.[16] The devices serve as a conduit for converting the sale of the other items the company sells into profits. Hence it is interested in developing an ecosystem that is not focused on maximizing the value of the platform itself, but rather enhances a different experience; the purchase and enjoyment of products that are sold through Amazon.[17]

Hence Amazon is only interested in Android to the extent that it affords a lower cost development platform and maintains its compatibility with the thousands of apps that add to, but do not detract from the main purpose of the device which is to drive sales to Amazon's website. Since any Android tablet could in theory purchase goods from Amazon, the strategic advantage from having its own tablet is the ease by which it can make that activity possible. By tailoring the user experience, Amazon can ensure that the purchaser of its tablet will look toward its offerings first. However, if that is all the tablet could do, customers may opt for a different one that may not serve as effectively toward defining the experience in a way that gives Amazon a competitive edge over rivals. As a result, it must still maintain some level of compatibility with the broader Android ecosystem.

Thus we see both the principle strength and weakness of the Android platform. It can serve as the foundation for accomplishing a proprietary set of goals, but it cannot stray too far from the standard on which it is based. If customers just wanted a proprietary experience, there is little reason other than price not to go with an Apple-based solution. However, if price is the more dominant consideration, then the lowest prices will always be offered by those who are able to tap into the greatest gains afforded from the division of labor, or have the deepest pockets and are therefore in the position to subsidize the cost of their devices. However, all this is going to do is trigger a competitive race to the bottom where no one makes any profits at all.

A similar tension between flexibility and control exists in game environments. The use of a game engine such as Source or Unreal can substantially reduce the time and cost of developing a game. Here the software platform becomes a tool for creating a unique user experience. What makes games different is they are marketed based not on their compatibility with other games, but on the uniqueness of their experience. The game engine serves as the foundation for user developed modifications (Mods) that can take the game in directions that the designers never imagined.[18]

In this sense a gaming platform is certainly different than the platform used by Apple which allows outsiders access only in so far as it enhances the Apple defined, controlled, and maintained experience. It is also different from the bifurcated Android approach. For those members of the Android ecosystem who derive their profits from the sale of Android-based hardware and software, enhancements are designed to make a richer and hence more valuable Android experience. This may take the form of additional functionality or an expansion in the current capabilities of the platform in order to generate greater value from the activities that emerge from use.

This then forms the essence of the difference between the game industry and personal device manufacturers. While game companies view standard software platforms as valuable tools for creating a unique consumer experience, they are willing to cede control of the user experience. Game companies take advantage of an expanded division of labor not only to reduce the cost and time to market but also to enhance and expand the user experience. By inviting user created mods, players are able to create a user driven experience that expands beyond the scope of the original game design.

Recognizing that what makes some play desirable is when the player can tailor the experience in a way that best appeals to their own individual interests; they can greatly expand interest in the game. As the pool of players expands, an individual will encounter more players with similar interests thereby creating a further expanded pool of potential modders or gamers willing to incorporate their mods into gameplay.[19]

As a result, we begin to see platform externalities emerge in game play.[20] As more individuals with similar interests begin to play and modify an existing game, the game and ultimately the user experience begins to change. As these changes are better able to capture the interest of similar minded individuals, there is additional interest and energy in applying additional modifications to the game. This leads to even greater interest and hence more players which eventually translates into higher revenues for the initial game developer.

Thus where tech companies derive the greatest potential profits from the control of the user experience, gaming companies have the exact opposite experience. By ceding control of the user experience to its players through the use of standard tools, it is able to employ an expanded division of labor to enhance the game experience. Through the use of standard tools, players are able to make the gaming experience their own. By personalizing the experience, it becomes more rewarding and hence gamers are more willing to spend both time and money within the game environment. This dynamic can be seen in Figure 2.3.

Figure 2.3

Success in the game industry suggests that we should question the current structure of the academic curriculum found in most institutions of higher learning. Generally a college education consists of a set of requirements designed to provide the student with exposure to a number of different disciplines spread across multiple departments. Layered on top of that is a more concentrated experience where multiple courses are taken within a single field. This education platform forms the foundation for the bachelor's degree. The institution develops standards that must be met if the student is to be certified with the conveyance of a degree.[21]

However, in a world where knowledge is constantly changing, the requirements of many majors seem as if they are stuck in time. This has led some to question the value of a college degree.[22] More importantly, given that the external environment is also changing and hence knowledge that was relevant 20 years ago may no longer be appropriate for today raises an entirely different set of issues. What is needed however goes beyond making the curriculum more responsive to the needs of a changing society or job market. It is about ushering in a new era of collaborative learning.[23]

Instead of thinking about the curriculum as a collection of self-contained units, we need to think about it as a learning platform. A platform that is not only more responsive to the external environment, but more importantly, one that is more receptive to the needs and desires of students. It is not about ceding control of the learning process, but instead is about adding a degree of freedom and flexibility that gives the student the ability to shape the experience in a way that enables them to advance their personal skill set in new and constructive ways. The central question is whether students are best served by blindly accepting a vision of how things are supposed to be from their professors, or are they, like gamers, in search of an interactive experience that is more personalized and meaningful for them?

It is easy to say that students are young and need the guidance of someone who is an expert in a particular field if they are to one day master a particular body of knowledge. However, while the university has an interest in turning out students who have demonstrated competency in a particular field, little of value can be accomplished if the student is alienated from the process. Students want to learn things that are meaningful for them and not for some abstract career that may or may not materialize at some point in the future.

By placing students within a one size fits all framework, what is lost are whatever benefits might arise from including them as part of the process. That is not to say that students should determine the curriculum or set their own standards for what consists of learning and what is not. Rather, it is creating an educational framework that welcomes student contributions and incorporates them into the curriculum.

It is not just a question of opening the door to the ivory tower, but turning the tower into a meeting house. In this new model, professors would construct a basic learning platform that can serve as the foundation for creating an educational experience. Control would still reside with the professor, but the nature and the flow of the experience would in part incorporate elements developed by the student.

The Power of Franchises

One response to a market that has become more competitive is to try and extend your reach beyond what has been considered to be the traditional customer base. If the customer for some reason cannot come to you, then you develop a means to go to the customer. In higher education, we see this occur in two ways. Some universities are establishing satellite campuses in other locations and even many more are expanding into e-learning in an effort to bring their brand directly to the customer.[24] It is the equivalent of creating a franchise consisting of multiple locations that provide the exact same service to a geographically dispersed customer population.

The appeal of a franchise is that it solves the problem of asymmetric information. Asymmetric information is a fancy way of saying "I know something you don't know." When you are traveling and enter a strange town looking for a place to eat lunch, the locals know all of the best places, but since this is your first time in town, you are unable to distinguish between the good restaurants and the bad. A franchise solves the problem because as long as you have previously visited one of its establishments, you will know exactly what to expect. Hence while a local restaurant may have better food, a menu more suited to your tastes, or offer selections at a lower price, you are not sure what to expect and because acquiring information is costly, you opt for the safe choice.

The value of a franchise is found in the consistent experience that is created. By ensuring that you will have the same experience regardless of where you are, the franchise has a great deal to offer despite the fact that it may not have the best food, prices, or most desirable options. Thus when a consumer chooses to eat at a franchise restaurant, she is purchasing a bundle of attributes that go beyond the size or taste of a hamburger. Because the consumer is purchasing a bundle of attributes, the franchises' number one priority is to ensure the consistency of these attributes from establishment to establishment.

This idea of consistency is not something limited to multiple locations. The concept of sequels has been effectively used by the motion picture industry to create a franchise. One of the longest running and most recognized is the James Bond franchise. The Bond franchise consists of 23 official films over a 50 year period (1962–2012) with six actors having played the role.

The movies are all built around the same basic formula. When someone goes to a James Bond movie, they have a fairly good idea of what they are going to see. However, it also effectively minimizes any confusion created by having multiple actors play the same role. By recreating familiar situations and having the films conform to a basic formula, the producers can avoid consumer confusion while meeting film viewer's expectations.

Having been successfully used for years in the movie industry, it should therefore come as no surprise that sequels would have a similar role to play in the games industry. One need look no further than Halo as a prime example of the power of a franchise. Many consider Halo to be the "killer app" that made the Xbox a successful gaming platform. Included in the series are: Halo: Combat Evolved (2001), Halo 2 (2004), Halo 3 (2007), Halo Wars (2009), Halo 3: ODST (2009), Halo Reach (2010), Halo: Combat Evolved Anniversary (2011), and Halo 4 (2012).The games have sold over 50 million copies with gross revenues in excess of $55 billion.[25]

What is different about the use of the franchise concept in the game industry is that the franchise is not something that is tightly controlled to ensure consistency and uniformity. Nor is it something to be protected to maintain the integrity of the character or story line. Rather than promoting consistency, franchise-based video games focus on familiarity. With video games, rather than purchasing a bundle of attributes, the player is looking to create an experience. Familiarity with the basic story, the look and feel of a virtual world, and game mechanics enables the player to advance more quickly to play. Hence the concept of a franchise serves a similar (but not identical) purpose. Where consistency reduces the problem of asymmetric information, familiarity reduces the costs associated with learning the basics. This dynamic is illustrated in Figure 2.4.

The value of the franchise is not consistency but familiarity. It is like becoming reacquainted with an old friend. Players don't require that everything must be the same. Rather they want to feel comfortable enough with the story, environment, or characters so that they can make changes. It is often easier to challenge oneself by altering the familiar rather than something that is new. Players do not want the same experience that is repeated over and over again, rather, they want an experience that will enable them to get a faster start so that they can more quickly advance to something that challenges them to do something new.

A flexible design that takes place within a familiar environment introduces freedom and choice into a pliable platform that does just enough to confer the benefits from creating a franchise, but not enough to limit the user experience. Because the franchise serves as a platform and not a prison, it becomes an extension of the individual. The end user becomes on a limited basis a co-creator and thus has a vested interest in the franchise. This creates a higher level of interest and a greater level of loyalty that becomes ever more important with the release of each new iteration of the game.

A loyal customer who has a vested interest is more willing to become buyer at $60 on release day. Moreover, since game play is

Figure 2.4

largely an experience good, previous players provide the most fertile pool for future customers with succeeding editions of a franchise game.[26] Thus a well-designed franchise never comes to a complete resolution in an individual version of the game, but is designed to have the player wanting more and thus willing to pay the price of returning and playing again in the next iteration of the game. Rather than weakening the franchise, inserting flexibility actually provides it with a new found strength.

What the games industry use of the franchise concept has to teach us is how to think creatively about turning a new customer into a repeat one that stays enthusiastic and engaged with each release of a familiar but somewhat different presentation of a basic concept. The goal is not merely to generate interest from a new group of potential customers, but more importantly, to convert them into an ongoing revenue stream.

This stands in stark contrast with many college and universities. Recruiting new students for a bachelor's degree program can be a very expensive proposition. However, rather than looking at an undergraduate student as a revenue stream that can extend beyond four years, upon graduation, those students are often just relegated to the advancement office as new prospects for fundraising. What is missing from this approach is the concept that the very high costs of providing an undergraduate degree can be spread over a broader audience. However, the best opportunity for spreading those costs is not by entering new geographic markets in order to compete for the same 18–23 year old student. It exists by turning alumni into lifelong learners and hence a potential partner for life.

Pricing

Every firm would like to have the problem where demand is outstripping supply. A shortage regardless of whether it is real or fabricated offers a firm the luxury of being able to raise prices or forces them to ration quantity in some way. For a highly anticipated game, those first few days represent a tremendous opportunity. Having been teased by a beta release, inundated with a marketing blitz, and overwhelmed by a feeling of anticipation as the result of a buzz that has swept over social media, game companies are in the best position to charge a premium for their new game. To take advantage of a narrow window created by all of the hype, a game company can engage in price discrimination. One example is the release of a regular edition, a special edition, and a collector's edition; all designed to create multiple value propositions at different price points.[27]

The willingness to pay a premium on release is heightened if the game has a significant multiplayer component. When the value of a game resides in the ability to play it with friends, then a gamer will need to buy the game when friends do and it needs to be played while the game is fresh and everyone is at the same experience level. Hence if a couple of friends buy it and start playing the game, there is pressure on others to purchase it as well if they hope to play with others while there is still interest in playing the game and everyone is roughly at the same experience level. Thus much of the work associated with price discrimination is done for the successful gaming company by its installed base of customers.

This is all well and good when the source of value is primarily provided by the game company. However, what happens when the gaming company provides a foundation for play, but much of the value is created by the players? Players recognize that an online multiplayer game that takes place within a virtual world created by a game company needs to be supported if for no other reason than the servers that host the game do not run for free and updates that provide a more robust structure for game play do not appear out of thin air. Hence they are willing to pay a monthly subscription fee in order to play. Yet competition between companies ensures that those fees stay relatively low.[28]

As a result, monthly fees are not necessarily the best way to generate profits. This is particularly difficult when the primary source of value created is not by the game company, but instead by the contributions of a small core of dedicated players. The challenge is in creating a pricing strategy that is low enough to encourage a strong user community while at the same time, is high enough to cover operating costs and leave some room for profit. In response to this challenge, a shift is occurring away from pricing strategies based on market power toward what we might call value-added pricing.[29] This dynamic is shown in Figure 2.5.

In this new model, the game company must entice a player to engage with its virtual world by either creating a strong marketing message that can reach a core group of gamers who will actually

Figure 2.5

pay money to acquire the software needed to play, or by essentially giving the software away in order to entice as many individuals to play as possible. Once a core group begins to create an exciting and interesting experience, word of mouth or a positive review draws additional players into the mix.

The principle challenge is creating a pricing strategy capable of converting the value added by players into a stream of revenue capable of generating profits. In response, game companies have engaged in a different form of price discrimination. For many, they have adopted what is known as a two-part tariff. What this essentially means is that the game company charges a monthly subscription fee for the right to play, and then offers for sale a number of in-game items that can boost player performance, prestige, or enjoyment.

Just because the player is the principle source of value creation in a multiplayer game environment, they often need tools, abilities, or accessories to advance play or gain recognition in a way that heightens the level of enjoyment that emerges with play. Thus we see more and more subscription-based games creating opportunities for players to purchase items designed to enhance play as means for appropriating some of the value created by its players.

The key once again is to focus on process rather than outcomes. While saving the world may provide the underlying motivation for game play, it must remain an elusive goal if players are to continue to pay their monthly fees. Hence while the end is never really attainable, pleasure or fun must derive from the process rather than ultimate success. There is not a desired outcome that defines the experience, but rather the parameters of an experience are established and rewards are structured around process-based achievements. Keeping players in the game for as long as possible generates the most fees and hence becomes one of the primary objectives of the game company.

Most of this does not come as a surprise to colleges and universities who have, for a long time, engaged in price discrimination to get the right mix of students. They use their market power to get some to pay more than others in order to create a blend of students designed to enhance the educational experience. This is done to create an environment that for some better reflects the real world, advances a certain set of values, helps to improve the financial viability of a particular institution, creates winning or successful athletic or academic programs, or generates a set of social connections that may prove to be invaluable at some point later in life.[30]

However, rather than viewing the educational process as a source of value creation that can motivate a rethinking of the pricing model, institutions still view themselves as entities that confer degrees, a set of support services designed to ensure that students reach that goal, and in some cases, the producers of research designed to increase knowledge for society as a whole. Thus the revenue model envisioned by most administrators consists of tuition to finance the cost of instruction, fees to defer the cost of student services, and research grants to offset the cost of creating knowledge.

It is not that there is something necessarily wrong with such a pricing model, but rather, it is one that does not recognize how new sources of value could be created and unlocked with changes in the learning experience that focuses more on process than outcomes. As currently structured, institutions of higher learning are limited in what they can charge not because of the degree of competition that exists in the industry, but because of their narrow view toward value creation that keeps them following traditional pricing patterns.

The Game of Chess (Again)

Viewed from a conventional business lens, the game of chess represents the same opportunities that currently exist in any industry. They include opportunities such as

1. providing the physical chess set itself along with the rules of the game;
2. offering instruction for better game play;
3. creating a place to play (whether physical or electronic) and opponents for continued game play;
4. generating innovation that keeps the game fresh and makes possible extensions that preserve or expand interest in the game;
5. efforts to place the game in a broader context (e.g., tournaments) that enhance the benefits associated with play.

Any of these elements present an opportunity for entry and the subsequent development of a successful business proposition. However, what is important to remember is that how enjoyable the game is to play depends not on the quality of the board or pieces. Nor does it depend entirely on the rules or anything that the initial designer of the game has done. Rather it emerges from the quality of the game play itself. Putting together two equally matched opponents who can challenge each other; thereby creating an experience that best fulfills the needs or desires of the players is the key to understanding the value creation process. It is something that emerges from the play itself and is not embedded within the game.

Thus what begins as a modest attempt to create a new business opportunity encompassing an old game, could, with the right amount of imagination, turn into a major business enterprise. The same holds true for higher education. However, the key rests not in the monetization of past practices but in creating a value proposition designed for a very different future.

CHAPTER 3

Gamification as a Business Strategy

If a rising tide lifts all boats, what should one do when the tide is falling and potentially may never rise again? Often when we read about the current crisis in higher education, the focus is on the curriculum. It is essentially a critique of current teaching practices and the growing disconnect between the requirements of the real world and current learning objectives. We tend not to think of higher education as a business, but rather as an institution that is exempt from the challenges faced by most other businesses. However, universities are not immune from the same market forces that guide other industries and an understanding of how businesses have evolved over time can provide us with key insights about why the game industry might provide higher education with the best path to a prosperous future.

To understand the potential of gamification as a business strategy, we need to look more closely at those forces that have previously shaped the business enterprise in general. In doing so, it will be possible to obtain a better understanding of how colleges and universities are going to thrive in a shrinking market. To accomplish this, we will see how the development of the modern enterprise has laid the groundwork for the creation of a new strategy based on the principles of gamification.

A new strategy for higher education that is not predicated on the abandonment of its bricks and mortar infrastructure, nor one that will require it turn aside hundreds of years of tradition. Rather, it will leverage existing advantages by strengthening the student experience in order to unlock existing value from assets that have been underutilized within the current structure of higher education.

The Structure of the Modern Business Enterprise

Some of the issues facing higher education today can be attributed to the development of the modern business enterprises in the twentieth century.[1] The production of large volumes of a single product drove down the cost per unit of output enabling the firm to enjoy what have become known as economies of scale. This fostered a common belief around the turn of the twentieth century that bigger was definitely better.

Of course, producing a large volume of goods only makes sense if there is a customer for each unit that is produced. As Adam Smith noted over a hundred years ago, the benefits from large-scale production are limited by the extent of the market; you can only produce large volumes if you have the customers to purchase all of that output.[2] By expanding their scope of operations beyond a narrow geographic region, firms discovered they could find customers in sufficient numbers to drive deep reductions in the cost of production. With the realization of economies of scope, firms were able to achieve ever larger economies of scale and as a result, greatly expand the amount of profit earned.

To secure the volumes needed to realize these economies, businessmen such as Henry Ford were forced to integrate into the production of raw materials and the distribution of finished products. If firms could not obtain all of the raw materials or intermediate goods required for the large-scale manufacture of a particular product, those economies of scale would remain illusory at best. Hence companies like Ford not only produced cars but also engaged in the production of glass, steel, and other important materials needed in order to keep its assembly line running.[3]

While physical capital was an important part of the production of goods like automobiles, over the course of the twentieth century, human capital has grown in importance. Intellectual property has replaced physical capital as the primary means for generating profits. Thus many of the more successful companies today do not manufacture anything, or if manufacturing is to be done, it is outsourced to a contract manufacturer.[4] Human capital has supplanted physical capital as the major source of value creation within many firms today.[5] Instead of needing to generate large economies of scale and scope to spread out the cost of an expensive physical infrastructure, it is more important today to try and spread the cost of human capital over the largest possible volume of output.

What has made this possible is the emergence of product platforms based on industry standards.[6] Platforms provide commonly accepted connecting points that promote greater specialization. A firm need only focus on developing and producing a single module that can plug into the platform, rather than having to produce every facet associated with a particular product.[7] By expanding the division of labor, additional value is generated that can be enjoyed by the developer and each company that contributes something to the platform.

Think about it in terms of vehicle navigation systems. Automobile companies try to compete based on a number of different factors. Styling, performance, and price are just some of the ways that automobile companies differentiate models within a family or between families of cars. More recently, technology, particularly in the area of navigation systems, has been an effective way to differentiate products and create additional value.

Prior to the widespread adoption of smartphones, car companies had the navigation space largely to themselves. Sure there were specialized GPS devices that could function as a substitute, but the use of external devices could not offer the same seamless integrated experience. As a result, customers were willing to pay a premium to have a factory navigation system installed in their vehicles.

All of that changed with the smartphone. As smartphones replaced built-in audio systems as the hub for their listening systems, it was only natural to extend the reach of the technology to also serve as a GPS device. As it became more common to connect an external device to an automobile's internal system, customers began to appreciate the additional functionality provided by their smartphone devices. Better maps with a greater level of detail, voice programmable features, and better integration with the user's life outside the automobile offered a superior value proposition.

To compete, the auto companies have had to embrace the technologies contained in smartphone ecosystems, while still exploring ways to take readily available technologies and turn them into a source for competitive advantage. Realizing that they will never have the resources to offer something comparable to Google Maps, automobile companies are now focused on improving the usability of open versus proprietary technologies. They have come to the realization that the source of their competitive advantage and hence ability to add customer value is not in trying to develop the best proprietary technology, but rather in the application of superior technologies that are embedded in generally available products. Competition has shifted from the technology itself to the quality of the user experience.[8]

Thus we see an interesting situation develop where instead of vigorously protecting their intellectual property firms willingly give it away or license it at a very low price.[9] They give it away because opening up a particular platform makes it more amenable to the creation of those family effects that may contribute more value than any monopoly power that might exist from defending a particular innovation from any and all who want to copy it. Sales increase not because the product itself has changed, but rather it has become more valuable through the efforts of others.[10] It has become part of a product ecosystem.

In markets where products are defined by membership in a particular ecosystem, the key is no longer to create the dominant product, but instead the dominant platform that can transcend a single industry. Thus what differentiates the firm in the twenty-first from the twentieth century is that capital is no longer seen as an investment in a bricks and mortar infrastructure that serves to make the labor hired by the firm more productive, but rather as a mechanism for reaching beyond the boundaries of the firm in order to leverage the efforts of others. By enabling firms to expand their scope outside the walls that have been created to house their own inputs, firms can capture the benefits associated with a further expansion in the division of labor. No longer limited by the resources they own or control through a formal employment contract, firms can harness the special talents and abilities of a broader range of contributors by leveraging the power of the crowd though the creation of an ecosystem.[11]

Higher Education as a Business

It is easy to think that higher education is immune from those forces that have driven the development of the modern business enterprise.[12]

After all, the social and economic benefits are substantial. Education not only increases the productivity of labor, but as importantly, contributes toward the development of a rich and vibrant culture.[13]

Both critics and apologists in the nineteenth century were troubled by the factory system and the toll it took on the individual, family, and society as a whole.[14] Working from sun up to sun down with not much more to show than enough to survive for one more day, it seemed that capitalism was just a new form of economic slavery. However, increases in productivity and the corresponding rise in wages changed all of that.[15] It became possible for life to take on a richness that transcended the economic necessity of work. Thus higher education became an important avenue for future economic prosperity through the development of human capital and a richer society by promoting the development of human knowledge and understanding.

Higher education was seen as part of a virtuous circle where growth in the creation and dissemination of knowledge led to social and economic gains that could in turn be used to fund further expansions. The industrial revolution had triggered a substantial increase in wealth making it possible for governments to make larger investments in public education. States made a conscious decision to invest in higher education because they believed that the tax dollars spent would be returned to refill state coffers as students entered the work force, moved up the ladder, and enjoyed good paying jobs.[16]

However, if education was to become an engine for economic growth, the knowledge that would be disseminated within its hallowed halls would need to be current and up-to-date. Moreover, just as Henry Ford needed to be assured a steady supply of tires, windshields, and other component parts in order to keep his assembly lines humming, the same was true for large public universities. Hence in a similar way, universities integrated upstream into research activities not only to enhance their public mission but also to generate content for their classrooms.[17]

Universities were quick to learn that knowledge creation is much more expensive than its dissemination. To spread the high fixed costs, universities expanded in size in order to capture economies of scale and scope.[18] In doing so, it was hoped that the university could become a cost effective means for both creating and disseminating knowledge. It would become an economical mechanism for creating new ideas and by opening doors to a larger population, create a pool of human capital that would effectively raise the rate of growth in the local, state, and national economy.

The lessons of modern industry have shown how higher education can achieve efficiencies by turning to those same management practices that had generated substantial economies of scale in private enterprise. Hence the structure of the education process shifted from an apprenticeship model based on individual instruction to a more universal model based on standardized courses that could be delivered economically via lecture to large numbers of students.[19]

Through a curriculum comprised of standard courses that were designed to deliver a tightly constructed quantity of knowledge pertaining to a specific topic, institutions could take a building block approach that would enable them to realize whatever economies of scale might exist in the education process. Scale could be achieved by delivering these standard building blocks to the largest possible audiences limited by nothing more than the size of the classroom. Universities could avoid the criticism of taking a one size fits all approach by allowing students to mix and match various building blocks in order to specialize in a particular subject.

Perhaps the best way to understand this transformation is to think about the rise of the modern textbook. A textbook is a low cost platform for delivering a set amount of information. It reduces the cost of acquiring, organizing, compiling, and delivering information about a particular subject. It greatly reduces the amount of time that a professor must spend in class preparation thus freeing up time to grade additional papers or offer supplementary lectures. In this way, it is similar to other platforms that standardize a process or body of knowledge in order to advance the division of labor and achieve economies of scale. Without the textbook and the invention of the lecture, it would be difficult to scale up the education process and obtain the requisite size required to make education affordable to a large number of students.

Learning Platforms and Ecosystems

New economic realities are prompting colleges and universities to look for innovative distribution channels that can help reduce the cost of delivering an education. This has led to a growing interest in the online delivery of course instruction in an effort to generate even greater economies of scale and scope. By eliminating the constraint associated with the physical size of a classroom, it becomes possible to deliver courses to an even larger audience dispersed over a broader geographic space. By detaching the delivery of instruction from physical time and space, it makes it relatively inexpensive for universities to expand their reach into new potential student populations. The ability to realize greater economies of scale and new economies of scope is the engine that is propelling the large expansion into online education.[20]

With the introduction of a potentially disruptive technology such as e-learning, it is perhaps not surprising that some are ready to proclaim the death of higher education as we know it. But what exactly is it disrupting? Is it a new distribution channel that offers the potential for replacing the traditional bricks and mortar college or university? Alternatively, is it instead a means for offering educational services to whomever wants them at any time and in any place?

Visions of universities freed from the tether of bricks and mortar, curricula no longer limited by the faculty who are in residence at a particular location, and a shakeout leading to a consolidation in the number of subjects that can be offered are all causes for concern. However, just as the development of new mediums for the delivery of games has not led to the end of traditional games, the same may hold true for higher education.

The true potential of e-learning is not in its effect on the cost structure of the university. Nor is it the new opportunities that are created for students to dip in and purchase those components needed to provide the training/learning that is necessary to accomplish a particular objective. Rather it is the potential for the creation of a digital learning platform with a supporting educational ecosystem. E-learning affords the opportunity to share the expertise of a faculty member with larger groups of students at their home institution, at other institutions within a system, or between traditional competitors who now find themselves in the role of collaborative partners.

Utilizing the flexibility created by e-learning, an entire curriculum can now be constructed around some obscure topic because a single institution no longer must hire all of the scholars in that field. What had not been financially viable in the past now becomes a significant opportunity because scholars from multiple institutions can be combined to offer a single degree program without having an individual institution bear all of the costs.

The creation of learning platforms offers a potentially new value proposition that can turn the disruptive force of technological change into a powerful one that can improve rather than weaken traditional institutions of higher learning. The future will not be found with institutions that offer a collection of courses offered by their own tenured faculty, but rather with the one that offers a coherent program made up of the contributions of a large family of scholars. While it may be true that in a competitive market comprised of online courses, the price of a single one may fall to its marginal cost, it will not be true of an integrated curriculum that is challenging to assemble, assess, and certify. The future will be all about the platform rather than the course.

A learning platform can turn out to be even more valuable if it becomes the foundation of an educational ecosystem. Such an ecosystem will consist of the contributions of not only academics but also practitioners, students, and others who have an interest in a particular body of knowledge. An ecosystem that is up-to-date and welcomes the contributions of those who have specific knowledge that has not been readily disseminated or is widely available could, with the right connections, enrich the learning platform.

Today, the role of a professor has changed in many ways from the originator of knowledge to a filter that assesses and evaluates the knowledge of others. Where in the past the student was exposed to ideas through the writings of their professor and the books that were suggested for them to read, today knowledge takes on many forms and can be found in a multitude of places. In some ways, the limited world of the academic has been widened to incorporate all of the knowledge that exists within society.

This change has created a number of issues. Instead of developing a curriculum based on the knowledge of a carefully selected group of individuals, it is now only limited by the extent of knowledge as we know it at a specific point in time. No longer is it about bringing together the right people within a limited set of choices. It is now about assembling the best set of ideas from a vast supply of choices. As such, something or someone is needed to make sense of the full extent of knowledge as it currently is embodied in a wide variety of media, sources, and individuals. Constructing an ecosystem based on a subset of ideas that exist from multiple sources, organized into a coherent and meaningful whole, and delivered in a manner that makes it understandable, has the power to make what students learn more current, meaningful, and of greater value. While the role of the professor may change, it becomes more relevant and plays a more important role when the scale and scope of learning expands beyond the limits of an individual institution.

Moving Beyond the Ivory Tower

Rather than thinking about bricks and mortar as the means for creating an ivory tower that stands isolated and apart from everything else, adopting a game perspective offers a different glimpse of how that tower can be converted into a village that plays a central role in a community. After all, the main role of an institution of higher learning is to serve the community by conferring various benefits that enhance culture, provide the glue for developing closer social bonds, advance civilization, and serve as an engine for economic growth. Gamification provides us with insights into how we might take all of this one step further.

One of the central concepts underlying the notion of a market economy is that specialization has the ability to divide labor into the smallest possible component. This is done in order to provide the best match between the requirements needed to perform a particular function and the capabilities required to carry it out in the most efficient manner possible. By dividing a problem into its constituent parts, one can take advantage of the different expertise and skills needed to handle each part. In the past, such skills and expertise were limited to a small number of individuals. However, by breaking problems down into even smaller parts, it became possible to micro target individuals who possessed the key to unlocking the smallest fraction of what was required to reach a more global solution. Moreover, by reducing the requirements of what was expected from an individual participant, it became possible to expand the pool of potential contributors. Hence complex problems were no longer the purview of a select minority, but rather entered a broader public sphere where individual limitation became less important because of the sheer increase in numbers of individuals who were now able to make a contribution.

This is the central idea behind what has become known as crowd-sourcing.[21] It is based on the principle that if you can expand the number of participants to the point where you can reach a critical mass, the crowd will possess a large enough variety of talents to solve complex problems. However, in order for crowdsourcing to be effective, some mechanism, shared set of values, or common objectives must exist that brings people together in sufficient numbers with the right set of talents.

In order for crowdsourcing to occur, three elements must be in place. First, something needs to draw people together. Second, something must identify the different skills and abilities in the population of potential participants. Third, something is needed to create a match between a particular aspect of the problem with the person who has the right combination of talent and ability to solve it.

While we like to think that crowdsourcing is something new, it is nothing more than a modern interpretation of an old idea. One can think of the emergence of the market as an example of crowdsourcing. Individuals come together in a central location to achieve an efficient allocation of goods or resources. The larger the number of participants, the greater the division of labor and hence the richer the mix that is brought to the market for trade. The power of the market as a coordination mechanism is based on Adam Smith's notion of the invisible hand. Embedded in Smith's concept is the principle that individuals do not need to be directed when it comes time to decide what to produce or how much to buy. Rather, within the context of a market, prices will adjust as if they were guided by an invisible hand and as a result, an efficient allocation will be achieved.[22]

However, the power of large numbers is not something that is restricted to the existence of markets. Think back to the emergence of the factory system and the gains in efficiency that accrued with a corresponding expansion in the division of labor. Through specialization, different skills and abilities were directed toward different steps in the production process in an effort to place individuals with specific skills into those job functions where they would be most productive. With an expansion in the size of the operation, more steps could be subdivided and with an expansion in the pool of individuals to draw from, more specialized talent could be brought to bear on even more specific aspects of the production process.

The difference between a product created in a factory and one that is crowdsourced is that in the former case, coordination is supplied by managers. In the latter case, it is provided by a structure that emerges spontaneously through the actions of the crowd.[23]

By its very structure, academia is the furthest thing one might find from the principles underlying the concept of crowdsourcing. Success in academia arises largely from individual achievement that promotes specialization in a single area. Years are spent gaining very specific knowledge for subsequent dissemination through publication in specialized journals. Reputations are not built on how many areas one can touch through their research, but instead, how deeply one can go with respect to a narrowly defined area within the context of a single discipline. Divided into academic departments populated by professors who have expertise within a particular discipline, courses are combined to create a major that forms that foundation for an education.

From the standpoint of the traditional structure of higher education, the power of the crowd has little to do with the provision of an education. A loose confederation of what, at times, seems like a collection of independent contractors, a university's success is often dependent on the accomplishments of each faculty member. Hence the focus is on supporting individual effort in the hope that sufficient numbers can be assembled under one umbrella to attract the best students, the most research dollars, and the largest alumni contributions.

All of this ignores the power of crowdsourcing and the additional talent that resides on campus in order to create new revenue streams for the institution. By bringing all of the talent to bear on real problems, it may be possible for universities to go beyond tuition as the major source of revenue. It is here that games as a crowdsourcing mechanism may provide a way to expand the mission of a university.

In discussing the efforts of a group of University of Washington researchers to tap into the power of the crowd, to solve what had been an elusive problem, using the game Foldit, Jeff Howe wrote in Slate Magazine:

> The best way to match talent to task, at least in the world of nano-biotechnology, isn't to assign the fanciest degrees to the toughest jobs, but rather to observe the behavior of thousands of people and identify those who show the greatest aptitude for the cognitive skills that task requires.... They are able, in other words, to match talent to task with exceptional efficiency. Not based on someone's CV, and not based on the magic of "self-selection," but rather through the thousands of data points generated by the gameplay.[24]

Crowdsourcing the collective intelligence that exists on a university campus may create a new role that can harness the resources of the institution to tackle meaningful problems. It would not only leave the world a little bit better but also build a stronger case for external support. However, it is one thing to say that a great deal of talent exists for crowdsourced solutions to emerge, while it is another to create the institutional support required to turn that into a reality.

Economists like to point to the market as a superior coordinating mechanism because price is all that is required to bring independent buyers and sellers together to efficiently allocate resources. However, when we talk about crowdsourcing a solution to a problem, it is the bringing together of skills rather than resources that becomes the path for reaching a desired objective.

Think about the firm that looks to hire a pool of talent with the appropriate skills to produce a particular product. Managers might scour resumes looking for particular experiences in a past work history or courses taken in a college transcript in order to gain some sense of whether a particular individual might possess the necessary skills or knowledge to make a contribution to the team that is being assembled. However, items on a resume serve as a proxy for what a particular candidate may or may not possess. Thus the extent to which he or she can make a particular contribution is filled with a great deal of guess work.

Contrast that with the potential of a game where play builds those skills that may be useful for accomplishing a specific objective. Whether or not a person has acquired the requisite skills is not the subject of guesswork, but rather would be open for all to see. Achievements are earned within a context that all would experience and could be evaluated in the present rather than the past. Most importantly, the structure of the game would create a framework where developed skills could be applied to specific challenges that by design, offer the potential to unravel a more global problem.

The design of such a game would need to incorporate the following elements:

1. A *meaningful goal* that serves to motivate the desire to solve a particular problem.
2. An *opportunity* to develop those skills that will be required to reach a resolution of the problem.

3. A means for *identifying* the myriad of skills and abilities that exist.
4. A *mechanism* for matching skills to requirements.
5. The *application* of skills to reach a solution.
6. A way to *celebrate* when the mission has been accomplished.

Examples of the power of games to create a disaggregated approach to problem solving are becoming more widespread. There is no reason therefore to think that they could not serve as a coordinating mechanism that could harness the talent of faculty and students to organically solve problems. However, to reach that point, games have to become part of the culture of an institution and integrated within a cohesive student experience.

Gamification as a Business Strategy

When thinking about gamification as a business strategy for higher education, we can draw an association between the various elements that define the student experience and those of a game. The curriculum could be conceived as being the equivalent of the pieces or objects of the game. It is a collection of courses that are arranged to provide a set of outcomes that prepares the student to become a more productive member of society. The learning platform is the equivalent of the rules that define how the pieces can be arranged and moved in order to generate various outcomes. It sets the pace, tempo and nature of play as it occurs. Finally, the educational ecosystem is the equivalent of the board, virtual world, or series of screens that creates an environment that stimulates the imagination and defines how play relates to the external world. Together, all three elements define the student/player experience, what they achieve, the skills they build, and the enjoyment that comes from play. The general structure is illustrated in Figure 3.1.

The goal of successful game design is to create meaningful play.[25] If only the same could be said of higher education, then perhaps it would achieve a greater level of success. Take a look at the current approach toward the student experience. While opportunities for social interaction are plentiful, they are not structured in a way that encourages skill building. Having some impact on the development of the student, they perhaps better represent a missed chance for enhancing the classroom experience.

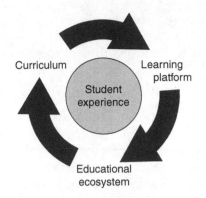

Figure 3.1

Opportunities abound outside the classroom. It could be something as simple as learning how to get along with a roommate, the other residents on the floor of your dorm, becoming part of an extracurricular club, or finding people to hang out with on a Saturday night. The entire campus can be viewed as a potential learning opportunity, but in contrast to the classroom, there is little direction, visible means of accomplishment, or an understanding of purpose. Left to fend for themselves, students can glean something out of the experience, but only scratch the surface in terms of mining what value exists in learning from the student experience.

There is no single assessment measure or objective standard for evaluating performance. As a result, it is difficult for the student to internalize success in a meaningful way. Coupled with the challenges involved in making relevant comparisons with others, it becomes very difficult for students to build self-esteem. Rather than one success building on another to develop a more knowledgeable and confident student, environmental factors instead have the exact opposite effect.

A sense of self is not developed in a social vacuum. With restrictions like the Buckley Amendment, it makes it difficult for students to achieve status among their peers and help to develop self-esteem.[26] Yes, while it is true that they might be recognized once a semester having achieved the Dean's list, for everyone else, there is little if any academic recognition. As a result, it should come as no surprise that students look to achieve status in other ways. How many beers one drank last Friday night, how many parties one has attended, the number of sexual conquests, or other such things take center stage by becoming measurable achievements capable of conferring status. It is not because they are more important, but rather because they are the only things that can easily be compared and hence form the basis for making relative comparisons. College students are not exempt from wanting to build self-esteem, they are just limited in terms of how that can be accomplished and hence in the defense of privacy, those socially less desirable characteristics achieve a disproportionate share of importance.

Using game design principles, university administrators can create an integrated experience that ties the classroom together with student life. Knowledge acquisition, rather than an end to itself, can become a means for enhancing the development of the individual and as a result, the quality of the entire student experience. Experiences that are able to engage multiple facets can lead to better learning outcomes and thus help to create individuals who are better prepared to make a significant contribution once they graduate. However, for many, this will require a rethinking of the modern university.

For those institutions that call themselves research universities, the name of the game has been all about expanding knowledge. Here the student is often merely a passenger along for the ride or a form of cheap labor to further the research aspirations of an individual professor. Gamification does not mean the end of the research university. Rather it provides a strategy for preserving the research university.

In an increasingly competitive environment characterized by skyrocketing costs, universities regardless of rank or aspirations will need to be more attentive to their student population in an effort to ensure that the value they generate is at least equal to the growing commitment to take on debt. Gamification is not a solution that merely layers on additional costs and therefore requires institutions to abandon something in return. Rather it is a strategy for rationalizing what they already do. It is a mechanism for taking organized chaos and turning into a means for generating additional value.

The Power of Bricks and Mortar

In an educational environment that is increasingly coming to be dominated by the disruptive effects of technology, it is easy to think of the physical infrastructure embodied in bricks and mortar as an outdated and outmoded cost center whose time has come and gone. However, jumping to such a hasty conclusion would involve making a giant mistake. We need just look at the strategy driving Valve Corporation to gain some insight into the very important role that physical infrastructure could play in a space that does not require any sort of physical presence whatsoever. In this way, it may become easier for nervous administrators to embrace rather than resist efforts to reach beyond the traditional boundaries of their institution.

Valve Corporation is a privately held firm that develops games such as Portal, Team Fortress 2, Half Life, and Left 4 Dead. With its social entertainment platform Steam, Valve Corporation is the largest distributor of digital games in the world. Finally, with the development of technologies like its Source Game Engine, Valve is powering not only the development of its own titles, but many others as well. Forbes magazine has estimated that Valve Corporation is worth somewhere in the neighborhood of three billion dollars.[27]

Recently Valve has announced its entry into the hardware business with the upcoming Steambox. Why are they doing that? To increase market share by offering a comprehensive solution would be one explanation. To solve technological hurdles that prevents some from participating is another possible answer. However, in an industry where the business model is to lower prices in order to gain market share, the problem is that the more prices are lowered, the greater the effort required to merely maintain whatever profits currently exist. The only way to get ahead is to increase the value proposition and the way that holds the greatest promise is by controlling the experience.

Valve is not entering the hardware business because it is a winning proposition. There already exists a long list of companies that have tried and failed to win the hearts and minds of gamers in the hardware end of the business. However, if it was just about hardware, then it would probably be only a question of time before this over reach comes back to haunt the company. It is not that one can make money off of the hardware itself, but rather the hardware creates new opportunities for avoiding the consequences of a downward price spiral.

In higher education, much of the learning experience actually takes place outside the classroom. Sure it is possible to recreate some of this within a content management system such as Blackboard. However, the experience only lasts for as long as the student is logged in. It is far from an immersive experience and is handicapped by the brief time the average student spends connected to this somewhat sterile environment. Think of the experience many have learning a foreign language. While a number of great interactive software packages exist and when coupled with a classroom where students can practice speaking to their classmates positive learning outcomes can be achieved, it all pales in comparison to an immersive experience where the language is spoken 24/7 within a backdrop of a rich culture and foreign atmosphere that helps to reinforce and provide meaning and context for the language.

In a similar way, a bricks and mortar university can have a significant advantage if it is able to leverage those assets to create an immersive environment that not only reinforces what happens in the classroom but also helps to shape the development of the student. Bricks and mortar serve a vital function when the goal shifts from mastering a body of knowledge to reshaping students into effective learners who have the requisite skills to acquire whatever knowledge is required to be successful both now and for the rest of their lives.

However, this can only occur if the bricks and mortar are assigned a role that goes beyond creating a desirable looking back drop. It is easy to sit back and proclaim something to be a strategic asset as had been the case when bricks and mortar were a required element for populating physical classrooms. However, with the rise of the virtual classroom, that is no longer the case. Rather than serving as a funnel that effectively keeps at bay the outside world, bricks and mortar will only have value when it contributes to the richness of an institution's learning platform in a meaningful way.

PART II

Gaming Fundamentals

CHAPTER 4

The Allure of Games

Our media-driven culture is constantly inundating us with messages and symbols that represent idealized types rather than actual human beings. Take, for example, the photo of your favorite celebrity who appears on the cover of a magazine. Rarely does the digitally altered/enhanced image that was taken under the most ideal of conditions match the way that person actually looks on a typical day under normal circumstances. Yet the reality that we create for ourselves is based on the images that we see and not the "truth" as it actually exists. Hence we strive to become something that is unattainable and we accept standards that are not very realistic.

For this reason alone, it should not come as any surprise that virtual worlds are so appealing to many. In a virtual world, a person is no longer constrained by their genes, circumstances, or socioeconomic status. They can become whoever they wish to be. The only limitations are the result of their time, willingness, and ability to fashion themselves into the persona that they have always wanted to become. They effectively can become a character that conforms to those social norms that they most highly value.

The same holds true for many college students who would rather sit in their dorm room playing games than going out and interacting with a world filled with constant disappointment.[1] While an abundance of options exist whether in terms of course selection, a leisure activity, or hanging out with friends, rarely is the student able to become the person they want to be. Instead, they are stuck with being the person that they actually are.

Life Stories

In the alternate reality game Evoke, players embark on missions in an effort to tackle meaningful real-world problems. To prepare the player for mission success, they undertake quests. These quests are designed to help develop an origin story. The origin story serves an important role in the design of the game. It serves as a framework that provides context for the acquisition of "super" powers. These powers embody the skills and abilities needed to successfully complete missions. Missions are the tool that the designers use to teach awareness of important social issues and empower the player to take positive action.[2]

The goal of Evoke and other similar games is to create what Jane McGonigal describes as "super empowered hopeful individuals." In her view of an alternate reality, gamers use their collective intelligence to solve real world problems. From her perspective, the true power of games is empowerment as reflected in the development of a set of skills and social conscience that both motivates and enables a single individual to make a difference.

For many educators, McGonigal's aspirations for gamers are consistent with their idealized conception of higher education. It is about taking young minds and giving them a perspective, exposure to ideas, and a conscience. It is about helping students embark on the formation of their own life story.[3]

For many, the development of a life story follows the same basic structure. That pattern is illustrated in the following sequence:

I want to establish a *place* for myself in the world.
That place has to have *meaning* and be significant to me.
To discover that place I must have the *freedom* to explore.
As I *journey* toward that place, I discover new things about myself.

In developing a sense of self, I *strive* to become a better and more successful me.
Success is reflected in the *achievements* I earn.
It confers *status* that makes me feel better about myself.
Gaining *self-esteem* makes me more confident.
Feeling more confident empowers me to challenge myself and *learn* even more.

While we might like to think of a life story as being linear in structure because it begins at birth and ends with death, it is instead a virtuous circle that merrily roles down the path of life. The pattern repeats itself over and over again as one milestone is reached and another appears in the not too distant future. Hence the development of a life story takes on more of the form of a virtuous circle. The concept of a virtuous circle is illustrated in Figure 4.1.

Economists are particularly fond of virtuous circles because they represent self-reinforcing patterns that lead to positive outcomes. For example, increases in planned spending prompts firms to expand output which in turn leads them to hire more workers thereby leading to further increases in spending. Guided by the invisible hand of the market, the economy grows as the circle expands.

The same can be said of the virtuous circle identified here. A greater sense of place leads to success that promotes confidence. Confidence empowers the individual to take more risks and as result, push themselves to explore and learn new things. As their knowledge about the world in which they live expands, they are able to develop a stronger sense of their place in the world and cultivate more secure identities. As their sense of self becomes more secure, they are willing and able to start the whole process over again. Thus, a stronger sense of self leads to increases in learning and an expansion of knowledge which in turn generate a greater understanding of self.

Virtuous circle

Figure 4.1

To better understand how a virtuous circle can turn students who develop a greater sense of self into better learners, we need to explore each component of the circle individually. By deconstructing the circle into its component parts, we can construct a better understanding of why games have such a strong appeal.[4]

Place

Who am I? For college students, this is perhaps the most important question as they strive in a period of four short years to not only gain a greater sense of who they are, but who they want to become. Establishing a place is the first step toward creating an identity that can serve as the foundation for building a life.[5]

It is not all that different from the online game that begins with the player creating an identity.[6] For some games, all that is required is a gamer tag (name) that serves as an identifier for the player. However, many games offer much more than just the choice of a name. In some games, players are able to create an avatar that can communicate more than just a name. An avatar is a digital representation of the player that possesses a particular look, expresses various characteristics, and can grow and develop over time. It can be a close representation of the player or it can be aspirational and embody those characteristics that the player wishes that she possessed.

Recent research suggests that avatars in virtual worlds provide an opportunity for an individual to "try on different hats" in an effort to enable players to assume characteristics they would like to have.[7] This enhances the enjoyment derived from a game because it gives the player the opportunity to act like the person they want to be rather than as they actually are.[8] For example, an overweight person can be thin, a shy person can be outgoing, a woman can become a man, a weak person can be strong, or a follower can now become a leader.

While we might like to think that this is nothing more than fantasy and hence does not have any influence on self-image, other research suggests the opposite.[9] Human beings have difficulty drawing firm lines between physical and virtual reality. As a result, they begin to think that the identities they create in virtual worlds are real. Dubbed as the Proteus effect, researchers discovered that individuals with avatars that were taller in height acted with more self-confidence.[10]

Even more striking was the observation that perceptions based on online personas also influenced real world behavior.[11]

The Proteus effect sheds light on why some players are willing to pay real money for virtual goods. Many game environments emulate the real world in that avatars perform some work, earn a reward and then spend that reward on virtual goods. Since behavior in their "second life" mirrors actions in the real world, it should come as no surprise that for many, the digital world becomes just as real as the one in which they normally live.

Meaning

Traditionally, a sense of purpose and meaning has become entwined in one's life story or the story of a particular social group or entire civilization.[12] Story can serve as the source of context to justify or legitimate one's actions.[13] It can also illustrate the road taken to personal success. Thus it is perhaps ironic that the student who is exposed during the course of their university education to many stories, is not really all that aware that they are in the process of constructing their own story with the power to provide meaning and a sense of purpose to their own personal journey.

Creating meaning and a sense of purpose moves hand and hand with the formation of what behavioral economists have referred to as an anchor.[14] When one thinks of an anchor, they generally think of a hunk of steel that is attached to a ship via a cable that when thrown overboard, holds the ship in place. When applying the concept to human behavior, it can be thought of as functioning in a manner similar to a compass. A traditional compass is a device that identifies which direction is true north. Once the compass has been anchored to that direction, it becomes possible to identify other directions as deviations from true north.

When each direction looks the same and it is difficult to determine which way is forward and which way is back, it becomes challenging to move at all. When life has meaning and individuals have a sense of purpose, they become empowered to take action because they now have a sense of which way is forward. However, it does not have to be characterized in such larger than life terms. The value of an anchor can be found in all facets of life. You often see it when it comes time to buy something at what is billed as a discounted price.

It is difficult to distinguish whether it is being sold at a bargain price without at the same time knowing the retail or what is commonly referred to as the reference price of a good (the price it is commonly sold at). This reference price serves as an anchor (basis for comparison) that enables the consumer to evaluate the quality of the "deal" that is being offered.

Just as life choices are easier to make with an anchor on board, the same holds true for students. Much is made of the influence of liberal thinking on college campuses and the vulnerability of young minds to the potentially corrupting influence of their professors.[15] Rather than debating whether or not there is a disproportionate liberal or conservative influence on college campuses, the more important point is to ask why it is so easy to influence the minds of college students. As a sense of self and place is being developed, students are at the same time struggling to obtain some sense of meaning and purpose. Thus, it should come as no surprise that the antiwar demonstrations in the 1960s started on college campuses. Nor should it come as any surprise that sustainability has become the dominant ideology on college campuses today.

In a complex and confusing world, we all need to have our lives anchored to some belief system that can help us to make good choices.[16] Without such an anchor, it is easy to see why many students appear as if they are adrift and hence either find it difficult to make choices or often select the wrong one. In fact, when it is difficult to determine up from down, the smart strategy is often to maintain the status quo because at least one (hopefully) knows that they are right side up.[17] Hence without some meaning to life, there is no reason to study and work hard because without a clear payoff, it is easy to do what is most enjoyable regardless of whether or not it amounts to much. Without a sense of where one is going, it becomes difficult to appreciate the ride, so it seems better to camp out and enjoy your time in the station.

Thus it should not come as a surprise that many students would rather spend the bulk of their time in a virtual world that is in part of their own making than the comings and goings of a college campus where they feel a little lost. In the virtual game world, it is not only easier to identify the good from the bad, but there is often some overriding theme that provides both context and meaning to the game. Hence one can more easily establish a place within a larger order where action has meaning and purpose.

Freedom

Each individual is different and the answer for one is rarely the same for another. Given that one size most definitely does not fit all, students must be given the freedom to explore a variety of options if they are to find the one that fits best.[18]

Human beings are naturally curious and seek out avenues for satisfying their curiosity by exploring their environment. George Loewenstein explains curiosity as the response to an information gap that exists between what one knows and what one wants to know.[19] When a gap exists between the two, this creates a level of dissatisfaction that promotes discovery and exploration. Discovering new things by engaging in exploration can alleviate boredom and create greater satisfaction.

That being said, too many possibilities can have the exact opposite effect. Individuals like having the freedom to pursue choices of their own making. However, if too many choices exist, this can lead to anxiety and ultimately inaction. Individuals can become frozen when they have too many choices. Unable to decide, they end up doing nothing.[20] Hence an ideal environment contains some freedom so that an individual can achieve a certain level of autonomy thereby making their own choices, but not have too many choices such that it becomes difficult to decide between alternatives.

The concept of there being an optimal number of choices can be tied back to Herbert Simon's concept of Bounded Rationality.[21] Simon believed that the brain was capable of acquiring and processing only so much information. Hence instead of using the entire information set, agents only use a portion when making decisions. Thus, human beings place natural boundaries on their thought processes in order to make the world a manageable place that does not lead to paralysis as the result of information overload.

The challenge for the traditional educational process is not that there is too much information out there (though this has become more of a problem in the age of the Internet), but rather that the traditional course utilizing a textbook and a fixed syllabus narrows the choice field too much. When the student is under the strict direction of the professor, there is not a lot of opportunity for self-directed learning. The lack of autonomy adversely affects the ability to form an identity and thus learning becomes more about the subject and less about the individual.

The advantage of virtual worlds is that they create a controlled environment that allows autonomy and freedom of action, but within prescribed limits that do not cross the bounds of human understanding. The virtual world has limits and as long as those limits are sufficiently flexible and capable of expansion, the player is not overwhelmed. More importantly, the player feels in control. This might potentially explain why game environments are preferred to real life. Choices become manageable as players are free to discover new things but are not so overwhelmed by the possibilities that they cannot act.

Journey

Identities are not created in a day, nor are they the result of one or two events. Rather they emerge as part of a long process. While we all might wish that life could be as simple as a Harry Potter movie where all it takes to reveal our true place in the world is to put on a sorting hat. Most only discover where they truly belong after confronting a series of challenges that helps shape who they are and ultimately serve as a vehicle for identifying what one is capable of achieving.

How human beings respond to the tediousness of life was the central focus of Tibor Scitovsky's *Joyless Economy*.[22] Scitovsky asserted that human beings are in constant need of stimulation. Sitting around every day with nothing to do may be restful at first, but soon, human beings grow bored. To alleviate boredom, they go out in search of stimulation.[23] Stimulation arouses those areas of the brain that generate pleasure. Pleasure then becomes the motivating force behind human behavior and the search for stimulation becomes the operating principle guiding the decision making process. Hence human beings do not make choices designed to maximize some hypothetical concept like utility, but rather choose those activities that are able to arouse the pleasure areas of the brain.

The fundamental distinction between Scitovsky's view and that of the standard economic model is that one can be said to be concerned with outcome while the other focuses on process. In the choice model used by economists, the utility one gains from something is obtained after the good is acquired and during the time that it is being consumed. The act of consumption creates enjoyment and dominates the decision making process. In the Scitovsky view of the world, pleasure is the byproduct of a process where stimulation arouses part of the brain leading to pleasure. It is engaging with those triggers that stimulate the brain and thus creates a positive outcome. Hence a satisfactory outcome (obtaining pleasure) cannot be viewed independently from the process (stimulation and arousal). Without stimulation and arousal, there is no pleasure.

This may happen during the consumption of a product, but it may also occur in anticipation of consuming the product. The fun of playing a game is in part the result of winning the game, but individuals do not win all of the time and yet continue to play. A well-designed game environment is one that is capable of providing the necessary stimulation to relieve the tediousness of life. It also contains an element of randomness so that even the most disadvantaged of players have at least the slightest hope of becoming victorious.

Games are effective at relieving boredom because they focus on both the process *and* the outcome. Hence it should come as no surprise that one of the reason students study so little is because they find it boring. It is boring because the educational process is focused on outcomes—(how much did you learn)—rather than on the process. Too little attention is placed on the search for knowledge as a means for providing the requisite stimulation to arouse the student in a way that makes learning an enjoyable process.[24]

Strive

If a person doesn't know who they are or what they want, it is difficult to find the motivation to do much of anything. For many students at the beginning of a life journey, it is unclear whether the payoff associated with hard work will exceed the cost of the effort involved. Without a sense of what is important, it is easier to choose to do nothing.[25] Is this the reason why many students appear to have a lack of motivation when it comes to making the best of their educational choices?

Game designers rely on the concept of flow to create a positive source of motivation.[26] A well designed game will create an experience that totally absorbs the attention of the player to the point where the game becomes a reality in and of itself.[27] When a basketball player can seemingly hit every shot regardless of where they are on the floor, we say that the player is in the "zone." His concentration is totally fixed on what he is doing and he reaches a rhythm where everything feels "right." Each basket adds to the point total of the team and serves as additional motivation to take the next shot. Success leads to even more success as confidence rises as the player gains an increasing sense that they can do no wrong.

Flow becomes the mental equivalent of the release of endorphins associated with a runner's feeling of being high. It may be the only time in a person's life that they feel that all is right with the world and hence look to recreate the experience as often as they possibly can. As a result, game play begins to displace other activities. After all, a virtual life where flow is abundant shines in comparison to the real world where it is difficult to achieve such a state of being.

Flow is something that is felt as part of the experience. It makes a person feel good about what they have done and by extension, about themself. Contrast this with the primary source of motivation behind the decision to earn a bachelor's degree; the prospect of future lifetime earnings. Yes, it is possible to remind the typical college student that the reason they are amassing a large amount of debt is because they will enjoy higher future earnings after they graduate, but that provides little solace and not a whole lot of motivation when it comes time to study on a Thursday night.[28]

It is difficult to choose to study instead of going out with friends when the payoff for studying is off in the future and the benefits of spending time with friends is immediate. However, if somehow academics could incorporate something similar to flow, the choice to study may have a fighting chance. That being said, if there are few opportunities within student life to actually experience flow, the whole point may be moot. As a result, we wind up in the worst of all possible worlds: economic incentives don't work and other psychological drivers such as flow are virtually nonexistent.

Achievements

If it was just about flow, then why do gamers often need some tangible sign of success? Perhaps because it has less to do with fun and more to do with the interaction between the forces underlying stimulus and response. In other words, it is all about the structure of rewards. As David Wong explains in his blog post *5 Creepy Ways Video Games Are Trying to Get You Addicted*:

Gaming has changed. It used to be that once they sold us a $50 game, they didn't particularly care how long we played. The big thing was making sure we liked it enough to buy the next one. But the industry is moving toward subscription-based games like MMO's that need the subject to keep playing-and paying- until the sun goes supernova. Now, there's no way they can create enough exploration or story to keep you playing thousands of hours, so they had to change the mechanics of the game, so players would instead keep doing the same actions over and over and over, whether they liked it or not. So game developers turned to Skinner's techniques.[29]

The reference to Skinner is of course B. F. Skinner whose pioneering experiments revealed that through variable reinforcement, behavior could be modified to conform to an external set of stimuli.[30] The basic idea behind the Skinnerian approach is that if an individual is rewarded for the things they do, then they will want to do them more frequently in order to earn those rewards. That being said, if someone is rewarded each time they do something, they will lose interest. Hence the key to getting someone to do the same thing over and over again is to vary when they actually receive a reward. It is not just reinforcement, but rather variable reinforcement that is the key to managing behavior.

The behaviorism of B. F. Skinner can therefore be viewed as the antithesis of the positive psychology underlying the concept of flow.[31] Under positive psychology, games are designed to make the experience fun. By creating the conditions that lead to flow, it is possible to get players engaged with a virtual environment to the point where play becomes their preferred choice for how to spend their leisure time. Under behaviorism, the play itself becomes secondary to the structure of rewards. What the player is expected to do in many ways becomes irrelevant as long as what they are doing carries with it some reward. The reward and not the experience itself becomes the motivation for continued play.

Yet like many things in life, it is rarely an either or proposition. Perhaps the best example of how flow and reinforcement can work together is found in the popular Guitar Hero series. Players hit color coded buttons as they play along to a familiar song. Experienced players no longer need to concentrate on the buttons as they become second nature and instead, attention can more fully focused on the music and being part of the experience. At the same time, points are earned each time the player pushes the right button and bonus points appear with special challenges that are randomly inserted into the music. By combining both flow and reinforcement, Guitar Hero creates an effective environment for learning how to play along with the music, while creating an experience that is addictive for some and enjoyable for just about everyone else.

Transferring the Guitar Hero experience into today's classroom however it is not a trivial exercise. Opportunities for experiencing flow are limited, reinforcement is somewhat haphazard, and few opportunities exist for immersion in something meaningful. A huge gulf exists between what happens in the classroom and what occurs on campus the rest of the time. Rather than working in tandem, student life often contributes to a lack of performance in the classroom while coursework is viewed as an impediment to achieving a successful social life.

Status

The concept of flow describes a process that balances a fine line between something that is challenging but not so difficult that it might discourage additional effort. There is a feeling of satisfaction that comes from a job well done or the acquisition of skills and abilities that enable an individual to do something they have never done before. Pride in terms of what one has accomplished and the ability to string one success after another can provide all of the motivation that is necessary to gain participation.

However, the extrinsic rewards associated with a job well done, manifested in the tangible form of a gold star, letter grade, point total, honorific title, or the ability to reach higher levels, are often downplayed because they are thought not to have as great of an impact as intrinsic rewards such as flow. However, extrinsic rewards can have a much greater impact if they are a means for gaining status.[32]

There is something special about being first. Whether it is as the first person to walk on the moon, earn a billion dollars, capture the flag or slay the dragon, status is often associated with having achieved a difficult goal before everyone else. Of course it is not just about being first. Often it is about being the best. Being the fastest runner at school can confer a certain amount of status. However, being the fastest in the state or the nation confers a great deal more. Of course, everything pales in comparison to an Olympic gold medal; a contest that only comes around every four years and pits the best against the best.

Everyone loves a winner and for a university that is grappling to gain recognition in a competitive market, the achievements of its faculty, students, and staff can confer status for the entire institution. Whether it is national championships related to an individual sport, the number of Nobel Prize winners on the faculty, or having the best food service at a college campus, each suggests that the institution has the "right stuff." By partnering with a winner, it is believed that you too can become successful.

While success by association can help someone feel good about themselves, it is not a very good substitute for success that is earned from one's own accomplishments. Yet this represents a serious challenge when it comes to the average student experience. While we like to believe that everyone is special, and indeed they are in their own special way, many are left out as the criteria for success is often limited to achievements in the classroom or on the athletic field. The grades in most classrooms follow a normal distribution and in athletic contests, there generally can only be one winner. Hence, the opportunity to gain status through achievement is only available to a select few.

Self-Esteem

When a person is placed within a peer group, suddenly the size of their star or the number of stars becomes important. Not because a larger star in some way supersizes an achievement, but instead because relative position now becomes something that matters.[33]

The significance of relative position is perhaps understood within the context of leader boards. A leader board is a device that both tracks the performance of individual players, and also makes it possible for a player to see how they are doing relative to others. Sure it is great to see that you have answered all of the questions correctly, but it becomes even more special when you discover that you were the only one.

The importance of relative position stems from the futility associated with trying to reach some absolute standard of excellence. No one is perfect and hence it is unrealistic to assume that it is possible to be successful in any and every endeavor.[34] Yet if it is not possible to succeed, then why try? Because in order to feel good about yourself, all you really need to be is better at something than everyone else. Hence gaining a superior relative position represents a lower bar, but one that is no less effective in building self-esteem.

While games solve the problem with leader boards, in life the basis for making relative comparisons is not as straightforward. For example, a natural candidate that could provide a foundation for making relative comparisons is the amount of money a person earns. Income is often used as a proxy for measuring the value of one's economic contribution and hence relative worth within a society. Yet how much a person actually earns is often something that is only known to a select small group of people. Hence it is difficult to display success when the fruits of that achievement are held in secret.

One solution to the problem is to use something else as a proxy for success. Thorstein Veblen, one of the early founders of the field of sociology, developed a theory of society that focused on conspicuous consumption as the means for making relative comparisons.[35] Wealth could be put in evidence not by publishing the balance of one's bank account, but instead, could be reflected in the car they drive, the neighborhood they live in, the clothes they wear, and so on and so on. By making a public display of what their wealth can afford to buy, success can be placed in evidence and relative comparisons made.[36]

However, as everyone puts their respective wealth in evidence, conspicuous consumption becomes itself a form of contest. As friends, neighbors, coworkers, rivals, and others place their wealth on display in the form of material possessions, a competition emerges to see who is driving the most expensive automobile, lives in the nicest neighborhood, or owns the largest diamond ring.[37]

As a form of hedonic adaptation, a person can only continue to feel good about themself if they are able to match each purchase by a peer with an even more expensive purchase of their own.[38] In this way, the measure of success is constantly changing as individuals engage in activities designed to outdo the other. It is as if the process of making invidious comparisons is equivalent to climbing a ladder where each step reveals another new step that is higher than the one before and must be continuously climbed in order to preserve a feeling of self-worth.[39]

Achieving a favorable position relative to others regardless of the basis for making those comparisons helps to build self-esteem. Higher levels of self-esteem create a stronger sense of self and lead the individual to feel better about themself relative to others. Thus while it is common to talk about happiness as the primary driver underlying game play, the concept of self-esteem offers an additional element capable of explaining what sustains interest in a game.

This becomes particularly relevant when trying to explain the large number of hours spent engaging in activities that appear to be similar to work. While happiness may play a role, under the surface, it is the ability to build esteem, and hence feel better about oneself and how a person fits in the world (whether real or synthetic) that serves as a prime motivator underlying game play. *I play because it makes me feel good about myself and that in turn makes me happy.*[40]

Compare that with the amount of depression found on college campuses.[41] Students are constantly challenging themselves and more often experience failure rather than success. Just compare and contrast the reward system found in games and the one that dominates the classroom. In a game, players start at zero and accumulate points that allow them to move up from level to level. In the classroom, every student starts with the equivalent of an A in the course. As they progress from assignment to assignment, they are constantly losing points and are placed in a weaker and weaker position. Hence for many students, taking a class is a matter survival: who can outlast a series of assessments that lead to a loss of points. The irony of course is that playing many games is a fictional matter of survival, but as the game goes on, the character being played gets stronger and stronger. In the classroom, many students unfortunately view their objective more in terms of not failing than achieving some form of success.

Learning

With all of the requisite elements in place, it is now possible to develop a deeper understanding of why games are so appealing. It is not just that games enable the player to develop a life story that is based on who they would like to be rather than who they actually are, instead it is that they help to develop a stronger sense of self. Why is this important? It is important because identity is an essential component of learning and success in learning helps the individual to grow and develop as a person.

The connection between identity and learning, however, is not straightforward and perhaps is best served with an example that has nothing to do with education, but instead has to do with the decision making process. Once we have a better understanding of how decisions are made, it will be relatively easy to show how a stronger sense of self can improve learning outcomes.

To draw a clearer connection between identity and learning we can adapt the Prospect Theory of Daniel Kahneman and Amos Tversky.[42] Prospect Theory attempts to develop a richer understanding of how individuals make choices in the face of uncertainty. Confronted by a variety of alternatives (prospects), the decision maker evaluates and organizes them with respect to some reference point. Prospects to the right of this reference point lead to positive gains, but those gains come with the assumption of risk. Prospects to the left of the reference point also entail risk and are associated with losses. Arguing that people are essentially loss averse, Kahneman and Tyversky show how prospects that minimize losses are chosen more often than those that hold the promise of maximizing gains.

Perhaps the best example that illustrates the concept of loss aversion and the use of a reference point can be found in the housing market. One of the characteristics that set housing apart from other markets is that prices seem to be particularly sticky downward. Home owners have a sense of what their property is worth (reference point) and are reluctant to accept an offer below that price. Where does this reluctance come from? Given that the purchase of a home is for many the largest financial decision they will ever make, they do not want to admit that they made a mistake by buying a property at a price that was higher than what their property is now actually worth. They would rather hold on to the property than force themselves to confront the fact that they made a mistake. In other words, they would rather stay in the house than take a loss.[43]

We can use this basic insight to show how identity plays an important role in learning. Instead of talking in terms of prospects, we can in its place speak about paths that one can follow in life. From the perspective of a student enrolled at a university, these paths might take the form of different majors. A premed student follows a radically different path than a business major.

In addition to the choice of a major, students can take different paths through their selection of courses. Unfortunately, some students select their courses not based on what might best help them develop needed skills or provide knowledge that will help them in their future career, but instead, because they are just an easy way to get a good grade. Why would a student take a class that offers no benefit other than the prospect that it is an easy way to earn a high grade? One explanation is that taking a challenging course entails more risk.[44]

At the most basic level, it represents risk to one's grade point average which might adversely affect the ability to get into a good graduate school or obtain a good job. However, at a different level, the risk associated with taking a more difficult course comes with the potential damage to one's self-esteem that might come with a lack of success. For example, a student might believe that they are good at critical thinking. However, as they fail in a course that focuses on that ability, they discover that they are not a very good critical thinker after all. The loss of self-confidence and the corresponding blow to their self- image may make them even more loss averse. Rather than continuing to challenge themselves, they might opt for safer choices that come with less risk of failure.

Once we acknowledge that there are different paths (prospects) based on the choices that a student might make and concede that some entail more and some less risk, we are partway toward developing a theory of learning based on Prospect Theory. All that is needed is something that is equivalent to the concept of a reference point.

How far along a student is in terms of their development as a scholar, the degree to which they feel secure in their abilities, and the extent to which they know their likes and dislikes, are all part of establishing a place within the order of things. The extent to which a student understands who they are and what they are capable of doing will help determine which prospects are more and which ones are less risky. For example, what appears to be a hard course to a freshman might appear to be easy to a graduating senior. Hence their place in terms of their development as a learner serves as an important reference point for the choices that they make.

A student will more likely take advantage of learning opportunities that have a higher payoff if the possible losses associated with those choices are smaller. Being in a better place as a learner does just that; it reduces the chance for failure and hence reduces the prospect that a choice will end with a loss. Being a more secure and accomplished learner therefore reduces the risk associated with those prospects (learning opportunities) that will pay greater dividends down the road. It as if Kahneman and Tversky's reference point slowly moves to the left as fewer paths represent a potential loss and the severity of those losses diminishes.

Closing the Circle

Identity can play a role in learning by better positioning the student to choose those pathways that will help them acquire the knowledge and skills that they need in order to succeed. More importantly, identity is not fixed in place. What serves as a reference point changes thereby opening up less risky paths that lead in a positive direction. As students learn more, their identities grow and develop and with that change, they become more likely to choose those paths that will lead to even greater success. All of this works together to create a virtuous circle that offers the potential of positive change for the remainder of their lives.

Thus the allure of games is that they help us learn about who we are and help develop the capabilities necessary to become the person we would like to be. Gamers accomplish this by creating a stronger sense of self that in turn reduces the potential losses associated with prospects that had once seemed to be very risky, but are now viewed as not such a big deal. By reducing the losses associated with trying something new, it becomes less scary to put one's self-esteem at risk. Advancing into uncharted territory is what learning is all about and with the appropriate preparation needed to confront the risks associated with possible failure, come rewards that that will pay a handsome set of dividends.

CHAPTER 5

Design Elements

We level up in games and level down in life. One view suggests that the individual is improving and advancing toward some goal. The other carries with it negative connotations more associated with failure than success. It is easy to think that is not nothing more than a difference in perspectives, but in reality, it has far reaching significance.

Is life a "struggle for existence" or an opportunity for "self-actualization?" Is the exam in school a means to affirm what we have learned, or a dreaded exercise in humility? Is a six-figure salary a sign of success or a sign of wasted potential? It all depends on how the numbers are framed.

The construction of an effective frame goes way beyond the look and feel of the game. Something as simple as the concept of leveling up suggests a positive ethos for play. The concept of failure is minimized as players are afforded multiple opportunities designed to empower and propel them toward success. It is all about making progress toward completion, or in the case of a subscription-based game, sufficiently engaged that the player is willing to tender the monthly fee required to keep their character alive.

All of this conforms to the results from various experiments in behavioral economics. The choices that individual actors make are not just dependent on whether they have all of the necessary information to make good ones, but also in terms of how that information is presented. Too many choices leads to inaction, the ordering of choices can affect outcomes, and the existence of a default option that relieves one from having to make a choice in the first place can all lead to outcomes that are inconsistent with the standard economic model.

Effective frames are a function of good design. When thinking about design elements and comparing them with game mechanics, it might be useful to think of elements taking place on the macro level while mechanics address the workings of a game on the micro level. Thus we address design elements in this chapter and move on to how to implement them in the next chapter when we discuss game mechanics.[1]

Learning Outcomes

Strong evidence exists that instead of preparing students for a successful future, we are instead casting them academically adrift.[2] When looking at the "crisis" in higher education, the conversation inevitably turns to a discussion of academics. Much is said about curricula that do not meet the needs of today's economy, academic standards that require little (if any) student effort and an environment in which life and not learning is fun. As a result, there is a growing disconnect between what students and their parents expect to receive and what is actually being delivered by many academic institutions.

Rather than trying to improve the learning process, many faculty members focus instead on the course requirements. They are steeped in the presumption that the solution to the problem is found in class attendance and more rather than fewer assignments. It is all about academic rigor and holding students accountable. It is about crafting rules and regulations that reign in student behavior and at the very least, deprive them of those distractions that make it difficult to acquire the skills and knowledge that we all believe are a part of any higher education.

History of course is littered with examples where an oppressive regime attempts to impose their standard of what constitutes acceptable behavior on an unwilling and unresponsive public. Requiring students to attend a class that they find boring, unenlightening, or a complete waste of time is one example of such an approach. While there is nothing to stop a faculty member from requiring that students attend class, read a particular book, or work through homework assignments on a regular basis in the name of academic rigor, it is not clear that any of it actually improves learning outcomes.

Rather than taking a professor mandated approach to student performance, gamification looks to affect learning outcomes by shaping the available choice set and providing the appropriate motivation to entice students to take the necessary risks in order to step out and learn something new. Learning can be a humbling experience and if we expect students to risk a serious blow to their feeling of self-worth, it is incumbent on those responsible for the construction of the learning process, to build in elements that lift up rather than tear down a student.

Constructing a positive learning experience requires the judicious use of the following design elements:

- *Choice Architecture* – A good choice architecture can frame student options and help guide the decision process.
- *Risk Management* – Many Students choose to manage risk in a way that is designed to minimize lossess rather than maximize educational gains.
- *Social Norms* – Students are strongly influenced by social norms that help to shape the choices they make.
- *Co-Creation* – By inviting students to become co-creators, they can assume more responsibility for the learning process.
- *Intelligent Obstacles* – Smart rather than dumb obstacles can turn students into engaged learners.

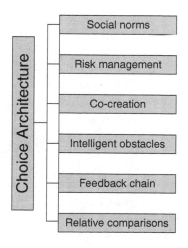

Figure 5.1

- *Feedback Chain* – A feedback chain sustains and strengthens the motivation to learn
- *Relative Comparisons* – Positive learning outcomes form the foundation for making relative comparisons that build esteem.

The elements are illustrated in Figure 5.1.

Choice Architecture

Individuals like to have some freedom to explore and discover new things. They also like to feel somewhat autonomous; as if they have control over events and to some extent their environment. However, too much freedom can lead to unhappiness as too many choices can lead to impotence rather than empowerment. For game designers, the challenge is to erect the appropriate balance between individual autonomy and active intervention in order to ensure a coherent and meaningful gaming experience. Recent research in behavioral economics suggests that providing unlimited choices does not create an environment conducive to achieving the best of all possible states of happiness. In fact, individuals are generally happier when they are given a limited number of options.[3]

A good choice architecture is not one where anything goes. Rather it is one that helps the decision maker to make good choices that lead to positive outcomes. Unfortunately, higher education is structured around a number of rigid rules that are designed to inform students about what they cannot do rather than empower them to make good choices. For many students, the first day of class is the best one. They can tell themselves that they still have all of the points available in the course. However, each exam, quiz, assignment, or paper is an exercise in leveling down. It is all about losing points in an effort to hold on to a high grade rather than leveling up to a state of mastery over the material. Most students are told on a regular basis that they are not very good—either in class performance, residence halls, or by the town police.

This insight forms the basis for the choice architecture approach advocated by Richard Thaler and Cass Sunstein in their book *Nudge*. What one takes away from this approach is the idea that human beings are never really "free to choose," and that this is not necessarily a bad thing. Advocating an approach they label as "Libertarian

Paternalism," Thaler and Sunstein believe that individuals should be given choices within a defined framework. How choices are framed can influence outcomes as much as the choices themselves. Hence it is not a matter of individual liberty, but rather setting the appropriate stage so that individuals will choose outcomes that further both individual and social interests.[4]

A great example of a choice architecture within a gaming environment can be found in Fallout 3.[5] Taking place in a postapocalyptic world, the player leaves Vault 101 (their place of birth) in search of their father in an effort to understand their place in a world dominated by the Enclave. It contains all of the elements found in a well-structured choice architecture. Those elements include

1. flexibility in the choice set;
2. a set of well-defined choices;
3. limitations in the number of choices;
4. the existence of default choices;
5. clear outcomes associated with individual choices;
6. consistency between choices;
7. tools for making better choices;
8. assistance for making complex choices;
9. the possibility for correcting bad choices;
10. feedback for updating choices.

The game itself is designed around what is known as open ended play. Players have the flexibility to pursue goals and objectives of their own choosing and are not required to follow a single path. The game is built around the choice of an initial skill set and play is designed to develop those skills. The choice of skills is given early on with a child's book entitled *Your Special*. SPECIAL is actually an acronym for the skill set (Strength, Perception, Endurance, Charisma, Intelligence, Agility, and Luck). From this well-defined set of choices, the player takes an exam at the age of 16 (Generalized Occupation Aptitude Test) to identify the three skills that will serve as the focal point for the rest of the game, thereby effectively limiting the number of choices.

An interesting element in the design of the game is the introduction of the concept of karma. Karma is a measure of the positive energy associated with doing good. It is an element that can affect the outcome of the game. Good deeds create positive karma and negative actions reduce the level of karma. With the use of karma, a player can see a clear outcome associated with their individual choices. In addition, the existence of positive and negative karma ensures consistency between choices. One set enables a player to build karma while another leads to a reduction in the amount of karma.

Because it is easier to gain karma than to lose it, the game affords the opportunity for the insertion of Thaler and Sunstein's concept of liberal paternalism. The existence of such a bias effectively nudges the player into doing good rather than engaging in evil activities. It is a way of promoting positive ethical behavior without mandating individual choices.

In addition to the karma system, the game includes tools for making better choices. One example is the Pipboy: a device that is used to monitor in game status. Tools also exist for assisting in the making of more complex choices. The VATS (Vault-Tec Assisted Targeting System) can be of great value when engaging in combat. It helps the player identify potential targets and the probability of success resulting from various engagements with enemy combatants.

Bad choices can adversely affect the health of the player, but opportunities exist for correcting bad choices and regaining losses. Finally, with the help of the status screen, players gain the feedback they need for making revisions to their choices as the game progresses.

Risk Management

Economists like to believe that most people are risk averse. What is meant by the term is that people in general do not like uncertainty and hence they would prefer to accept a sure thing with a lower payoff than assume the risk associated with a higher, but uncertain one. A great example of this type of behavior can be found in the relationship between employers and workers.

Instead of selling their services on a daily basis to the highest bidder, many workers choose instead to bind themselves to longer term contracts with a single company. The reason they are willing to do that is because they are risk averse. Many people prefer the sure thing of knowing they have a job tomorrow and what that job entails, rather than accept the risk as a contractor that there may be no work to do, or they may have to work at a job they do not like.

Guarantees with respect to security, retirement, and health benefits enable firms to lock-in valued employees.[6]

Within academia, this type of risk aversion is most prominent in the tenure system. Some like to think of tenure in terms of a set of golden handcuffs. Once a faculty member receives tenure, they in essence have a job for life. Only with the financial failure of the institution will they ever again be subject to the vagaries of the job market. Hence from the perspective of risk aversion, it is hard to do better than that. Of course, tenure does not come without its price. Once one receives tenure, it is not something so easily given up. Hence most faculty members will only leave to go to another institution if they are given tenure as part of their new employment contract. However, since tenure represents a large commitment over an uncertain period of time, many institutions are reluctant to grant tenure to someone who has not demonstrated that they can get along with existing members of a department and that they will in some way continue to be active. Hence the concept of golden handcuffs; on the one hand a faculty member has job security, but they pay for that with a lack of job mobility. The lack of mobility has the additional consequence of depressing salaries because for many faculty members, there is nowhere else that they can go.[7]

However, if we think that faculty members are good managers of risk, they are often outdone by their students. For many students, required courses are thought of as complex pools of risk that are best approached not by a great deal of study, but rather through risk management. Students want as many assessment opportunities as possible during the course of the semester in order to reduce the risk associated with not feeling well on the day of a test, or minimizing the loss of points the comes with studying the wrong content. The more exams, homework assignments, projects, and extra credit opportunities the better because in tandem, they create a risk management system that minimizes the damage associated with one, or several missteps.[8]

Creating a large number of assessment opportunities such that risk becomes almost negligible, or an employment system that eliminates the largest source of anxiety once tenure is obtained, can have unintended consequences. We like to think that creating a secure environment leads to risk taking by eliminating many if not all of the consequences associated with failure. However, the opposite can just as easily occur. In the absence of risk, the concept of taking a chance has little meaning. Thus someone with little experience with risk can be easily overwhelmed with the inclusion of just the slightest bit of uncertainty. Rather than embracing risk, it is instead rejected because it is very disconcerting when confronted by something that is unknown or where there is in which they have limited (if any) experience.

It is not about eliminating risk, but rather managing it. Players tend to get bored if they are not challenged and outcomes are certain. The key to good design is to allow randomness to enter the game space without placing the player's self-esteem at risk.

Game designers understand this principle very well. At the most basic level, one can allow risky outcomes while minimizing risk to the player by creating a safety net. In games, this net can take the form of a do over. Make a fatal mistake and your character dies; only to be reborn again so that play can continue.

Nonfatal failure is one way of encouraging risk taking, but it is not really a risk management strategy. Offering a variety of ways to get to a desired end or multiple modes of assessment so that no single event has too much significance is another. Yet both of these strategies, while minimizing risk, does not promote success. Instead, they merely reduce the consequences of failure.

A more effective risk management strategy is one designed to reduce the chances of failure by increasing the probability for success. Take for example a game like L. A. Noir. The player assumes the role of Cole Phelps, a war hero turned detective during the golden era of Los Angeles at the end of World War II. The object of the game is to solve crimes and as a police detective, it is done by interviewing suspects. The game utilizes a revolutionary technology called MotionScan that is able to accurately convey facial nuances. Multiple opportunities are given to learn how to evaluate a suspect and as the player gets better at detecting whether suspects are lying or telling the truth, the player becomes more successful at solving crimes.

By offering both multiple opportunities and a means to develop the skills needed for success, risk management is embedded in the gaming environment. As a result, the player can focus on success rather than minimizing the costs associated with failure. It becomes a game element that enhances rather than detracts from learning.

Creating an environment that promotes success supports efforts designed to try something new. This represents an important step toward eliminating the tendency that most individuals have to remain content with the existing status quo. Status quo bias, as represented by the desire to stand pat with existing skills or circumstances, is perhaps the largest impediment to learning.

It represents a particularly serious problem for higher education where the willingness of prospective students to shoulder an ever higher debt burden is directly related to the prospect of obtaining a good and higher paying job upon graduation. Living in an economy that is becoming more and more reliant on innovation as a strategy for gaining or maintaining a competitive advantage means that employers are increasingly going to be looking for graduates who embrace rather than reject change.

Social Norms

When economists conceptualize choice problems, they like to conceive of economic agents as if they were Robinson Crusoe on a deserted island. The benefit of taking such an approach is that it greatly simplifies matters. However, recent work with experiments in both the lab and the field suggest that decisions are not made independently of the context in which they are made. For example subjects have been observed who contribute to a public good even if there is no benefit to them; are willing to give up resources in order to punish others who do not contribute to the public good; and they give unto others even when there is no reasonable expectation that such behavior will ever be reciprocated. This research suggests that the choices made by experimental subjects are, in part, conditioned by social norms that exist outside the laboratory environment.[9]

The influence of social norms is evident in the latest fashion trend on college campuses. Leggings have become the predominant fashion trend on campus. Coupled with a tall pair of leather boots and a long baggy shirt, many women look like they would be as comfortable playing a character in a medieval role-playing game as they walk from class to class. If you asked a woman on campus why she wears leggings, she would probably tell you that they are just as comfortable as sweat pants (a previous fashion fixture on campus) but look a lot better.

It may very well be that half the female population woke up on the very same day and had the same fashion thought. However, we see this behavior in other contexts as well. The field of behavioral finance has spent a good number of journal pages trying to explain why the typical investor does not buy low and sell high, but rather buys when everyone else is buying and sells when everyone else is selling. The desire to follow the herd seems at odds with the simple rule of how to make money in financial markets. However, the fact that individuals do not feel comfortable as outliers, but rather conform to whatever the investing norm is at the time, can explain in part the wide and persist swings in various markets.[10]

Thus social norms are an important design element in both games and life. They can not only lead to the creation of entire value systems, but can also play a large role influencing behavior. If the norm is to go out drinking on a Thursday night rather than studying, then a good number of students will put their books aside regardless of the consequences.[11] In fact, the strong role that norms can play in effecting behavior is best seen in the game League of Legends.

League of Legends is a free to play online multiplayer battle game developed by Riot Games. It averages over 12 million players per day with as many as five million playing concurrently at any moment in time[12]. Players are placed into evenly matched teams at either sides of a map in an area with the object to destroy the other team's nexus. Success depends not only on individual ability, but also on the performance of the team. The important role played by the entire team in achieving individual success, however, has created a great deal of bad behavior.

Lacking in positive social norms, League of Legends is notorious for its "toxic culture."[13] In an attempt to reduce bad behavior, Riot Games has resorted to the use of bans to try and mitigate bad behavior on the part of its players. However, when a player can just register with a new account and start all over, the ban is not a very good long-term solution to bad behavior. Nor does it reform a bad person and turn them into a productive member of the community.

The need to discipline behavior in order to improve the game culture however runs the risk for Riot Games that it will alienate players and they will flee to some other game. This could have serious financial effects because the company generates a considerable amount of revenue from in-game micro transactions. For the game to be financially successful, it needs as many players as it can support who are so engrossed in the game, they are willing to spend money to advance their play. Hence the difficult position for the company, is that those players who are most likely to make money for the game company are also the ones who are most likely to be banned from play.

In an effort to reduce the magnitude of the problem, Riot Games has instituted what are called reform cards. When a player behaves badly, they are judged by the community through the workings of a Tribunal (the equivalent of a court system) and handed down a punishment in the form of a reform card. The card details exactly where the player went wrong and by identifying the source of the problem, there is an opportunity for players to learn the difference between acceptable and unacceptable behavior. The important point is that the system is not based on the judgment of the game developer, but rather, it is based on community standards that are created and communicated via the Tribunal system.

Can this be the reason why many attempts to end college drinking on campus have failed? Rather than an idea that emerges from the collective student body, it instead is one that is often imposed by the university administration. No one likes to be told what to do, whether it is college students or gamers. Contrast this with efforts to infuse sustainability as a set of values on many college campuses. It is both a value system and a social norm. Students recycle not because they are told to do it, but rather because it is consistent with their value system, one that is pervasive and part of the culture.

Co-Creation

The rise of social media has done more than turn today's undergraduate student into a multimodal consumer of information, it has also turned them into storytellers who share their lives on a daily or even moment by moment basis. Such a shift in how students live their lives creates an opportunity for rethinking the age old debate over whether we should turn students into active learners or just teach them how to become better passive listeners. Just as it is somewhat futile to expect students to more carefully listen to stories they don't really want to hear, or actively learn things that have no meaning or significance to their lives, it may be possible through the use of Service Dominant Logic and the concept of Value Co-Creation to rethink the entire learning experience.[14]

We can view Facebook for example as a product of this new Logic. The company provides a framework that offers both constraints and helpful nudges for how best one might display content. It provides a host of tools that facilitate the content creation process. Users use those tools within the defined framework to create pages that in combination, tell a story. Stories are then shared within the community that emerges as friends get friends to join and post their own pages. The stories could not exist without the framework and tools supplied by Facebook and the company's website would be nothing more than an empty shell without the content generated by its community of users. Hence value emerges from a co-created process that has the user learning more about themselves and their friends while enhancing feelings of belonging within a community of peers.[15]

Co-creation as part of learning is not about ceding control of the educational process to the student, nor is it about joint knowledge creation, rather it is about creating an experience environment in which students can have an active dialogue and co-construct personalized experiences that will facilitate the learning process.[16] It is about creating an environment where a student can take abstract constructs and turn them into relatable concepts that have meaning for them.[17]

From a service-dominant logic approach, the student learning experience can be identified as the core service provided by a university.[18] As part of a co-created process, the student is in part a productive resource and in part a producer of value. The student brings their existing knowledge, learning skills, and desire to succeed that in turn can be combined with the knowledge, teaching tools, and experience of the instructor to create a coherent and comprehensive learning experience. As a co-creator of their own learning experience, the student becomes partially responsible for the quality of the experience as their role shifts to one of learning partner.

All of this is not, of course a surprise to game developers. When it comes to game play, the individual is not only the consumer (they purchased the game or a subscription to the game in order to participate), they are also co-creator when it comes to the production of the game experience.[19] As the coproducer of the gaming experience, the player experiences the satisfaction associated with developing those skills required to reach higher levels, making a positive contribution as the member of a group, or saving the day from some threat.

To gain a sense of the importance of the co-created gaming experience, one need only look at the pricing model utilized by many game companies. They use a form of price discrimination that is no different than other forms of media-based entertainment. Regardless of whether we are looking at video games, movies, music, or TV shows, some consumers are willing to pay a higher price to be one of the first to hear, view, or experience entertainment. To accommodate this interest, media companies release their products at a high price to capture the additional value that consumers perceive to exist with a new release. They then have a program in place that lowers the price over time to capture more price sensitive consumers who do not ascribe any importance to being one of the first.

This standard price discrimination strategy, however, experiences an interesting twist when it comes to multiplayer games. In a multi-player game, much of the experience depends on who is playing at the same time. Friends generally like to play with friends and hence if all of the gamers you know purchases the game when it is first released, the value to be gained is not only a function of the quality of the game, but also the shared experience with friends. Hence it is not a question of being first to purchase a new game, but rather to buy the game as the same time as your friends. If everyone you might play with buys a game within the first release of the game and you want to maximize the value created through a shared experience, then you will pay a premium to obtain the game at the same time as your friends.

Thus in the case of multiplayer games that generate much of their value through a co-created experience, gaming companies find themselves in a superior position to charge a premium. Moreover, as a community grows and develops, the quality of the experience can extend the life of a game beyond the point where many have gone off to new challenges.[20]

This of course is no different than what many residential colleges try to do through their admissions process. It is perhaps most apparent in what are known as the Ivy League schools. The value of the experience is greatly enhanced by one's contemporaries both inside and outside the classroom. By being able to attract a higher caliber of students, courses can be taught at a more advanced level. As importantly, where learning about a particular subject or life in general is a shared experience, the value that is created is very much dependent on who participates.[21]

Intelligent Obstacles

Standardized tests have a bad reputation because average test scores seem to rise but the average level of skills actually falls.[22] Teachers are accused of teaching to the test and students are branded as having improved their test-taking skills, but at the expense of actually learning anything of value.[23] We have become outcome driven, but at the same time have lost sight of what outcomes we truly desire. The purpose of an exam is to assess learning and not to become an end in and of itself. Yet for the average student, exams are viewed as nothing more than an obstacle to moving on to the next stage of their journey.[24] From this perspective, exams are nothing more than a dumb obstacle. They rarely contribute to learning, but rather are something that must be endured if one is to reach their goal (graduation).

Compare that with a game like Angry Birds. In one sense, each round is the equivalent of passing an exam. The player is given objects to shoot at some construct in order to free the birds. If you are successful in destroying the cages, the birds go free and you can move on to the next round. Fail to figure out how to destroy the cages and you get stuck in place. In the most general of senses, this is the equivalent of passing a series of tests in order to move up to the next grade in school. Fail the tests and you repeat the grade (course) until you figure out how to demonstrate sufficient competency that you are then allowed to advance.

However, in games like Angry Birds, the exam or challenge is not just a means for assessing learning. It becomes the principle mechanism for teaching the player those skills that are needed to overcome the challenges that stand in the way of success. Gaming is perhaps the best representation of the concept of learning by doing.[25] The player learns those principles and develops those skills needed to succeed. Overcoming an obstacle is both validation of what they have learned, but also contributes to the overall learning experience. Assessment therefore becomes a means to an end and not the end itself.

Perhaps the confusion between learning and assessment can be traced back to the basic economics of the industrial revolution. Around the turn of the twentieth century, an idea known as Scientific Management was in fashion in business circles.[26] Largely the result of work by Fredrick Taylor, Scientific Management was all about promoting efficiency; how to produce something with the fewest number of steps. The key to implementing those principles was to construct a system of measurement that could form the basis for continuous improvement. All of this was designed to produce goods at the lowest possible cost. It was believed that in a competitive environment, only the most efficient would survive, let along thrive. It was an economic form of the concept of the survival of the fittest.

Thus it should not come as a surprise that education might take on some of the characteristics of Scientific Management (sometimes referred to as Taylorism). Examinations become a means for measuring success. Grades are assigned in order to evaluate where improvement is needed. Those whose grades are below the median are assigned remedial work in order to improve their scores. Failure to improve had the unfortunate consequence of being held back a grade.

Yet if work and school are based on efficient work processes, the same cannot be said for play. Game designers understand that a game that truly engages the player is one that consists of a number of challenges that are just beyond reach, but not too difficult to discourage someone from playing the game. This approach of engaging the player by placing artificial hurdles in her path is not, however, consistent with how we have traditionally envisioned efficient work processes. The traditional approach to work is to organize activities in a way that enables you to produce the largest amount of output in the smallest amount of time.

What we have learned from gameplay is that the use of intelligent obstacles can lead to greater rather than less productivity. While players may spend more time overcoming unnecessary elements, they derive a sense of accomplishment that provides further motivation. While it may take more time to accomplish a particular objective, players are more motivated to complete a task and thus spend less time trying to avoid a particular activity (think procrastination).

Consequently, if we are to try and incorporate game design principles into an educational environment, we need to replace existing dumb obstacles with intelligent ones. It may very well be the case that students retain information much better if they are constantly being quizzed. However, as more and more time is spent on testing whether knowledge has been retained, there is less time available to actually teach something. More disturbing, it is not clear that after a certain amount of time has elapsed, whether the students retain much at all.[27]

All of this begs the question of whether it is all about retaining facts or should it be about teaching students how to critically think. Everyone likes to talk about developing critical thinking, but will a short quiz that students can respond to using clickers in the classroom or as part of an online learning environment actually improve critical thinking? How can a mechanism used to assess performance serve the same function as an intelligent obstacle found in a game environment?

Feedback Chain

Feedback is the equivalent of a double edged sword. One side builds confidence making it easier to take a risk and try something new. The other side undermines confidence, thereby leading someone to wish that they had never tried in the first place.[28]

If one compared the introductory economics textbooks of today with those 30 years ago, the difference would go beyond the explosion of color, boxes, applications, and the use of technology. The theory itself has been greatly simplified in order to make it more accessible to the average college student. As a result, rigor has been politely shown to the exit and the textbooks themselves have shrunk in size to reflect a new reality that relies less on algebra and graphs and more on simple ideas.

This stands in stark contrast with many video games that have their users demanding higher and higher levels that are more and more challenging with higher degrees of difficulty. How can this be? Why are college curricula being dumbed down while video game companies are being besieged with requests to create ever more advanced challenges?

The difference can be found in the role that feedback plays in the two environments. In a gaming environment, feedback is an element designed to build confidence. Rather than tearing someone down, it instead helps to build them up. A lack of success has less to do about any failings as an individual and everything to do with what skills still need to be developed in order to complete a level.

Feedback is about more than creating a single loop. Rather it is about constructing a series of loops that form a chain capable of providing the support needed to continue making progress toward the completion of the game. It ties together why certain skills are needed and how they can be utilized to advance play. It helps to reinforce the strong cause and effect relationship between skill acquisition and success. Good feedback takes on the form of helping the player understand why they need to improve their performance at a certain activity.

Knowing that players will fail on a regular basis, successful design uses those failures to build confidence so that players are more willing to take a chance in order to advance to the next level of play. However, feedback is only an effective tool if it supports and builds confidence. It must be seen as the foundation for a better future rather than validation of a past that many would rather forget. In other words, it is about choices rather than abilities.

Take the introductory economics student who cannot solve a simple algebra problem. As a result, they do poorly on the exams and eventually flunk the course. Did they fail the course because they are not smart enough to successfully complete the problems assigned on the exams, or is it because they made poor choices? The answer to that question could be the difference between someone who becomes alienated from the learning process rather than a person who picks themselves back up and tries again.

Those poor choices can be nothing more than spending the night before the exam with friends rather than studying. It could be that they never learned how to properly study. Alternatively it could be that they did not take the right courses that are needed in order to be successful. The important point is that it is easier to accept a lack of success that is result of past choices that were less than ideal rather than some fundamental failing that cannot easily be fixed.

Unfortunately, in higher education, failure to pass a test or an entire course is seen as a failure of ability rather than previous poor choices that now are making it difficult to succeed. The conclusion that students reach when confronting failure is that there is something wrong with them rather than a problem with the past choices they have made. Once again, this is where games shine. They have been designed from the ground up to provide the needed skills to succeed, multiple opportunities to try and try again, and often offer multiple avenues for reaching the same objective; all within a framework design to support risk taking with few recriminations. It is a much different environment. It is one that builds confidence so that players can and will succeed.

Relative Comparisons

Without some absolute standard, it becomes difficult to determine what actually constitutes success. A number really only comes into focus when it can serve as a basis for comparison. Once the high or low score is identified, or the mean or the median are known, it becomes possible to get an idea of one's performance relative to others. As a result, it becomes possible to use relative position as a measure for success.[29]

It is this concept of relative position and thus the development of self-esteem that serves as the foundation for what, in the gaming industry is known as points, badges, and leader boards (PBLs). PBLs are the gaming industry's way of combining rewards, recognition, and relative position. Of course one does not have to look to the game industry to see how PBLs can be used effectively to generate personal success. Perhaps the best example has little if anything to do with games.

Weight Watchers is built on game principles (though few may actually call it a game). Goals are set based on weight reduction. To make progress toward that goal, the Weight Watchers client gets points for making good food choices. If they limit the number of points, they are rewarded by being able to eat a treat. More importantly, successfully managing points brings the client closer to achieving their goal. Success is measured in pounds lost and going to a group meeting allows a participant to put their weight in evidence and compare their success (weight loss) relative to others. If the same people attend the meeting regularly, they become the relevant peer group and relative comparisons become even more meaningful and significant.[30]

Like any successful gaming model, it is all about process rather than outcome. Players move closer to achieving a goal, but final resolution remains elusive. Success is not defined in terms of some stated outcome, but rather results from engaging in play. Players express their autonomy by choosing what they do. They become powerful by mastering different challenges. Self-esteem is built as their online identities grow, develop, and experience success. Very concrete symbols exist that serve as measures for success and each time they play, these symbols serve to reinforce a positive self-image.

One appeal of gaming environments is that they are designed to make such relative comparisons easy. Take for example the role of hats in the game Team Fortress 2.[31] As of this writing, there are a total of 297 different hats available in the game. All but a very small number are purely cosmetic and therefore have no role in advancing game play.

Given that most hats do not enhance play, it is perhaps surprising that a market exists inside the game where hats can be exchanged. Some are quite rare and command extraordinarily high prices.[32] The interesting question is why hats are so valuable when they appear to serve no purpose. Actually they do serve an important purpose when you view them as symbols of achievement.

While everyone can wear a hat, not everyone can wear the same hat. The more expensive the hat, the better the symbol for success. In order for success to be meaningful, it must be put into evidence. If it wasn't hats, it would be something else. In fact, the more inconsequential the item, the better signal it provides. It is one thing to have a better weapon that leads to greater success in the game; it is something else to be able to demonstrate to the other players that you have been so successful, you can afford to purchase something expensive that does not advance game play whatsoever. A hat, or some other inessential item, becomes a source of status by enabling the player to put their success in evidence through the wearing of the hat. Thus, those hats that are in short supply command higher prices, not because they are needed to advance game play, but instead, because they serve as better symbols for success.

Now think about how students make (or don't make) healthy eating choices. In the dining hall, a mix of healthy and unhealthy choices exists. If the goal is to promote student health, then it is important that they make healthy choices. To facilitate the decision process, it is relatively easy to provide information about portion size and number of calories. However, information alone is not going to lead to good choices.

What is the reward for making a good choice? How will those rewards be recognized? How can earning those rewards lead to the achievement of status and a superior relative position? Is it any wonder then that there is such a thing as the Freshman 15 where it is presumed that the average first year student living away from home will gain 15 pounds? Unlimited food is made available but the necessary support framework does not exist.

Learning Environments

It is easier to look to the past rather than the future for the solution to problems that exist in the present. The past is familiar and for most, some part represents "the good old days." We like to selectively remember those hardships that for one reason or another were easily overcome. Hence we fondly remember those days of having to walk a mile in the cold and snow to get to school, when mathematical calculations were made using slide rules, or computers were programmed using punch cards. We then chastise the current generation for having things much easier and think that all it would take is to impose similar hardships in order to improve performance.

Of course, the world has changed a great deal over the course of the last 50 years and hence it is not clear that trying to return to the way things used to be done makes any sense. The real promise of game design is not that it redefines those timeless issues that have plagued humanity from the start of time, but rather that it affords a different approach to building a pathway to the future. It is about preserving cherished values such as choice, but seeks to craft a context that helps ensure that they are made intelligently. It is not about creating a free-for-all where anyone can do anything they want at any time. Rather it is about effectively channeling behavior into productive activities that lead to positive outcomes. It is not an assault on freedom, but rather a way of empowering individuals, so that they can stand up on their own and accomplish anything they so choose.

CHAPTER 6

Structural Design

Many individuals who spend countless hours in a game environment choose to do so because they get to become who they would like to be, rather than being stuck in an identity that was not of their own (conscious) making. It is all about constructing a life. The difference is that within the confines of a game, we are able to start with a fresh slate and choose from a set of characteristics, abilities, and skills that are subsequently refined through game play. In the real world, however, we are rarely free to choose as nature and nurture work within the level of the subconscious to place invisible limitations on what we can and cannot become.

Outside the game environment and in the real world, we are who we are. We are not constructs created for success in an idealized world of our own choosing. However, how would life be different if instead it was more like a game? While it may be true that some things are beyond our ability to choose, that is not the same as saying that an environment could not be created that would help us overcome those barriers that stand in our way of becoming the person we wish we could be. While it is true that much of the dye has been cast by the time one can make mature and reasoned choices about their life, with the use of the appropriate game mechanics, it still may be possible to bring out the best that exists within a person.

How do we then reinvent ourselves to be who we actually would like to be in a world where we must play the hand we are dealt? If we were playing a card game like poker, it might be as simple as discarding a few in order to rebuild the hand. Unfortunately, life does not work that way. However, just as poker is based on a set of rules and mechanics that determine the nature of play, the same could be said for life itself. It is just that in life, the mechanics are somewhat less obvious and not necessarily organized in a way that promotes improved outcomes.

Many college students see themselves as a stranger in a strange land on the first day they arrive on campus. This is not all that dissimilar to the experience of the gamer entering a new virtual world for the first time. The challenge for both is to create a life worth living: one that has meaning, is rewarding, and is satisfying. Something that is often easier said than done. However, by exploring those elements that when combined create a life, we can construct a framework with the relevant game mechanics capable of empowering a person to make positive changes in their life.

Constructing a Life

It is often said that the more things change, the more they stay the same. Patterns formed in childhood serve as guideposts that ensure we travel the same path (though in different contexts) over and over again. Thus it is not surprising that many prefer the freedom (or at least the appearance of freedom) that exists in a game environment. In a game, a person can choose an avatar that embodies all of these characteristics they would like to have and spend the rest of the game developing various skills and capabilities that turn desired elements into a reality, or at least into something that gives the appearance of being real.

However, what appears to be relatively easy when playing a game swiftly turns into the near impossible when it comes to life in the real world. All of a sudden, we no longer seem free to choose anything as we resign ourselves to living the hand that appears to have been dealt. Nonetheless those same mechanics that facilitate the formation of a life in games also exist in the real world, albeit in a more scattered and haphazard fashion.

Who we are and how we fit within the world all revolves around identity. Feeling secure in who we are and what we want enables us to take risks when making external connections. These risks are not insubstantial and can serve as an impediment for building a successful and satisfying life. For example, the risk of rejection is very real when attempting to connect with new people. Another can be found in terms of the risk of feeling dumb as a part of any attempt to connect with new ideas.

Creating a strong identity helps to build a reputation that serves as the external touch point for making connections with other persons, places, or things. As social animals, human beings thrive when feeling connected. These connections form the basis for establishing relationships that can be crucial for learning to take place. For many, it begins with the bedtime story that many parents read to their children every night. The story serves as a guidepost for exploring the wondrous persons, places, and things that exist within the pages of a good book. It extends later on in life to the stories we construct as we develop new connections that help fashion those experiences that enrich our lives.

Our experiences both shape and are shaped by who we are. They accumulate to both reinforce who we are and to serve as building blocks that help to construct a meaningful and rewarding life. More importantly, they form the basis for achieving success. Experiencing success is perhaps the best motivator for taking the risk associated with trying something new.

Often success begets success and as experiences begin to pile up, a person's own story begins to take shape. One way of thinking about life experiences is that they are the equivalent of lines on a resume that serve to remind us where we have been and form the foundation for making the case that we are ready and qualified to take the next step.

The major steps for building a life are identified in Figure 6.1.

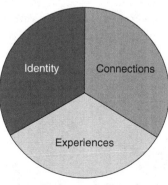

Elements of a Life

Figure 6.1

To understand the how the development of a reputation, social relationships, and a resume becomes the outward manifestation of who we are as a person, we need to explore in more depth the role played by identity, connections, and experiences. Looking more closely at each element will enable us to see how the mechanics found in many games designed to advance play, or indistinguishable from those same mechanics that lead to the development of a life.

Identity

How many nights does a young child go to bed wishing they were smarter, more athletic, thinner, or prettier? In fact, the list could probably go on and on. Of course, one of the benefits of a game environment is none of that matters—you can be whomever you have always hoped to become. A person can change gender, race, age, and size. With the creation of an avatar, in a matter of minutes a gamer can start the process of assuming the identity of the person they have always wanted to be.

Selecting an avatar is of course only the first step toward constructing an identity capable of serving as the cornerstone of a real or fabricated life. There are in fact many facets to the concept of identity. Three of the most important are what we will call: Compass, Competence, and Comparisons.

If life is a journey, then it can be valuable knowing whether or not one is moving in the "right" direction. Just as a compass can tell north from south and help guide a traveler to their destination, we all possess a similar compass that helps us determine right from wrong, good versus bad, and what should and should not be done.

Who we are is often defined in terms of what we do. To affirm our identities and create a positive sense of self, we strive to achieve a feeling of accomplishment through our actions. The tangible outcomes associated with mastering a set of skills, successfully grappling with the intricacies of a particular task, or overcoming the obstacles found in a challenging environment, all serve as touch points for both reinforcing our created identities and motivating continued play. Having mastery over a concept, technique, skill, or set of facts can help to propel an avatar along a particular path. More importantly, being competent at something helps to foster positive feelings about oneself.

Success frequently only becomes meaningful when individuals are able to compare her achievements with those of others. A person might feel good about her efforts, but the extent to which they believe they have been successful is often influenced by relative comparisons. It is when a person likes their position relative to others that their behavior is reinforced and feelings of contentment arise. Relative position is a foundational element for building self-esteem and thus plays an important role in how we feel about the identity that we call our own.

All of this sounds straightforward unless you are a student at an institution of higher education. Away from home for the first time, many students encounter difficulties adjusting to their new environment. Plagued with homesickness, overwhelmed by their new found freedom without parental constraints, or encountering difficulties in managing their coursework, the freshman experience is often more about confronting one's lack of competence than attaining mastery over anything. Even more problematic is that many successes are not shared because of privacy concerns. Hence even when positive opportunities exist for developing self-esteem, university rules and regulations work against creating an environment that promotes feelings of self-worth.

While we might like to think that a compass is the result of good parenting, competence follows from hard work, and comparisons are made possible with positive outcomes, all of this is easier said than done. Notwithstanding the challenges, the mechanics that exist in games or in real life have an important role to play in the formation of identity. Some of the more important components related to identity are illustrated in Figure 6.2.

IDENTITY		
Compass	Competence	Comparisons
Theme	Mastery	Measurement
Belief	Confidence	Success
Reinforcement	Progression	Self-esteem

Figure 6.2

Compass

An important mechanic for developing a compass is the use of narrative to create an overarching theme that can serve as the context for play.[1] A good story forms the basis for some underlying epic drama capable of taking gameplay from the doldrums of everyday life and creating an entire alternate reality. One example of this kind of drama can be found in a story structured around the triumph of good over evil. Within this context, overpowering evil can become something honorific and as a result, actions that contribute to the goal helps to solidify a sense that one is moving in the "right" direction.

What exactly constitutes the right direction hinges on the adoption of a belief system that is designed to support the overarching theme. Whether emerging from a belief in a supreme being, a set of ideals, or something else, such a system forms the foundation for drawing a distinction between right and wrong. By associating these stories with a higher power, for example, they take on a greater meaning and hence exert a stronger influence over a particular belief system. It helps to fix our place in the cosmos and give our lives meaning.

Rituals are another example of a mechanic designed to affirm the underlying belief system. They might be nothing more than the playing of the national anthem before the start of a sporting contest, or in the tossing of a coin prior to the start to determine which side each team will defend or who begins the game with possession of the ball. This opening ritual pays homage to the notion of fairness as the ritual is designed to demonstrate to the crowd that neither team will start the contest with an unfair advantage. The playing of the national anthem confers honor to the contest by suggesting that the game is part of something larger than a mere contest between two teams.

While rituals are designed to buttress an underlying belief system, an additional element is often introduced to reinforce behavior that is consistent with a set of beliefs. One often used mechanic designed to provide reinforcement within the context of a game is the idea of a bonus. Bonuses can be used to create a variable ratio reward structure.[2]

If, for example, a person knows that they are going to win at a game every time it is played, they eventually will grow bored with the whole endeavor. On the other hand, if the outcome is uncertain and hence winning is a reward that occurs without regular frequency, then they will become more interested in trying and trying again to see if this time (at least) they can prevail. In this sense winning is a bonus that occurs without regular frequency.

Competence

Games are designed to enable the player to assume the role of "master of the universe." In other words, they can choose a role to play, get better at playing that role as the game progresses, and if they are particularly good or lucky, can save the day. Good game design has the player building skills that enable them to both advance play, but more importantly, feel good about themselves. We all like to feel in control over what is happening and where we are going. Control stems from competence as the abilities developed enable the player to leave less to chance and more as the outcome of their actions.

It is all about developing mastery over a set of ideas, skills, or actions. Gaining competence can come as the result of learning, doing, or being part of something. In each case, whether the player has mastered stage of a game is determined by their success or failure at some assessment mechanism.[3] Passing a test, overcoming a challenge, or reaching a goal are all examples of ways that players can build self-confidence.

Confident players are ones who are willing to not only take the next challenge but also look forward to developing new skills and abilities. Confidence, however, can easily be gained or lost. To reassure players that they are making progress toward the successful completion of a goal, mechanics such as a point system are used as sources for continuous feedback.[4] The number of lives left, the health of a character, and a whole host of other measures serve to affirm that the player is achieving success and hence moving in a positive if not *the* right direction. They exist at every stage and serve as constant reminders of a job well done and serve primarily as a mechanism that reinforces behavior.

It can be a long time from start to the finish of a game and waiting that length of time without reinforcement can easily discourage a player from continuing. Hence one mechanic that is often employed is the concept of a level.[5] The completion of a level serves as an intermediate step where progress can be assessed, reinforced, and rewarded. Levels tend to be progressive with each one representing a higher degree of difficulty. This helps to foster a growing sense of accomplishment and helps to reduce the level of frustration. It also makes it easier to couple rewards with specific activities. Players know exactly what a reward is for and levels make it possible to earn achievements sooner rather than having to wait until later. Hence they serve as a constant source of motivation.

Comparisons

The advantage of using something as simple as points or levels is that they can easily be measured and thus turn into achievements. When a certain number of points have been earned or a new level reached, the accomplishment is often codified in an achievement that can take on the form of a badge, trophy, or award. These achievements are a mechanic that serves as tangible forms of recognition that demonstrates mastery associated with development of a skill or competency.[6]

It is not just about recognizing success with an achievement, it is also about putting that success into evidence. Badges are one type of symbol that serves as an effective way to demonstrate to the others their accomplishments.[7] As importantly, they can also serve as a means for comparing performance.

While there can be a great deal of satisfaction associated with earning a badge or winning a game, victory or success takes on greater significance when it serves as a basis for making relative comparisons. These relative comparisons not only foster a healthy competition but also serve as a mechanism for gaining status and ultimately achieving self-esteem. Hence a leader board, for example, can do much more than merely assist a player keep their eye on the prize and serve as a continuous source for motivation.[8]

Connections

For some, a good crossword puzzle on a Sunday afternoon is their concept of heaven. Often a solitary endeavor, a feeling of satisfaction is achieved when all of the boxes are filled in with the correct answer. Of course, technology has changed all of that with the development of social games like Words with Friends. Rather than a solitary endeavor, word puzzles can now do much more than provide a challenge for a single individual. Playing with friends or strangers for that matter adds an entirely new dimension to what many have found to be a far richer experience.

Challenging oneself can be satisfying, but challenging others can turn satisfaction into feelings of superiority. It is one thing to overcome the challenge created by a game designer and it is quite something else to place your skills at work against a live opponent. Completing a puzzle can be much more rewarding when it turns into a contest between equally matched opponents. Victory confers status, provides external validation of one's abilities and contributes toward building self-esteem. It also provides the individual with an opportunity to join a community, develop collaborative skills and form relationships. The outcome is the acquisition of a set of skills, relationships, and experiences that lead to even greater feelings of personal satisfaction.

From this perspective, playing games like Words with Friends is not all that different from what happens at college. While getting an A on an exam can be a satisfying accomplishment, it becomes more special when it is shared with others where it can be acknowledged as something special. Pleasing oneself is important, but when others are even more pleased, it heightens the satisfaction associated with the experience. Students form relationships to test their abilities, become part of a community, and generate future opportunities for success. Much is dependent on the connections that are formed in a relatively short period of time (generally four years).

One way of thinking about these connections is to combine them into three groupings: Pals, Peers, and Profession. These groupings also can serve as a structure for understanding how mechanics can

CONNECTIONS		
Pals	Peers	Profession
Common interests	Common characteristics	Common objectives
Touchpoints	Social norms	Information sharing
Mutual support	Collaboration	Competition

Figure 6.3

be used to foster relationships that have the power to transform a simple gaming experience connected to one's entire life. In combination, they all contribute toward gaining a sense of place and provide a springboard for jumping off into the future. These groupings and their associated mechanics are illustrated in Figure 6.3.

Pals

Friendships that are based on common interests and shared interaction fall within the category of pals. In a multiplayer game environment, friends or other collections of individuals that share common interests often form groups capable of advancing game play. Sometimes these groups are referred to as clans, thereby suggesting ties that transcend simple friendships. More importantly, the concept of a clan suggests a common purpose and set of goals that can only be achieved if everyone in the group works together.[9] The concept of a clan is an example of a mechanic designed to bring together individuals with shared interests.[10]

In order for groups to form, some mechanism must exist that opens up touch points between current or prospective members. A clan is only as strong as the ties that bind it. But they are ties that are not available to everyone. A clan is a close-knit group formed around common characteristics, mutual acquaintances, shared experiences, or communal interests. In order for the clan to be effective, there must be a mechanism that both facilitates the making of connections and serves as a gatekeeper to exclude others. Creating private areas that are not open to everyone, the use of private information that is available to only a select number, or keeping membership a secret are all examples of mechanisms designed to exclude others from participation.[11]

If anyone can join the clan, then it becomes less effective at what clans do best: provide mutual support for its members. Mutual support offers comfort and serves as a respite from interactions with what can be a stressful environment. Close-knit groups serve as the foundation for the formation of tight personal relationships and make shared experiences possible. Mechanics that serve to foster the clan and the concept of mutual support can be found in similar modes of dress, attendance at the same events, or emerge in the form of shared activities.[12]

Peers

As individuals begin to make connections outside their comfort zone, emphasis shifts from Pals to Peers. Peer groups are collections of individuals with common characteristics. They begin to emerge when a critical mass of similarly situated individuals develops through the extension of one's reach beyond close associates. For example, fraternal organizations, associations, or clubs tend to be comprised individuals that share similar characteristics like race, academic success, social interests, or pedigree.

Many games use organizational forms like guilds as a mechanism for the type of social cohesion needed for effective teamwork.[13] In older times, guilds were organized around common economic functions. Today, peer groups are similarly organized around commonalities, but those points of intersection expand beyond economic concerns.[14]

Guilds or peer groups are part of a broader social system that can have a strong influence on behavior. Human beings have a desire to belong to something that brings them into contact with similar people and thus naturally tend to form groups. What emerges within these groups are social norms that both guide behavior and provide a means for measuring performance. For example, if everyone else has reached level 5 within a specified period of time, then the norm is that everyone who wants to become a member should be able to do the same. Social norms form the foundation for conventions that serve as mechanisms for establishing standards for behavior and achievement.[15]

Perhaps the greatest influence of social norms on individual behavior is that they lead to collaboration between the members. Having common goals and objectives nurtured and guided by norms is an effective mechanism for getting individuals with similar interests to work together. This form of collaborative behavior can advance gameplay or lead to a higher level of success in life.[16]

Profession

If life is truly about the survival of the fittest, what is the best way to ensure that you are more fit than everyone else? Eating right, getting plenty of exercise and generally just about anything that will improve one's physical and mental health will make a positive contribution.

However, the concept of being fit extends beyond the individual. Being fit also means taking advantage of those around you who can offset any weaknesses and extenuates existing strengths. Being a part of a team that shares common objectives can make an individual vastly more effective at surviving or actually prospering.

In some games, movement to the next level only becomes possible with teamwork. In others, the experience is heightened or becomes more valuable with membership in a group. In still others, being part of a group may not be necessary in order to advance an objective, but rather serves as a support mechanism to provide a sense of camaraderie through a shared experience.

To form teams based around a common objective, some type of mechanic is needed to get the word out that a group is forming, is in need of a new member, or that someone is available to join an existing association. Professional associations, like many personal ones, are formed from a matching process which often takes place using mechanisms such as message boards, online forums, or specialty websites.[17] By creating a central location for matching interests and abilities, information can be efficiently shared.

The outcome of this matching process is the formation of teams that are often in competition with each other. In life as in games, often scarcity is used as a mechanic designed to ensure that there is not enough to go around and hence there can only be one winner.[18] Alternatively, in the absence of scarcity, the winning team is generally the one that amasses the largest number of points, scores, vanquishes the source of evil, or in some other way manages to save the day.

Experiences

We all need to learn at least some basic skills and knowledge in order to make a positive contribution in anything we choose to do. Fortified with the means for creating success, we embark on a life that consists of experiences designed to accomplish personal success and in many instances, assist in the success of others. Often this occurs in conjunction with those choices made to ensure one's livelihood. Work and the corresponding professional success that is achieved is one of the primary means that individuals create a positive self-image and build esteem. The three components are illustrated in Figure 6.4.

EXPERIENCES		
Learning	Life	Livelihood
Co-creation Risk management Frustration	Uncertainty Flexibility Victories	Internships Awareness Skills

Figure 6.4

Learning

The concept of learning has changed dramatically in recent years. First there was passive learning. Think of a student who sits in a lecture hall and passively listens to the professor pontificate on a particular subject. Passive learning then turned into active learning as students were given a role in the learning process that required them to do something more than just sit back and listen. However, merely turning students into active learners who are working on problems that are of little interest did not do much in terms of engagement. Thus, active learning gave way to personalized learning where lessons were made relevant to the student. All of this, however, has been transcended by the current interest in adaptive learning. Here, technology is used to identify deficiencies and customized content can be provided to correct any lack of student understanding.

What is missing from all of this is the type of learning experiences that exist in many games. Sure, within the structure of many games learning is all of the above: passive, active, personalized, and adaptive. However, what makes learning through play different is that it is based largely on what we might call a co-created experience. The player has a great deal of input into how they learn, when they learn, and what they learn. Most importantly, learning emerges from the play itself. The game motivates the desire to learn as advancement is often dependent on the development of skills or knowledge. It is the interaction between the player's pieces or character and the game environment that fosters learning.

The completion of quests provides one type of mechanism for building needed skills and demonstrating one's prowess to potential allies, opponents, or group members.[19] Alternatively, traveling around the board in games like Monopoly creates opportunities for learning how to allocate scarce resources, build a dominant position relative to others, and negotiate when things turn sour.[20]

When outcomes are less than certain and a lack of success can significantly lower self-esteem, learning seems more like an exercise in loss aversion rather than a positive experience designed to enhance knowledge or build skills. Mechanics like levels that are designed to break a game down into stages or small chunks can be used to reduce the stakes associated with learning a given concept.[21] As a result, failure can be contained, resolved, and overcome without placing the player in a position where the best alternative is to just give up and stop play.

By design, the essence of gameplay is not to accomplish a particular task in the fewest moves or the shortest amount of time. Games are interesting because they are challenging—obstacles must be overcome if the player is to advance and ultimately win the game. To minimize potential player frustration, game designers pay careful attention to pacing.[22] The goal is to challenge the player enough to get them to take the next step while not requiring so much that they become discouraged and stop trying.

Life

Many of us take comfort in having a plan. There is something reassuring about having a sense of where you have been and where you are going. For some, the exact nature of how we are going to get from point A to point B is not really what is important. What we really want to know is how it is all going to end. Does the journey come with a happy ending or will it end in frustration and failure? As long as it all turns out the way we would like, or better than whatever we can imagine, then the path and, along with it, the plan are not all that important.

However, all of this may come to naught because nothing is certain. An often used mechanic in games and something that appears in every life is an element of randomness.[23] In a game, randomness may be the key to preventing boredom. If everything was known with certainty, there would be little point for many to play. Think in terms of sporting contests, while we always want our team to win; there is something extra special when that win comes in the last few final moments of a contest whose outcome was anything but certain. In a similar fashion, life itself becomes more interesting when the outcome of the various challenges that must be overcome is far from certain.

While we would all like to take comfort in knowing that everything will end the way we would like, what exactly constitutes a happy ending is subject to change. As life is experienced and one challenge after another is undertaken, exactly what we want or how we would like things to change often does not stay the same. As a result there is often more than one path that leads to an outcome that is subject to change. The existence of multiple paths is an example of a mechanism utilized by game designers to impart some flexibility in design that keeps players engaged as they adapt to random events or changes in their own desires or ambitions.[24]

Regardless of the road traveled, what is important is that the end leads to a victory of some sorts. Success can be fleeting unless it is embodied in something of substance that can endure through time. Winning the Super Bowl has more significance than winning a league championship. A league championship has more importance than winning an individual game. Winning a game endures for a longer period of time than having a great practice. The concept of an epic win used by game designers represents a mechanic that turns success into something more. It serves both as the crowning achievement of one's life and to a certain extent, forms the foundation for justifying one's existence. It is a mechanic that gives meaning to both actions and outcomes.[25]

Livelihood

The current fashion in higher education is to incorporate some sort of experienced-based learning in the curriculum. It is not only designed to send a signal to potential employers about the viability of a candidate, but it also brings an uncertain future into the present. An internship or apprenticeship can serve as a mechanism for helping the student understand what the future holds and thus bring that uncertain future that is far away into the very real present.[26] By helping students see what they are working toward, they may adopt a different perspective about the present.

It is really about building an awareness of what is possible. We typically know only what we are told or what we are able to glean from our limited experiences. Very much the product of how we are raised and where we have been raised, it is difficult to think outside of that "box" in order to gain a greater understanding of what is possible. To build awareness and encourage players to explore their virtual game environment, many designers use an open world or what is sometimes referred to as a sandbox approach. Here freedom is used as a mechanic that allows players to discover more about themselves and the world around them in order to empower them in a way that creates greater awareness and new opportunities.[27]

However, just opening up someone's eyes to a broader range of possibilities will do little if they do not have the skills required to capitalize on those opportunities. This perhaps points to the largest difference between learning in games and life. Games are for the most part all about skill building. Sure a backstory can provide a much needed background to provide a rationale for why a certain set of skills are necessary, but the learning is focused more on acquiring the abilities necessary to overcome the various challenges that stand in the way. College on the other hand is more about mastering a body of knowledge and the development of the requisite skills required to do that are left largely to the students themselves to figure out.

Hence we see a fundamental difference between games and higher education. In games the focus is on skill building and various mechanics exist to walk the player through the development process in a manner that leads to success.[28] The acquisition of skills places the player in a position to succeed regardless of what challenge they might face. Overcoming various challenges promotes learning and by the end of the game, a player has not only mastered a set of skills but also acquired the knowledge necessary to be successful within the game environment.

In contrast, academics seem to be slaves to their discipline. Having been trained to master a certain body of knowledge, they view their job as one of imparting knowledge on the young minds that enroll in their courses. Knowledge transfer becomes the focus of the learning experience with an implicit assumption that students already possess the requisite skills required to absorb new ideas. For students that don't, it becomes someone else's problem or is left to the supposition that the student probably chose the wrong major because they must not have a natural aptitude for the subject matter. Thus students are not taught within the discipline of their choice how to master the concepts needed to obtain the knowledge necessary for success. Skill building is either relegated to specialized courses or to computer programs that use repetition to achieve some type of rote learning.

Mechanics

An award-winning game is often based on a great story, amazing graphics, and an incredible user experience. That being said, it is the mechanics that guide the player and shape the nature of play that is really the unsung hero of any well-designed game. It is about assisting the player to achieve their best while keeping them engaged and motivated to remain in the game.

Similar mechanics could be used to enhance the student experience. In the classroom where the lecture still prevails and PowerPoint presentations have become the preferred method for delivering course content, we see various mechanics in play. Examples include the amount of text on a given slide, the way that bullet points can fly across the screen, or the use of pictures to break up the monotony. Yet even if all of the rules are followed, slides can never replicate the spontaneity that can exist when using a chalkboard to communicate.

Just as random play in a well-designed game is never truly random, a chalk and talk based lecture can create the illusion that knowledge is being created as part of a shared experience in real time. The lecture is not something that has been given multiple times from the same set of dusty notes, but instead is a unique experience that is new and fresh. Mechanics are not a substitute for good design. Rather they are the mechanism for turning great design into a vibrant and meaningful learning experience.

PART III

Transformation through Gamification

CHAPTER 7

The Classroom as a Game Space

To understand the true potential of gamification, we need to think about why games appear to offer such an attractive learning environment. When human beings play, they can often imagine that they can be whomever they want to be. They have a hand in shaping the environment in which play occurs and therefore feel empowered in the belief that they can positively effect change.[1] They have some control over the outcome and what it takes to succeed is more easily understood. Within the context of a game, they can sometimes become the person they always wished they could be and in many ways, there is nothing more gratifying.[2]

No longer are they unattractive or overweight. They can be smarter than they normally perceive themselves to be as they carefully select a form of play or a game that lends itself to their natural skills and abilities. They can form social relationships that have a shared purpose in an environment where it is easier to understand right from wrong. They can be the hero and no longer just one of the anonymous masses.

What is being suggested is that it is not about winning or losing, nor is it about how you play the game. Rather, it is about who you become as you engage in play. While it is always nice to win, the underlying premise here is that people play because it makes them feel good about themselves.[3] They feel good because they are able to assume a persona that brings out the best they have to offer. It is the development of a positive self-image and it is the feeling of empowerment that comes when they place that persona in action. They can become the hero that saves the day, the person who is sought out by others, or an important part of something that can at times become larger than life.[4]

Feeling good about oneself motivates the individual to try harder and achieve success. The key from an educational perspective is to connect a sense of self to positive performance in the classroom. The goal is for the student to see how learning can help them become the person they hope to be.[5] Hence the focus shifts from the mastery of a body of knowledge to personal growth and development. Knowledge becomes a tool that helps a person discover more about who they are and what they are capable of achieving rather than some abstract end that may have some benefit in a future that is hard to imagine.

Gamification of the Learning Experience

Who we are is often defined in terms of what we do. To affirm our identities and create a positive self-image, we strive to achieve a sense of accomplishment through our actions. The tangible outcomes associated with mastering a set of skills, successfully grappling with the intricacies of a particular task, or overcoming the obstacles found in a challenging environment, all serve as touch points for both reinforcing our created identities and motivating continued play.[6]

Gamification is often thought of as being nothing more than the addition of Points, Badges, and Leaderboards. However, the process of gamifying the learning experience can contain so much more. Taking a more holistic approach, the gamification of the learning experience contains the following elements:

- **Narrative**
Many games rely on narrative to advance play. We fall asleep listening to stories as children, imagine ourselves as imaginary heroes or heroines when we play make believe, and craft stories about ourselves within the broader context of social media.

- **Identity**
Games often allow us to become the person we would always like to be and at least temporarily, forget most, if not all, of our own shortcomings. We tend to see ourselves in the characters that we create and their successes become our own.

- **Co-Created Experience**
Within many games, the player has an important role in defining the experience. The player is not a passive participant, but rather becomes an active contributor to what, how, and why play advances.

- **Skill Development**

Individuals like to feel that they are in control of their actions and to some degree can influence outcomes. Mastery comes from the ability to confront any possibility and succeed.

- **Leveling Up rather than Leveling Down**

Games are designed with the idea that the player advances with each new development rather than minimizing as many losses as possible along the way. It is about empowerment rather than failure.

- **Frustration-Free Learning**

Good game design is focused on making the experience challenging enough to be engaging, but not so difficult that it becomes frustrating.

- **If at First You Don't Succeed**

It is not about try, try, try again. Rather it is about being able to self-edit—the ability to go back and fix things that you now realize could be done better.

- **Opportunities for Building Self-Esteem**

A well-designed game will offer a series of well-crafted experiences designed to help the player feel better than when they started. It is designed to make a person feel good rather than bad about themselves.

- **Healthy Competition**

Whether it is against other players, some performance standard, or an imaginary opponent, competition often brings out the best in each of us.

- **Relative Position**

Relative position can be an effective mechanism for building self-esteem. Games often contain mechanics that make it easy for a player to compare their performance relative to others.

- **Peer Feedback**

People seek approval in the form of feedback. Often the most effective feedback comes from peers.

- **An Experience that Encourages Risk Taking**

Learning often entails taking a risk. Feeling more secure makes it easier to try something new.

The Journey Approach

The principle challenge in gamifying the learning experience is that many students seem to be more interested in averting losses than achieving success.[7] Whether they are trying to prevent losing points on an exam, looking foolish answering a question in class, or selecting easy rather than difficult courses to take, it is more about averting losses than gaining success.[8] Thus in order to create a successful learning experience, it must be designed to build students up so that they are more willing to take a risk and try to learn something new. It is about replacing fear with achievement.

These principles are incorporated into what we will identify as the Journey Approach. The Journey Approach is based on the premise that learning best takes place when it is part of a co-created process. Students are no different from anyone else: they do not like to be told what to do. Rather, they are looking for assistance in reaching goals that *they* establish along a journey that takes them where *they* would like to go. They want the freedom to explore, a variety of pathways to choose from, and the tools needed to help them succeed.

The concept of taking a journey works well in the current environment where the rise of social media has done more than turn today's undergraduate student into a multimodal consumer of information. It has turned them into storytellers who share their own personal journeys on a daily or even moment by moment basis.[9] As a result, story has taken on a significance that has gone far beyond a means for entertainment or a method for disseminating knowledge.[10] The stories we tell about ourselves create a form of expression that helps to develop a sense of identity and place within a social fabric consisting of friends, relatives, and peers.[11]

Thus it seems only natural that if a student, having invested heavily in the development of this human capital (the ability to tell stories), is growing accustomed to using story as a form of personal expression, that it may make sense to also use it as a tool for learning. Instead of asking students to develop a skill set that is divorced from what they employ in their private lives, more successful learning outcomes may be achieved with a melding of their personal and professional lives.

Using story affords the potential for transforming the concept of active learning into a co-created learning experience.[12] While the construction of a story is a form of active learning, it is not the result of completing exercises that have little meaning and often seem disconnected from the object of what it is we want the student to learn. Rather, the student has a role to play and by achieving success within the parameters established, gains a command of the material required to advance.

The co-creation approach provides the student with a framework for crafting her own choices, offers assistance for selecting the best one, and finally, affords an opportunity for the student to see and experience the consequences of her choices. It is the narrative that ties all of the choices together and by closing off promising storylines or expanding the length of the story (because poor choices were made), the student experiences first hand which choices truly work toward achieving a desired goal.

Within the journey approach to learning, mastering a body of knowledge becomes the means to an end and not the end itself. For the hero to save the day, she must have a firm grasp of basic concepts and utilize them in a way that good can triumph over evil, or in the case of economics, scarcity can be held in abeyance or be overcome altogether. The journey can consist of a series of challenges designed to both create a deeper understanding of important concepts and help the student to gain a sense of mastery over the material.

In this context, learning becomes a part of establishing an identity within the context of the experience.[13] In that sense, learning within a course mimics the way learning is done as part of everyday life. It is not an activity distinct from one's life, but instead becomes an integral part of what naturally occurs on a daily basis. Thus the journey approach encompasses the following principles:

- **A Positive Learning Environment**
There is no reason to assume that students are any different from anyone else. The challenge therefore becomes one of creating a learning environment where a set of positive values can be generated in order to encourage and rationalize behavior that furthers a set of learning objectives.[14] If the environment can be created in a way that allows the student to visibly grow and develop over time, the experience will have more meaning and hence stand a greater chance of forming a lasting impression.[15]

- **Bite Size Chunks**
Ideas must be encapsulated in blocks that are challenging, but not to the point where they become discouraging.[16] Students must have

some freedom to explore and exert some level of control over what they learn and how they go about learning. Some challenges require working together and the completion of challenges must confer some type of a reward and an opportunity for displaying that reward.[17]

• **Process rather than Outcomes**

By comparing games to current educational practices, there are both subtle and substantial differences that cannot be reconciled merely by using a different vocabulary or including an instruction manual so that students can better understand the game comparison. Most college courses are outcomes based rather than providing the process-based experience found in games. Students are assigned a certain amount of knowledge to be learned and are rewarded based on how well they master that knowledge. Thus while they might become more proficient in solving problems, interpreting readings, or analyzing situations, a connection is missing between their greater understanding of a particular subject and what it means in terms of who they are or how they stack up relative to their peers. Students feel only marginally more powerful, and in many cases, are just as confused about who they are or what they are capable of doing.

• **The Importance of Context**

Most disciplines of study can be applied to situations that students experience every day in their own lives. The difference between an 18-year-old freshman and a 40-year-old executive MBA student is context. MBA students are more familiar with events in the world that they live in and have a relatively longer experience set that better enables them to place basic economic ideas into the appropriate frame of reference. While many textbooks understanding that their students have little familiarity with the events of the day try to compensate by including boxes that attempt to place an idea within a current event, often these events are unfamiliar or uninteresting to the average student. Without a rich set of life experiences, it becomes difficult for undergraduate students to not only learn but also apply basic concepts in a meaningful way.[18]

• **An Overarching Theme**

It is hard to build toward a goal when you don't have one and it is challenging to set goals when you are lacking in purpose. We are all striving to achieve a sense of place within the cosmos in order to give our lives meaning. We are purposeful beings who create goals in order to organize our actions.[19] Therefore, one way to

facilitate the learning process is to create an overarching story line capable of providing a rationale for why a particular set of concepts is important. Students will be more engaged if they think that there is some larger purpose to their study and if the tasks or challenges that have been developed as part of the learning process are designed to reinforce some sense of meaning.[20] This can set the stage for generating an epic win either at the end of the semester, the end of one's college career, or for later in life.[21]

• **Rethinking What It Means to Be an Active Learner**
Active learning is not the result of completing exercises that have little meaning and often seem disconnected from the object of what it is we want the student to learn. Rather, it is a co-created experience where the student has a role to play and by achieving success within the parameters established, gains a command of the material required to advance.

The Hero's Journey

The goal of the Journey Approach is to transform students from being passive listeners into active story makers. By tapping into those universal themes that are embedded within a familiar story archetype, students will be able to appreciate that any subject is not built on some foreign set of concepts that offer little meaning, but instead shares many of the same elements stories that they have already seen or read.

Perhaps the best known story archetype is that of the Hero's Journey created by Joseph Campbell.[22] It shares the foundation for many journeys like Dorothy in the Wizard of Oz, Luke Skywalker in Star Wars, and can be even found in the biblical story of Moses.

As students undertake their own "hero's journey," they encounter challenges that must be overcome using the important subject-related concepts that they learn along the way. As their character achieves success, the student begins to think of learning as a positive force for both individual and social change. By adopting the role of the hero, they can establish an identity within the context of a story that can take on epic proportions; thereby contributing to a sense of self-esteem. It is not just about learning important concepts but is also about empowering a student so that they can make progress along their own personal journey. It is designed to place individual action within a social context; thereby helping students understand that a single individual can truly make a difference.

The basic Hero's Journey archetype can take the following form:[23]

SETTING THE STAGE

1. The Fundamental Problem

Our hero grows up in a familiar environment and has never been in a position where they had to think too much about the nature of things. While problems exists, they take on the form of just the way things are and have always been.

2. The Call for a Solution

Something goes wrong. This creates a problem of such severity that it has the potential to dramatically change the familiar and comfortable world. As our hero becomes increasingly aware of the magnitude of the problem, they become motivated to overcome their ignorance in order to become a force for positive change.

3. Avoiding the Call

Change can be scary and our hero experiences a growing awareness that any solution will alter the world as they know it. A growing sense of dread becomes overwhelming and as a result, they refuse the call thinking they can stubbornly hold on to the past.

4. Acquiring Skills, Tools, and Knowledge

As the ramifications of the new normal becomes more apparent, our hero realizes that if events are allowed to run unchecked, then the past will be lost regardless and the future will be even worse than the present. This new realization enables our hero to hold their fear in check and to take the first steps toward acquiring the means for becoming an agent for positive change.

THE JOURNEY BEGINS

5. Entry into a New World

Newly committed to become a force for positive change, our hero journeys to a new world where they can enhance their understanding of the fundamental problem and explore

potential solutions. A new world brings with it a fresh perspective for developing a deeper understanding of how to overcome the problem leading to the destruction of everything our hero knows and cares about.

6. Friends, Enemies and Challenges

As our hero explores new ways of thinking and doing things, they are confronted with new challenges. Friends become rivals and rivals are empowered to stop our hero from achieving success. Our hero has no choice but to experiment with new things and modes of thought in order to eventually solve the fundamental problem.

7. Uncovering New Knowledge

After much trial and error, our hero begins to come to the realization that the answer to the fundamental problem was there all along. As the veil of ignorance that had kept them in the dark for so long starts to fall, our hero begins to see that a solution exists after all. Honing their skills, our hero continues to refine her understanding of how change may become a force for good; she comes to the growing realization that the future can become a place that is better than the past.

8. Facing the Ultimate Challenge

Nothing is ever easy and a threat emerges that could possibly prevent our hero from making it back with the solution to the fundamental problem. Something threatens to take it all away and our hero must overcome what they hope will be the final challenge.

THE ROAD TO VICTORY

9. Formulating a Solution

Emerging from the ultimate challenge, our hero is now ready to solve the fundamental problem. Empowered with this new understanding, our hero is now prepared to return home and save the day.

10. Encountering One Last Challenge

On the way back, our hero is confronted by one last challenge that forces them to question whether or not they have actually uncovered the truth and really formulated a solution to the fundamental problem. What emerges from this last challenge is the final piece of the puzzle that brings everything into perspective.

11. Mysteries Revealed
With all the pieces finally out in the open, our hero has a chance to reflect on what it all means. They are finally able to place the fundamental problem into the larger picture.

12. Celebrating Victory!
Our hero returns home and saves the day changing their world in a way that makes it better.

Creating a Storyline

Every good story contains at least one continuous thread that weaves together the various characters and events that become the lifeblood of a good tale. While the hero's journey provides a framework for how the journey unfolds, it does not mandate the storyline that is woven through the various stages. In fact, that is why Campbell's mono myth is so powerful; it offers a scaffold that can easily be erected and shifted from one story line to the next.

One continuous story line can be used to provide meaning and a sense of purpose to the hero's journey. A problem leads to conflict, conflict creates a series of challenges, and as those challenges are overcome, some form of resolution is reached. By breaking the journey into distinct stages, each stage can follow the same general structure. Stories can then be created within a much broader story to form a series of "bite size chunks" that eventually can be combined to create an entire "meal."

As part of a co-created learning experience, it is the engaged student who is part owner of the process and thus supplies the basic story line. In this way, the journey becomes a meaningful experience rather than a requirement they attempt to fulfill with the least amount of pain. In the case of a class in economics, the only requirement would be that the story line is based on the lack of something. After all, most of modern economics is about addressing the fundamental problem of scarcity: there are too many wants and not enough goods and resources to satisfy everyone. However, to provide meaning and give the story a larger than life feeling in order to set the stage for an epic win, it should be of major significance. Examples of potential story lines include

- Climate change has turned the Earth into an inhospitable environment where life no longer exists as we know it.
- The world runs out of fossil fuels and technology has not kept pace and as a result, conventional energy no longer exists.
- A population explosion has placed strain on the ability of the planet to feed all of its inhabitants.
- A global, national, or local community becomes ruled by a powerful dictator or group of mega corporations that enrich themselves at the expense of the general population.
- A pandemic has decimated the population thereby creating a serious challenge to a society that has relied on the division of labor.
- An electronic pulse has rendered electronic devices inoperable and a new society must cope without the benefits of electricity or anything that is not self-powered.

Story Elements

Once a story line has been created, it needs to be populated with story elements. To be effective, these elements should be similar to the ones that are used to create real-life stories on a daily basis. Having spent most of his academic career exploring the role that life stories play in the development of a sense of self and place, Dan McAdams offers the following seven elements that he has found are common to most life stories.[24] They include

- **Narrative Tone**
  Each story embodies an emotional tone that expresses a feeling of optimism or pessimism. It can be up lifting and full of hope or a sobering look at one individual's perception of reality. From the perspective of a student constructed story, this can take the form of the hero who is challenged along the way and at the very end of the day, manages to grasp victory from the jaws of defeat.
- **Imagery**
  The imagery used to develop a story provides a sense of who our hero is and what they are capable of becoming. It provides a sense of the environment in which they operate and provides context

and color to the challenges faced and (hopefully) overcome. Used properly, it can provide depth and richness to the story.

- **Theme**

The theme provides a context for our hero's journey and forms the basis for the underlying story line that establishes the path to be taken and the challenges that need to be overcome. It sets the stage for an adventure that can be larger than life and one that culminates in an epic win.

- **Ideological Setting**

Every hero needs to stand for something good in their efforts to triumph over evil. The ideological setting provides a value system that injects meaning to the purpose driving our hero forward. It can makes us want to care about the story and serve as a means for reaffirming a sense of justice.

- **Nuclear Episodes**

Nuclear episodes are those points in the story where the hero discovers some fundamental truths and as a result, becomes a stronger and better person. As part of a hero's journey, these episodes become the various stages where challenges are encountered and difficulties are overcome.

- **Imagoes**

The hero becomes the idealized personification of the story creator's sense of self and hence becomes a model for powerful action. Every hero has a trait or special ability that sets them apart and provides them with what is necessary for success. They also possess some fundamental weakness that creates its own set of challenges and introduces the possibility of failure.

- **Endings**

We all like a good story to have an ending where issues are resolved. Within the context of the hero's journey, good may triumph over evil, or a fundamental problem that seemed unsolvable is brought to a successful conclusion.

Challenges

Every good story has the central character facing various challenges. Within the context of a co-created learning experience, overcoming challenges within the context of a broader story or theme can

Figure 7.1

accomplish two very important goals. Successfully meeting the rigors of a challenge can have a profound effect on the development of identity. It can help the student feel more secure in their ability to learn new things and develop new skills. Secondly, secure students are ones who are more willing to take risks. By becoming less loss averse, students will push themselves to master concepts that they previously found intimidating and reluctant to tackle. As a result, overcoming a challenge becomes a very important element when designing a co-created learning experience.

The nice thing about using a story archetype like the Hero's Journey is that it organizes the learning process into individual steps that can serve a similar function to levels in games. In a game, at each level the player is confronted by a single or series of challenges that consist of an obstacle that must be overcome in order for play to move forward. By developing the appropriate skills, the player is able to put herself in a position to overcome the obstacle in order to reach some objective. Overcoming an obstacle and reaching some objective demonstrates mastery and forms the basis for creating a rewarding experience for the player. The structure of such a challenge approach can be found in Figure 7.1.

- **Action**
  Instead of inserting the student in a passive role where their job is to absorb knowledge as it is presented to them, they are instead placed in an active role. Actions involve skill development by

using concepts to overcome obstacles that stand in the way of making progress toward the completion of some goal.

- **Obstacles**

While the shortest distance between two points is a straight line, life would not be very interesting if all we did was to try and economize on the time spent performing various activities. Through the use of intelligent use of obstacles, skills can be developed, actions can take on greater meaning, and concepts become less abstract.

- **Concepts**

Homework problems, much to the surprise of many students, often incorporate concepts from the textbook that are needed in order to solve a particular problem. What is often shrouded in the context of an abstract problem is uncovered within the journey approach as concepts become a means for taking action in order to overcome those obstacles that are blocking the path forward toward reaching some objective.

- **Skills**

More often than not, students spend the bulk of their time trying to memorize rather than acquire the skills they need to develop an understanding of the material. What they don't understand is that with the right skills, concepts become easy to understand and apply, obstacles can easily be overcome, and the actions they take will end in success.

Achievements

Achievements serve as a means for assessing learning outcomes and as a basis for determining relative position. Thus they play an important role in providing those intrinsic and extrinsic rewards necessary to motivate student learning. Students want to know not only how they are doing in relation to some absolute scale but also how they compare relative to other members of a class. It can be disheartening to learn that you missed a number of important concepts on an exam, but one can take solace if their performance was significantly higher than the rest of the class. Both contribute to self-esteem.

It is important to pay close attention not only to how a narrative-based learning environment is constructed but also how outcomes are assessed and rewarded. The key is to embed achievements directly into the learning process. By enabling students to earn achievements as they learn, they will feel better about themselves, thereby keeping them engaged and motivated.

A class based on the Journey Approach can be divided into a number of smaller journey teams. For example, in a class of thirty students, there might be five journey teams. Each team serves as a mechanism for peer feedback and as a platform for engaging in healthy competition. Trying to be the most valuable member of a team, or part of a winning team can be a powerful source of motivation.

The 12-step journey process can easily be divided into thirds in order to create opportunities to recognize and acknowledge student achievements. After four stages have been completed, a pause can be inserted into the journey so that students are given an opportunity to combine the elements they have developed into a coherent narrative. By sharing their narratives with other members of their journey team, an opportunity is created for peer-to-peer learning. Each member of the journey team would comment on the work of the other members and vote on who wrote the best narrative, had the best character, or assign awards for other attributes like best use of the course concepts to overcome a particular challenge.

Points would be assigned and a leader board constructed to track the performance of each student. Within a team, students would be vying against other members to win various prizes, earn points and make it to the top of the class leader board. In this way, a healthy competition is created to help motivate students to perform at their best. Students would be given the opportunity to revise their work at any time and hence based on the feedback they received, could improve their narratives before embarking on the next stage of their journey. As the journey moves forward, students continue to earn achievements and points as an additional opportunity for evaluating their work comes after the completion of the next four stages.

With the end of the journey after the completion of the last four stages, one last opportunity is created for assessment and achievement. The person with the most points from each team after the submission of the final narrative could be designated as a superhero and therefore eligible to enter one final competition that will determine the best story in the class. The person who becomes the best of the best would be crowned as the "ultimate hero."

However, just as in life where success depends on personal achievement, but is often assisted by the help of others, each member of the team that produced the ultimate hero could receive bonus points to reflect their contribution to the success of the eventual winner. After all, it was peer feedback that contributed to making the ultimate hero's story the best of the best. Thus, those who played an important role in achieving final victory would have their contribution acknowledged. By doing so, each student has an incentive to not only work hard for themselves but also for the other members of their team. It is way of empowering each to help the other while still preserving the benefits associated with individual achievement.

Gamification and Classroom of the Future

The gamification of the learning experience is designed to shift the focus away from exam performance and toward developing those skills and talents necessary to understand, utilize, create, and communicate ideas. It is flexible in design so that students have an opportunity to personalize the learning process while still offering enough structure so that they do not get easily frustrated. Rewards are internally generated rather than externally given as part of how learning is assessed. Most importantly, learning is not viewed as something distinct from the rest of one's life, but rather becomes an integral part of day–to-day living.

If we want students to gain mastery over specific material, we need to provide them with a set of choices that gives them some control over learning process. This choice needs to be more than whether or not they choose to study on a particular day or how much time they allocate to the process. They must be provided with real choices that affect how much they learn or what they learn as a result of the actions they take. Students need to be placed in a learning environment where choices lead to actions that have consequences that affect real outcomes. By seeing the consequences of the choices that they make, students do not need to wait for external validation from a professor, but rather experience success or failure as choices are actually being made.

Confronted on a regular basis by their lack of knowledge, it should come as no surprise that students are less than enthusiastic about studying. Studying merely reinforces a negative self-image. The key to greater student engagement is to empower them to become active learners who can develop those skills needed to become the masters of their chosen academic discipline.

Rather than thinking of ways to motivate students to do their homework or make modest improvements with respect to their exam scores, gamification should have loftier goals. Exam performance is only one measure of what we really want; the development of a true understanding of the course material that stays with the student beyond the end of a particular course. We want students to learn *and* retain the ideas and concepts associated with a body of knowledge. To accomplish this goal, we can use game mechanics to strengthen the development of personal identity, establish a foundation that demonstrates the usefulness of the material, and serves as motivational elements that contributes to the retention of key ideas.

CHAPTER 8

Creating a Game-Based Student Experience

The typical freshman at a residential college or university is assigned a dorm, a roommate, and a course schedule. Their first friend is (hopefully) their roommate. The first peer group often consists of the people who live on the same floor of their dorm. They might become acquainted with one or two others in their classes (particularly around exam time), and they may or may not join a student group. If they are not too homesick (at least at first), they might even be persuaded to attend a campus event or two.

The point is that their reach starts out very small and slowly expands as they become better acquainted with the campus and more comfortable venturing out. Over time, their circle of friends extends beyond the dorm and involvement in curricular and extracurricular activities grows. Unfortunately, much of it occurs in a somewhat haphazard manner. It is the equivalent of building a giant sandbox and waiting to see what emerges. For some, this is all they need to create a rewarding and fulfilling experience. However, many want, and in fact, need more.

Taking a sandbox approach that leaves many students on their own to fashion a valuable and rewarding experience outside the classroom, stands in stark contrast to the academic experience. Rather than taking a wait and see approach hoping something positive emerges, academics take on more of the characteristics of a linear game. A linear game is one that is designed around a specific goal or set of objectives. The player progresses through a series of challenges that lead to the successful completion of some initial goal.

The equivalent from an academic perspective starts with the student (usually) declaring a major. After taking some foundational courses, she eventually move into courses that are more advanced and tailored specifically to her major of choice. Having satisfied a list of requirements, the student then graduates with a degree. All of this follows a basic linear progression and all students follow the same pattern.

Thus when we look at the student experience in its totality, we might think of it as if the typical student is simultaneously playing two games. She is playing an academically based game that spells out a linear progression with all of the individual steps carefully constructed and specified from start to finish. At the same time, she is playing what we might call a "student life game" where as long as she does not violate any student policies, she can effectively do whatever she wants. It should therefore come as no surprise that the two "games," or what we might identify as separate tracks within a single game, are somewhat disjointed and operate independently. As a result, what happens along the academic track has little to do with what happens along the broader student experience track.

However, when you stop to think about it, something doesn't quite make sense. Professors and administrators do not seem to trust the judgment of students when it comes to their academic experience. They map out majors with specific requirements, impose performance standards for remaining in a major, and then do not bestow certification upon a student until they are assured that all of the requirements have been fulfilled. Yet those same professors and administrators expect those same students to have good judgment when it comes time to make decisions that encompass the remainder of the student experience. Universities do not skimp on providing the necessary accoutrements required for creating a desirable student experience: nice dorm rooms, exceptional dining, state–of-the-art fitness facilities, stadiums and theaters hosting a variety of events, a carefully selected student body, and the list could go on and on. However, once in this carefully crafted environment, students are afforded a level of trust and an assumed degree of competency that is at odds with their academic experience.

At the same time that students are struggling to master a body of knowledge that will prepare them for whatever career might follow after graduation, they are grappling with a set of fundamental issues. Who am I? What do I like? Who do I want to become? How will I get there? Where do I want to end up? These are not easy questions to answer under any circumstances. It becomes especially challenging when, at the same time, much is left to chance when the student exits the classroom.

For some students who are able to find their way, the student and academic experiences become self-reinforcing. As a result, the subsequent value that is created more than justifies the price of tuition. However, many others wander aimless through their four years. For those who must still bear many of the costs without gaining all of the possible benefits, finding oneself becomes a luxury that few can afford.

If the purpose of a residential college experience is to provide value that extends beyond the classroom, then institutions must develop strategies that help students connect their experiences into a coherent whole. By failing to help students develop a narrative, the rationale for why bricks and mortar institutions can charge a premium will go by the wayside.

The Disrupted Student Experience

It is almost impossible to scan the popular press without hearing about the disruptive effects of technology. For higher education, the focus has been primarily on what happens (or no longer occurs) in the traditional classroom. The explosion of online courses, debates about the efficacy of the use of technology such as clickers in the classroom, or the excitement associated with "flipped" or "inverted" classrooms seems to get most of the attention.[1]

However, the disruptive effects of modern technology have now reached way beyond the academic side of the higher education experience. Just as technology has become a force leading to change in the classroom, it is playing an equally disruptive role across the entire student experience.[2] Technology is creating fundamental changes that are affecting how students interact with each other and the world around them.[3]

In the early days of the World Wide Web, individuals would create entire websites to tell their personal story or sell a product. Unfortunately building a website turned out to be a resource-intensive and time-consuming process. In response, blogs emerged as a way to reduce the costs of creating a presence on the Web by relieving the burden of having to create a comprehensive infrastructure to tell simple stories about oneself. Yet even managing a blog can be a resource-intensive experience. While software tools exist that make it easier to display content, the burden of generating all of the content still rests on the shoulders of the blogger. Thus it should come as no surprise that Facebook, where the equivalent of blog entries could be reduced to simple posts and pictures, would come to dominate.

Even so, developing a full-fledged Facebook site still requires a considerable commitment of time. Thus enter Twitter. By reducing posts down to 140 characters, Twitter made the process even easier. When combined with other services like Vine and its six second videos, words are no longer a required component for self-expression.

The ability to be in constant contact through social media sites, such as Facebook, Twitter, Instagram, or Vine, is making it more difficult rather than easier to develop meaningful relationships.[4] It is more challenging to form meaningful social relationships when the majority of those interactions take place via abbreviated text messages or videos about inconsequential matters.[5] Without the ability to weave a narrative that links all of these posts together, it can be challenging when trying to form deep relationships with each other.[6] The consequence of all of this is that students are becoming a generation of posters rather than storytellers.

In the rush to share every aspect of our daily lives, what has become misplaced is the context in which all of those events have taken place.[7] We have lost sight of the underlying narrative that forms the glue that holds all of these different snippets together. Our posts are now devoid of both context and meaning.[8]

Posts have become the equivalent of badges that are put on display through social media in order to build social capital and hence gain self-esteem.[9] The more things that one does and the more impressive they are perceived to be (based on my sense of what others view as important or significant), the better a person can feel about herself. However, what games have taught us is that the effectiveness of a badge in building self-esteem is only as strong as the accomplishment associated with how the badge was earned. Taking part in an activity is not the same thing as accomplishing something.

When posts replace accomplishments as the primary mechanism for building self-esteem, it should come as no surprise that it is difficult to construct a narrative that is able to turn actions into accomplishments and accomplishments into a story. Insecure in terms of who they are, digitally savvy students may be more plugged in and hence exposed to a wider range of information and experiences, nonetheless are having more and more difficulty making sense of it all.[10]

The Potential of Big Data

Through gamification, a student experience can be created that supports students in the construction of their own personal narratives. However, the start of the process begins not with game design principles, but rather with the big data approach more commonly found in data-driven Internet-based companies like Google. It is all about the collection of large amounts of data about individuals and the subsequent use of analytics to understand actual behavior. It has ushered in a world where the concept of pay for performance has been elevated to a whole new dimension where every web page, click, and purchase can be tracked and credited where credit is due. These analytics are designed to assist companies in understanding how web traffic can be converted into a revenue stream capable of sustaining a business.

The true power of the Internet is that for the first time, businesses can know exactly what works and what doesn't. It has become possible to observe actual human behavior in real time and respond by altering the mix of incentives, opportunities, or choices available. By understanding that a similar environment can be created on a college campus, it is now possible to collect "big" data and develop a similar set of analytics. This will have a profound effect on the choice set and the mix of incentives that can guide the student experience. As a result, technology that at one point was thought to be so disruptive that it may lead to the end of the residential student experience, can instead serve as a foundation for continued prosperity.

One opportunity that clearly exists can be found in the academic portion of the experience. At many larger universities, it can be challenging to support multiple sections of an introductory course that in concert, enroll a large number of students.[11] With current technology, it is now possible to track attendance, student performance on assignments and exams, and identify even before they are examined, what students understand and where they seem to be lost. Through the collection of multiple data points across a number of variables, it is possible to create a dynamic study plan that changes from week to week as a class unfolds. It enables targeted support so scarce resources can be deployed where they are needed and not wasted in solving a problem that doesn't exist.

Taking a big data approach to the allocation of academic resources however only begins to scratch the surface of what is needed to improve learning outcomes. Providing support is only a useful endeavor if students are actively seeking out help because they want to learn. Yet experience suggests that most students are interested in doing only the minimum of what is required to achieve a certain grade. For many students, the concept of earning a grade by learning the material has been lost.[12]

To try and understand why students appear to be more interested in grades than learning, we can utilize Daniel Kahneman's modern approach to dual process theory embodied in his concept of thinking fast and slow.[13] Simply identified as System 1 and System 2, Kahneman proposes that there are two processes that controls human behavio:. System 1 requires little effort, is often first to respond to the slightest form of stimulation, and is capable of making responses at lightening speeds; System 2 on the other hand is slower, is more contemplative, and often waits to collect all of the available information before suggesting a response.

Unfortunately, there is only so much mental effort or attention that can be devoted to meet the needs and wants of a particular individual. Thinking can require a great deal of effort and hence to not overtax the brain, it becomes necessary to economize on the use of mental resources. Hence we can think of the decision making process as one that seeks to use System 1 as much as possible so that mental resources can be conserved and used for those really important decisions that require a great deal of thought by System 2.

The concept of a brain that thinks both quickly and slowly can help to develop a better understanding of the choice problem facing students. The college experience consists at the most basic level, of academics and socializing. In an effort to become as happy as possible, students need to allocate their scarce mental resources between socializing which relies primarily on System 1 and academics that, depending on the difficulty of a particular course, might place small or significantly larger demands on System 2. Easy courses, or one ones that have a large number of assignments that require little more than memorization, primarily utilize System 1. Those courses that require critical thinking, significant writing, or the application of concepts, place large demands on System 2.

Hence we reach the crux of the problem. The more classes a student takes that require the use of System 2, the less effort/attention is left over for social activities. Since social activities have more of an immediate reward than academics, students have an incentive to use their limited effort/attention for social activities than academics.[14]

Hence they look for courses that place fewer demands on System 2 and for ones that can more easily accommodate the limited capabilities of System 1. This leads them to take a course from the easy professor rather than the "best" one. Alternatively, they select courses based on the amount of writing required, the number of exams, or how easily the material can be memorized; all in an attempt to minimize the amount of effort that is required.[15]

It is not that students are being irrational and shortchanging their own future by easing the load. Rather, they understand that in a world of asymmetric information, grades serve at best as a noisy signal that often has little if any meaning. Think of it this way, the goal for many students is a job after they receive their degree. Because it is difficult for employers to assess the intelligence or motivation of job applicants, they use signals like grades to help weed out potential candidates. Knowing this, students follow their own self-interest by focusing primarily on getting good grades. While it is nice to believe that there is a strong connection between grades and learning, often that is not true.[16] As a result, they believe they can have it all. They can conserve the amount of effort they expend on coursework, so that they can focus their attention on having a good time, and through careful course selection, achieve good grades.[17]

Hence, if we care about learning outcomes rather than grade point averages, the big data approach to education can only take us so far. It may improve the allocation of time or resources, but not have anything to do with turning unmotivated students into active learners. As a result, data and their corresponding analytics, while providing a necessary foundation for the gamification of the academic experience, only serve to take us part of the way.

Gamifying the Student Experience

Game designers create game environments that extend way beyond look and feel. Their designs determine when, where, and how players interact. They offer a range of choices and tie consequences to the choices made by the player. In other words, the designer determines a priori how play will unfold within the constraints they have devised to advance a story or make the game more interesting.

University administrators could exert a similar degree of control if they so desired. It is not much of a stretch to think of a college campus defined by its architecture, buildings, and grounds as serving the same function as a virtual game environment. The parallels get more interesting when you start to think of a college campus as an artificially controlled environment that can serve as the foundation for a game called the student experience. That game could share many of the characteristics found in any off-the-shelf video game created for the Xbox, Wii, or Sony PlayStation.

Because video games take place in a digital environment, it is easy to capture every move, event, or interaction. Data can be compiled, processed, and through the use of various status indicators, give continuous feedback to a player. With all of this information at their disposal, players can easily keep track of how many lives they possess, whether or not they have collected any superior powers, and get a general sense of overall health. All of this serves as an indicator of whether or not they are in a position to undertake a new challenge, need to gain additional strength, or must acquire those necessary skills or tools required to advance to the next level of the game.

Given that a college campus exists as a similar environment that contains much of student life within a well-defined set of boundaries, it is possible to collect, process, and disseminate information about the student experience in very much the same way as a game environment. All of the raw material needed to design a choice architecture capable of improving student decision making is already in place. Just as continuous feedback improves game outcomes, a similar case could be made for improving student ones.

Take, for example, the making of healthy choices. These could take the form of what students put in their bodies (food), whether or not they are active (exercise) or even something as basic as how much rest they get (sleep).[18] Since many freshmen live on campus, eat in the dining hall, and rely primarily on what is available on campus for recreation, the core elements are in place to recreate the game experience. Missing is the data points, recorder, display, and decision trees that exist in a virtual game environment.

Being able to capture the relevant data, mine it, and return it in a meaningful format is not beyond the capabilities of existing technology. Currently every campus has some mechanism to keep track of the number of times a student visits the dining hall. It would not be much of a stretch to use the same access card or some type of device similar to a smartphone to record the choices the student makes once they enter the dining hall. Tapping or scanning a QR code at each food station would make it possible to collect data on the food choices each student makes. The same card (device) could be used each time the student enters the fitness center and uses a particular machine, room, or engages in a particular activity.[19]

There is no need to stop there. A class schedule could be entered into a program with building locations. The number of steps between buildings could be used to enhance their activity profile. If they take a campus shuttle instead, information could be entered from that as well. How many times the student goes to the health center, whether or not they have purchased something from the vending machine down the hall, just about anything that affects the health and well-being of a student could be collected. Actually, the possibilities are endless. The point here is that control of the campus environment makes it possible to collect data and all of that information could be used to create a health index for an individual student.

To make use of all of the information that can be collected, a university could create a personalized portal that exists for each student every time her or she logs onto the campus network. A health indicator could appear on the front page enabling a student to check their current state of health and readiness to take on new challenges. It would empower students to make healthier choices, but moreover would enable them to receive support for the choices they have made or will make.

The power of data can be extended in a number of different directions. Take, for example, institutions that keep in close contact with their alumni. Tracking an alumnus' employment history, career choices, and achievements could form another important element in the development of a choice architecture. Matching what a graduate has done with their history as a student on campus opens the door to creating career profiles.

It would become possible to match success in a particular career with the choices that were made while a student. Course selection, major, skill development, or extracurricular activities could all be used to construct a profile. Such a profile could form the foundation for the construction of a status indicator capable of providing a student with a sense how well they are making progress toward achieving a particular career goal. If the indicator shows that a student is not making good progress, suggestions could be offered based on what other students at the same institution with similar aspirations have done. It is not about requiring that students do certain things, but rather it is about empowering them to make better choices.

Another example is the case of allocating time to studying. Many textbooks now come with electronic learning platforms capable of tracking everything the student does: from how much time they spend studying, to their success (or lack therefore) in mastering individual learning objectives.[20] With the increasing utilization of devices such as clickers in the classroom, similar technologies can monitor whether or not students come to class or understand what an instructor just got finished saying. In combination, data could be collected capable of creating a study profile. Such a profile could serve as the basis for creating some type of study status indicator. An indicator of this type could provide the student with a simple measure of whether or not they are on track, whether they are improving, and where they have strengths or weaknesses.

A Data-Driven Student Experience

The promise of big data is that used appropriately, it can empower and motivate students to make better choices. In addition to providing real-time information about the current status of various metrics, data collected could be used to create benchmarks for identifying social norms and determining relative position. By enabling students to see how much time others spend studying or the average number of calories consumed each day, they can get a better sense of whether their choices fall outside what would be considered as "normal" behavior.[21]

By making students more aware of their own choices and those being made by the peers, it becomes possible to nudge behavior in a positive direction. Students would possibly study more if they were aware of how little time they have spent or knew that everyone else was putting in more effort. By channeling the power of data, status indicators and benchmarks, rather than rules and regulations, could play a large role in helping students make better choices.

The structural elements contained in such an approach are illustrated in Figure 8.1.

Student data could be collected using wearable technology (watches, bracelets, or glasses), or in the form of a device (smartphone, tablet, or just about anything that can be clipped on to something else). The key is to have something that automatically collects the data, thereby eliminating the need to manually enter anything. If calories, footsteps,

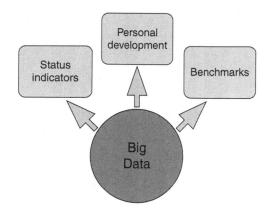

Figure 8.1

hours in bed, or any other type of data must be manually entered, the probability of that being done would most likely be close to zero.

Hence in order for this approach to work, everything must be tied into the data grid. Energy usage in a dorm room could help to determine sleep patterns. How many hours a student is logged into an electronic learning platform could provide a measure of how much of their time is allocated to studying. Results from the various activities within the learning platform can provide a measure of student performance. The possibilities are endless.

Various status indicators could be constructed and available in a personal student dashboard. The indicators would measure things like health or academic performance. They could also serve as indicators that a student is in trouble. If they are not attending class, have not completed their assignments, have stopped eating in the dining hall, or spend a great deal of time in the dark; all may be early warning signs that a problem exists. The real power of a data-driven approach is when students are given the opportunity to create their own indicators capable of monitoring their progress toward reaching a goal. At the most basic level, it could keep track of the progress being made toward fulfilling the degree requirements for a particular major. At a more advanced level, it could monitor skill development, progress toward reaching a career goal, or even the number of achievements earned across a variety of different activities.

In this way, students would be provided with continuous feedback in real time. The consequences of various actions could be immediately detected and the value from making a midcourse correction would become immediately apparent. Sometimes all that is required to change behavior in a positive way is to see the adverse consequences that result when poor choices are made.

Data collected could also be used to create benchmarks that would enable a student to see how they are progressing relative to others. These benchmarks not only serve as an important piece of information that enables the student to track performance but also as a means for establishing relative position. Success builds self-esteem when it is placed in evidence. Hence these benchmarks could also serve as a leader board capable of creating a healthy competition among students. By creating meaningful subdivisions within the student body, it becomes possible to have a multitude of winners who can subsequently take pride in their accomplishments.[22]

All of this is well and good, but the data-driven approach really shines when it becomes an important tool for personal growth and development. For example, as students log into their personal portal each day, a dashboard pops up that displays a variety of status indicators. Along with information about their status, a set of options can be dynamically generated based on their current status and previous history. For example, alerted to a decline in their overall health, some suggestions might pop up tied directly to what is contributing to the problem. Maybe they have started eating too many deserts at meal time, or perhaps they have reduced their level of physical activity. The power of a data-driven approach is that students can not only monitor their condition but also see the consequences of their previous choices.

For some, just knowing the source of the problem may lead to an instant correction. For others, it may not be so simple. Suppose the decline is because the student has become less active. With knowledge of the things they like to do, suggestions can be made about how they can get back on track. It could be as simple as a list of activities that are happening on campus on a particular day, information about groups that are meeting that share similar interests, or even finding a partner to play tennis or just go for a bike ride. It is about using the environment to collect data and with that data, providing the student with choices tailored to their needs or interests.

That being said, it is possible to create something even more powerful. It is not merely to make information available to improve decision making, but it is also about changes in the choice set. In other words, a data-driven system can do more than just provide a static list of individuals who have shown a similar interest. It can actively seek out participants and create potential pairings or groups.

Take for example the scheduling of tennis matches. By monitoring how often students play and whom they play, it would be possible to identify those students who are having a problem finding potential partners available during the same time blocks on a particular day. Alternatively, it could suggest possible partners who might have more in common than just tennis and use the sport to bring people together who might form deeper friendships. It could even take things one step further. If there are a number of students who would like to play and do not have partners, it would be possible to create a group of players who might form a club and organize a series of matches between the members.

The real power of taking a data-driven approach is not in crowning victors in artificial categories that mean little, but rather in creating meaningful opportunities where students are given an opportunity to participate and through their involvement, earn success. If on the other hand, success seems just beyond their reach, other opportunities can be generated that enable the student to grow, develop, and improve so that one day they can enjoy their own personal victory.

Narratives as Pathways

Game design, in combination with the collection of big data, can provide the student with options that would enable them to pursue a path capable of providing context and meaning to their student experience. It is not about turning education into a state of anarchy where anything goes. Rather, like any well-designed game, direction along with the appropriate "nudges" are embedded in game. In terms of the student experience, we can think of the various paths that emerge as part of the learning community created by faculty, staff, and administrators.

The difference is that the student experience emerges not from the idealized view of administrators or as the result of the "way we have always done things," but as a result of real-time interests. Pathways become student-driven and emerge in response to choices that are made by the student rather than the institution.

We can think of a pathway as a map that helps to direct a student toward some ending point. It relies on the student to take an active role and make a contribution as part of a co-created process. In that way, the student becomes responsible for a series of outcomes that have little to do with grades and much to do with accomplishment.

As a result, learning is no longer a function of whether professors or courses are easy or hard. Instead it emerges in response to a set of life experiences. Learning is turned into something that is real, observable, and of value. It offers an alternative to an endless series of posts or texts that, in their totality, contribute little toward developing strong personal ties or a better understanding of self.

Perhaps the best illustration of the concept is to think about Dorothy in *The Wizard of Oz*. The Yellow Brick Road certainly served as a path from the land of the Munchkins to the Emerald City where Dorothy hoped to learn the secret for making her way back to Kansas. There was much more however to the story than a young girl travels to a new world, follows a predefined path and ends up at a destination that helps her achieve her goal. As she travels along the Yellow Brick Road, Dorothy makes friends, becomes part of a team, overcomes various challenges, and in the end, attains what her heart most desires.

Hence the pathway chosen by Dorothy is more than just a roadway; it is an entire story where the shy, uncertain, and unconfident girl becomes an assertive, knowledgeable, self-assured, and empowered young woman. It is interesting that the film is not called the *Adventures of Dorothy* or something like *Pathways to Home*. Rather it is called *The Wizard of Oz*. While Dorothy is the central character of the film, Dorothy's journey is about more than the wayward adventures of a young woman. It is part of a much larger story that conveys a broader meaning.

The Wizard of Oz is a metaphor for the power each of us has instead to transform ourselves into the person we most want to be. It is a story about the power inherent in all of us to obtain that which we truly want. When Dorothy taps the heels together of her red shoes and proclaims "there is no place like home," it is forming a strong connection with family and friends and not about a particular farmhouse. Kansas for Dorothy represents a state of mind rather than a physical place.

Thus *The Wizard of Oz* is a potent story that teaches us about the power that resides inside each and every person. It also serves as a model for how students might follow a path and construct a narrative that is capable of bringing sense and meaning to their experience.

CHAPTER 9

The Future of Higher Education

The foundation of any game lies within what is called the Magic Circle. The Magic Circle defines the space and establishes the binding constraints that will give rise to many of the challenges the player will face. It can be dynamic, but any changes occur in a controlled manner. The rules help to fashion what is possible and what is not. They also provide guidance in terms of how one navigates the various challenges and possible strategies for success. Objects are the parts of the system that take on the form of variables that move, change, or are eliminated as events unfold. Finally, the players move objects according to the rules to generate outcomes. This all culminates in the creation of a game.

The equivalent of the Magic Circle when applied to the student experience can be thought more broadly in terms of the concept of space. Learning communities are not defined by what occurs within a classroom, but takes a broader macro perspective and looks at the totality of the student experience. Extracurricular activities, life in the dorm, and how one spends a Saturday night are all potential components of a broader experience that can be just as important as what takes place in the classroom. Space can be defined as narrowly as the borders defining the physical footprint of a geographical location, or can be thought of more broadly in terms of the myriad of relationships that a university has established with the larger community. The most important point is that rethinking our conception of space creates awareness that powerful areas exist outside the traditional classroom for promoting learning.

Just as the rules establish the various parameters defining game play, something equivalent must provide guidance and shape the learning process. The traditional view of education has the professor imparting knowledge to students through the process of lecture.[1] This model is currently being disrupted by e-learning as more and more courses transition to an online environment. In contrast, within a game environment, guidance is provided not by a single figure, but is embedded in the mechanics of the game. Learning takes place through an interactive process that includes confrontations with a hostile environment, other players, or artificial impediments.[2] Learning also takes place through collaborative efforts designed to solve joint problems for individual achievement or social advancement.

However, the gamification of the learning process does not signal the end for professors. Just as it was feared that machines would replace workers in the twentieth-century factory leading to widespread unemployment,[3] the reverse was true. Someone needed to construct all of those machines and as productivity skyrocketed, a growing demand for machines ensured that widespread unemployment failed to materialize. There is no reason to assume that the same will not hold true for academia. While it may be possible to take a class online in almost any subject, students will still need assistance in selecting the classes to take and how the concepts they learn in those classes can become something meaningful. It is not that professors will become superfluous, but rather that their roles will change.[4]

A shift in the role of the professor will help usher in a fundamental change in how students learn. Just as players learn from one another as they band together to solve a joint problem or compete in order to succeed, peer-to-peer learning under the guidance of a professor will become more pronounced.[5] The power of an effective learning community lies in its ability to turn students into teachers as they access common building blocks and through a shared experience, combine those blocks in new and innovative ways. The role of instructor will become one that helps students identify the appropriate blocks and then creates an environment that encourages them to take risks. Knowledge emerges from the contributions of the many in pursuit of a common objective. The value created by the higher education institution is not in the training, certification, or reputation of the instructor, but rather in the quality of the learning environment.

Helping students realize their strengths and weaknesses and then providing extra work so that they can improve in those areas where their performance is below expectations, may improve learning outcomes. However, it fails to address the reasons for the poor performance in the first place. Weaknesses can only be turned into strengths if the will is there to keep doing the same thing over and over again until one finally gets the hang of it.

While the old adage "if at first you don't succeed, try, try, again" may lead to better results, why would someone keep trying to do something that frequently ends in failure? We all like to do more of what we do best. It makes us feel good about ourselves and helps to build self-esteem. Constantly confronted with our failures, rather than try, try, again, many prefer to just call it a day. If we want adaptive learning techniques guided by big data to improve learning outcomes, we need to help students feel more secure and connected to their academic experience.

Without purpose, it is hard to figure out which direction is forward. Without meaning, it becomes difficult to choose one action from another. Without a path, it is easy to just wander around aimlessly. Hence if we want to "fix" higher education, it is about providing students with the means to construct a narrative that enables them to understand who they are, what they need to do, and most importantly, why they should do it.[6]

Alienation and Anxiety

With the transition from an apprentice system designed to impart specific skills to a system of higher education based on a more general training model, the twentieth century can be described as the age of human capital.[7] More flexible and easier to transfer, those general skills associated with higher education became more important in a period of skills-based technological change.[8] In a period where the demand for general skills has outstripped the supply, the premium associated with a bachelor's degree has risen dramatically.[9] On the other hand, more recently when the supply of skills has outpaced demand, the premium appears to have tapered off.[10] Thus some economists have viewed changes in the standard of living and the benefits associated with higher education as a race between education and technology.[11]

However, the shift from an apprentice to a more general education model has not been all benefits without any corresponding costs. There is a dark side to the shift to a more general education model. This "dark side" mirrors to a large extent the shift that occurred with the rise of the factory system.

One of the concerns associated with the growing division of labor during the nineteenth century was the threat of alienation.[12] When goods were produced predominately by hand, the local artisan could take pride in what they produced largely from their own efforts. However, with an expansion in the division of labor and the corresponding rise of the factory system, workers became removed from the products that they produced. Instead of being able to hold up the fruit of their labor and take pride in what they had created, they instead could merely boast that their contribution was to be found somewhere within a combination of interchangeable parts.

A similar shift occurred in higher education. As knowledge became more general and its scope of applicability widened, it became more and more disconnected from a specific application.[13] Many careers became disconnected from the subjects to be studied and hence learning lost some of its meaning. Moreover, the transition from a personalized learning experience to a more standardized one characterized by large lecture driven courses, further removed the student from both the professor and the subject matter. When a student is one of five hundred sitting in a lecture hall with a professor they will never meet, an assessment mechanism that is not tailored to their own learning style, during a time when they often wish they were somewhere else; it is easy to see how they might feel disconnected from the education process. Hence it is not much of a reach to conclude that many of those same forces that led to alienation on the factory floor might have the same influence in the classroom.[14]

Feelings of alienation in and of themselves may not be a problem as long as the demand for degree holders is outstripping supply and therefore graduates can feel confident that a job is waiting for them upon graduation. However, coming out of the recession of 2008, the prospects of obtaining a job, let alone one in a graduate's preferred area, has become less certain. There is a real fear that the economy is no longer capable of generating new and high paying jobs at a rate that can keep pace with the supply of college graduates.[15] Moreover, the problem has been compounded by a lingering fear that the knowledge and skills being taught are no longer relevant for the needs of a more competitive and dynamic global economy.[16]

The anxiety associated with launching a successful career in today's economy is perhaps exemplified by the experience of Apple. We applaud a company that over and over seems to be able to develop entirely new product categories with award-winning designs capable of dominating the market. We idolize the company's founder despite the fact he is no longer with us and anxiously await each new product announcement to see how the company will once again change our lives. However, each new transformational device raises the bar and makes it that much more difficult for a single company to follow up with another market changing invention. Yet we have come to expect a company like Apple to be able to do that year in and year out.[17]

The need for continuous innovation has placed ever greater pressure on universities to produce graduates capable of making a contribution toward something that currently extends just beyond the current frontiers of knowledge. Yet in a global economy where competition is reducing the margins of existing products to the point where they are just profitable, the only way to satisfy hungry investors looking for ever higher rates of returns is by turning the imagined into something that is very real. As long as institutions of higher education are able to keep pace and supply qualified graduates, Apple and other companies stand a fighting chance of success.[18]

While some institutions of higher learning are at the cutting edge, and in some cases are actually one step ahead of the private sector, many are struggling in a difficult budgetary environment to keep things afloat.[19] Yet as the skills required compared to those being delivered stretch further and further apart, students are faced with growing levels of anxiety. When the jobs that are available require skills that they don't possess, students become anxious about their future and begin to question the value of their substantial investment in an education that may no longer be able to pay sufficient dividends to justify the expense.[20]

Hence it should come as no surprise that many seek to escape by transforming the collegiate experience from one that prepares them for a successful future, to one that instead represents more of a hedonistic ride to a good time designed to last for four years. The failure of higher education is not necessarily that it is teaching the wrong things, or the right things in the wrong way, but instead that it has become an exercise in anxiety and alienation rather than an established pathway to success.

A Culture of Learning

Singling out students for making a rational choice that places fun ahead of their future is not all that unusual. Just look at the following statistics related to credit card debt. Thirty nine percent of all Americans carried some amount of credit card debt in 2012. While the average credit card balance of college students was $755, the average for low and middle income households was $7,145.[21] If credit card debt can be used as a proxy for measuring the intensity of desire for immediate gratification, then students are not alone in their willingness to ignore future consequences in order to increase present enjoyment.[22]

It is easy to take cheap shots at Millennials and attribute the failings of academia to an entire generation.[23] However, they are just as much a product of society as those who instruct, staff and administration institutions of higher education. The desire to do only the minimum of what is required to pass a class, jump through a hoop, or satisfy what they perceive to be an unreasonable demand is not something that happens at birth and mysteriously manifests itself 18 years later.

The simple solution might appear to be that colleges and universities just need to increase the level of academic rigor so that grades more adequately reflect what a student has learned.[24] As an additional bonus (positive externality), creating a more rigorous academic experience would most likely reduce the amount of undesirable social behavior that takes place on campus.[25] However, in a limited resource environment where schools and individual departments must compete for every tuition dollar, there is a greater incentive to not make things any more challenging than the other departments or competitors in an effort in to feed the bottom line.[26]

Offering high grades in exchange for enrollments that preserve the flow of funds to an individual department may represent a winning strategy for the individual faculty member or department chair, but it does little to enhance the reputation of the institution or prepare a student to have a successful career. In the current environment where a bachelor's degree is viewed as a required stepping stone to a better job or a higher salary, graduation rates are being supplemented by the percentage of students who obtain a job and rankings are now influenced by average starting salaries of graduates.[27]

While giving out high grades may create a false sense of success, it does little to resolve the underlying feelings of anxiety. Such feelings call into question whether a degree is worth all of the additional years that will be needed to service the tens of thousands of dollars of accumulated debt. It is not a question of returning to the days when academic rigor was the norm rather than the exception (if those days ever actually existed). What is required instead is to create a culture of learning.

If learning is to become a preferred choice, it needs to be something capable of generating intrinsic rewards (flow) and extrinsic ones (self-esteem). When an individual is doing something that makes them feel good about who they are, they become motivated to try harder and give things their best effort. It is about real accomplishments rather than meaningless symbols that don't reflect much of anything.

Institutions of higher learning are failing not because they lack in rigor, but because they are not motivating students in a way that inspires them to reach out and achieve more than a passing grade.

The problem will only be solved when students demand more from their professors rather than less. When they are no longer willing to settle for an easy A and instead are ready and willing to take charge of their own education.

Student Empowerment

Growing complexity in the academic environment is a reflection of similar changes in the world outside of academia. If we are truly preparing students to be successful in a life they create after graduation, then students need to become capable of evaluating opportunities and making smart choices. A feeling of empowerment relies on more than skill or knowledge acquisition. It is a call to action. It resides in the ability to choose a path, achieve some success along the way, and make progress toward some end point.

If we design an educational experience in which learning is an essential part of personal growth and development, we could create empowered individuals who would be better positioned to make a contribution upon their entry into the "real world." However, to create such an environment, we must recognize that learning above all is about taking risks. Trying something new always carries with it the risk of failure. Hence every time a student is asked to learn something new, they are putting their self-esteem at risk. Yet without learning how to manage personal risk, it is doubtful that many students will be able to successfully make the transition from a highly structured educational environment to an unstructured employment situation.

Empowering students sounds simple, but it is actually very difficult. It requires that professors create opportunities rather than requirements. Administrators and staff must offer guidance rather than rules. Most importantly, it depends on the creation of a learning environment where choices exist that challenge but do not overwhelm. An environment capable of responding to personal growth and development where new challenges emerge as old ones become irrelevant.

Education as an Emergent Experience

Game designers often use support rather than structure when creating a game environment. They attempt to create an experience where achievements, meaning, and purpose from the play itself. Rather than completely dependent of the vision of a team of designers, it instead is a player-driven process. Perhaps the best example of this type of game are Alternate Reality Games (ARGs).

ARGs are designed to foster the creation of a narrative from what appears to be random or disjointed pieces of information.[28] They bring gamers together in an effort to collectively solve puzzles in an effort to advance some particular story line.[29] Because ARGS do not take place in a self-contained environment, the success and enjoyment derived from the game depends on the collaborative nature of the participants. Without collective interaction, there is nothing to push the game forward and it eventually stops. Sometimes referred to as procedural narratives, the underlying story is no longer embedded within the structure of the game as a reflection of the vision of the designer, but is something that emerges as a game character encounters one challenge after another.

To foster collective interaction and freedom of movement, ARGs use a variety of different kinds of media. Blog posts, print, television, email, and conventional telephone lines are all potential avenues for connecting players, distributing important information about the game, and creating an environment of total immersion in game play. Communication is essentially viral in that it takes on a life of its own as players choose between various media in order to communicate with other players.

Something similar is already occurring on college and university campuses today. Common value systems are emerging that become a part of every facet of the student experience. For example, a popular value system adopted on many campuses today revolves around the issue of sustainability.[30] Fears that society is moving along a trajectory that will one day lead to the end of the human race is prompting calls for smarter choices. People, profit, and planet is the new mantra designed to place individual decision making into a broader and more informed context. The challenge for university administrators is to create a variety of touch points capable of providing meaning and a sense of purpose for every student.

A New Definition for Student Success

If students are to become part of a broader narrative capable of combating feelings of alienation, then a different measure of success is needed. One that is not exclusively defined in terms of individual achievement. Rather than just focused on the individual, a new standard needs to emerge that reflects the collectivist approach found in games that rely on teamwork to advance play. A concept of achievement that can be shared among all participants in an effort to combat a problem that in turn, is also shared by everyone.

That is not to say that individual achievements would no longer be an important component used to motivate individual action. Rather, a hybrid approach is needed where self-esteem is developed as both the result of individual achievement *and* collective action. ARGs are designed to create engaged and empowered individuals, while building an awareness of problems that exist that can only be solved when very specialized individuals work together for the collective good.[31] People play ARGs and similar types of games because they want to believe that they are part of the solution to a problem that is larger than life. They need to believe that their participation might make a meaningful difference in discovering and/or implementing a solution to some epic problem capable of taking on mythical proportions.[32]

The same holds true for students. They are no different from gamers who choose certain games to play because they are able to feel a part of something that, at least within the context of the game, makes a meaningful difference. It is also no different from what we expect from our students when they graduate; to become engaged and productive members of society. If we do not teach them how to become part of something larger as college students, can we really expect them to know what is required when they advance to the next stage of their life?

An Expanded Role for Faculty

The success of any game that depends on emergent play depends to a large extent on the flexibility of the design. Players must be free to pursue play as it emerges. Hence a variety of pathways must exist. They must be flexible enough to serve as guide posts rather than binding constraints. It is not about stifling freedom, but rather allowing freedom to emerge by creating an environment that helps shape and support choices.

Pathways need to be constructed, populated with adventures and filled with opportunities for earning achievements. What this all means is that the traditional role of a faculty member will need to change. They are no longer just creators and disseminators of knowledge. They need to become an integral part of the creation of pathways. A choice of pathways that are available for students to pursue as they take control over their own life. The future of faculty members is not as lecturers, but rather as learning experience designers that create pathways available for students to choose from as they construct their own personal narratives.

A Community of Learners

One popular pathway thought to lead to professional success has been the incorporation of internships into the student experience. Grounded in a belief that much can be learned by doing, internships are more and more becoming a recommendation and in many cases, a requirement for graduation. This has necessitated a change in student assessment and a shift toward the construction of student portfolios. Recognizing that there is more to the four-year experience than the grades earned in classes, the portfolio approach seeks to capture a wider range of accomplishments.[33] However, what is often missing is a corresponding narrative to tie the elements together. Without some guiding set of principles that helped shape the choices that went into the selection of elements that comprise the portfolio, it is difficult to see how the whole can be greater than the sum of its parts.[34]

The construction of a cohesive narrative is not a function of learning by doing, but instead emerges from learning by example. Outside of the classroom or an internship, when a student wants to know how to do something, they often log on to the Internet to see how others have done it. Most questions are general in nature and not all that idiosyncratic. Hence there is a high probability that someone else has encountered the exact same problem or wondered about something very similar. In turn, there is a high probabilty that someone has provided the answer.

In this way, the Internet represents possibly the best example of a learning community. Members contribute to the community though the stories they tell about challenges overcome, how to solve problems they have encountered, or the successes they have experienced. In return, when they have a need to learn how to solve a problem, learn something new, or overcome an obstacle, a rich cache of examples exists just waiting to assist.

The same could hold true within the context of an institution of higher education. It is not necessary for faculty, administrators, or institutional culture to teach students how to construct their own narrative. Rather, all that is needed is that students (and alumni for that matter) be given an opportunity to tell their story and post it in a repository that will store it and make it easy for others to find.

By providing a forum for sharing stories, students can learn how to construct their own narrative.[35] By seeing what others have done, it becomes possible for them to imagine what they might be capable of doing. Half the battle is in discovering the vast array of possibilities. The other half is knowing what to do once you have discovered it. It becomes aspirational as students gain a glimpse of what is possible.

It is learning by *relevant* example. It is about real-life stories rather than some hypothetical that may or may not ever come true. It shows what is realistic and helps to temper expectations for some and opens the eyes of others.

As institutions of higher learning become repositories for the stories told by their students and alumni, they will start to be evaluated by an entirely different set of criteria. Institutions will no longer be judged by the quality of their applicants, or faculty, or facilities. Instead they will be judged by the quality of the stories that are told. Those institutions that provide the foundation for their students to construct compelling stories will be the ones who are best in a position to gain a competitive advantage.

A New Organizational Structure

To generate a nexus of pathways, universities must turn toward the development of learning communities that are firmly situated within an educational ecosystem. The development of an ecosystem can provide many of the benefits associated with having a diverse curriculum without bearing many of the costs. Ecosystems allow companies to hollow themselves out by enabling them to access much need competencies without having to make permanent commitments. As such, it becomes a potential strategy for meaningful cost reduction.

In addition to cost reduction, placing a learning community into an ecosystem expands the division of labor resulting in an increase in the quality of the educational experience. Rather than relying on just the resources that a single institution has at its disposal, it can draw from the collective wisdom that exists both internally *and* externally. Without tapping into these new sources of knowledge creation, universities run the risk of becoming irrelevant.

The largest benefits from an expanded learning community center around peer–to-peer learning. There is no reason to restrict peer-based learning to the boundaries of an individual college campus. This is of particular importance in an economy where there is increasing pressure for even greater specialization in order to develop new ways of generating value. Where a single campus or academic program may not be able to support the development of very specialized knowledge, expanding beyond a single border may create an interest group sufficiently large to generate a meaningful educational experience.

What is missing are organizational forms designed to foster connectivity. This will require structural changes that are designed to increase accessibility. However, if such changes are ever to be imagined, let alone implemented, a massive cultural shift will need to take place before serious work can begin on a new type of organizational structure. The insular nature of many colleges and universities will need to give way to a different view that is more outward rather than inward looking.

All of this is not going to mean fewer professors, but actually more. In order to achieve professional success, a professor carves out a small niche area in a larger field and uses their mastery of a manageable amount of knowledge to push forward the frontier. However, their ability to attract a student body that is sufficiently large to support their narrow area of specialization is rarely achieved.[36] As a result, faculty members must spend a large portion of time teaching subjects that are more general in nature. By adopting an ecosystem approach, professors will be able to access students with specialized interests in sufficient numbers to justify teaching courses that are tailored to what a faculty member knows best. By creating the equivalent of campuses without borders, universities will be able to supplement the resources available at their core campus with additional expertise that exists across a range of campuses.

A Partner for Life

Creating a learning community that extends beyond the physical borders of an individual campus carries with it other advantages. Tapping into specialized knowledge does not have to be restricted to just professors at other college campuses. Alumni who are solving real problems in new and innovative ways on a daily basis can become a resource. For that matter, institutions can develop professional networks that serve to both hire its graduates and provide much needed insight and knowledge to ensure that their students are well positioned for a future in a particular field.

Thus it becomes even more critical for institutions of higher learning to recognize the importance of creating a successful franchise. Changing demographics and growing competition in the higher education space will make it even harder and more expensive to attract students to campus. Having already borne those expenses, does it really make sense to spend the same or growing amounts, to recruit over and over again within a declining pool? Rather, it makes more sense to develop strategies designed to increase revenues from their existing student body. Not by raising fees and tuition for a particular program, but by developing relationships that transcend a particular degree program. It is about increasing the amount of revenue received over the lifespan of each student.

Students who become alumni represent a future stream of revenue that is not restricted to the relatively short period of time when they first arrived as an undergraduate. However, to keep them coming back for more, universities need to become more like game franchises where each successive iteration offers enough value that they will want to shell out money to play again and again.

This of course will be no simple feat for the institution that has turned outside its hallowed halls to enhance its curriculum or reduce costs. Yet the value offered by an institution does not have to reside within the boundaries of its campus. Having created a nexus of relationships with a variety of experts in multiple fields, the value provided by an institution of higher learning will be found in the ability to create entry points where *both* students *and* alumni can access the appropriate knowledge or develop the necessary skills to be successful at any point during their career.

Game Design as a Source of Competitive Advantage

All of this unfortunately runs counter to the traditional strategy adopted by many institutions. Residing in the steadfast belief that the solution rests in improving the quality of the signal that is sent to prospective students, parents, and employers. From this perspective, rankings are all that seem to matter. However, a growing gap has emerged between the additional benefit associated with the value that is attributable to a "superstar" faculty member, a new and innovative program, or an upgrade to facilities and the corresponding costs.

Spending on college campuses is subject to the same diminishing returns found in a business enterprise. Moreover, increased spending on higher education may be crowding out other types of investment for society that may have a larger impact of developing human and social capital.[37] Hence there may be real limits to what makes sense for society as a whole to invest in higher education.

Just like any race to the top, it becomes difficult to stop; even if a point is reached where it no longer makes any sense. However, at some point, colleges and universities will need to wake up to a future that is no longer being shaped by past discussions about the appropriate mix of tenured professors and nontenured lecturers or online and offline courses.[38] Rather, cost reduction will be achieved, and greater value added, by adjusting the mix of internal and external faculty. Instead of trying to provide depth in a specialization internally, institutions will more and more seek to supplement what they currently have with external experts who can be brought in a targeted basis to fill a particular need for only as long as it is required.

The university of tomorrow will seek to create a nexus of pathways designed to help guide students in their effort to find a meaningful (and successful) role after graduation and satisfy the desire on the part of business and society to find graduates who can help generate increased wealth while making the future a little bit better for everyone. Education is more than just acquiring a better understanding of learning theory or the neuroscience of the brain. It is not about engaging in the hand-wringing associated with lower math scores and the perceived paucity of young people interested in the sciences. Instead, it is about unleashing the power of game design to create a learning experience that taps into the power of play. It is about creating an environment where we choose to learn; rather than finding that we need to learn because there are no other choices.

Notes

1 The Coming "Perfect Storm" in Higher Education

1. Economists at Xavier University have created what they call The American Dream Composite Index. The Index can be found at: http://www.americandreamcompositeindex.com/adci. A coalition has been formed called The American Dream 2.0 to improve college access, affordability, and completion. They can be found at: http://americandream2-0.com/

2. Economists like to talk about the option value created by higher education. For example, completing high school gives one the option of attending college and enjoying higher lifetime earnings. The value of this option is one of the positive returns associated with a higher education degree. For an extended discussion, see Heckman, James J., Lance J. Lochner, and Petra E. Todd. 2005. "Earnings Functions, Rates of Return and Treatment Effects: The Mincer Equation and Beyond." National Bureau of Economic Research, Inc, NBER Working Papers: 11544, Cambridge.

3. Looking at a snapshot of the economy in November 2013, the Bureau of Labor Statistics reported that the unemployment rate for those with less than a high school diploma was 10.8 percent, high school graduates was 7.3 percent, some college or associates degree was 6.4 percent and bachelor's degree and higher came in at 3.4 percent. "Employment Status of the Civilian Population 25 Years and Over by Educational Attainment." US Bureau of Labor Statistics. United States Bureau of Labor Statistics. Last modified December 6, 2013, http://www.bls.gov/news.release/empsit.t04.htm

4. Oreopoulos, Philip and Kjell G. Salvanes. 2011. "Priceless: The Nonpecuniary Benefits of Schooling." *Journal of Economic Perspectives* 25 (1): 159–184.

5. Frame, W. Scott and Lawrence J. White. 2005. "Fussing and Fuming Over Fannie and Freddie: How Much Smoke, How Much Fire?" *Journal of Economic Perspectives* 19 (2): 159–184.

6. This is a process known as securitization. The role it played in the financial crisis is discussed in Peicuti, Cristina. 2013. "Securitization and the Subprime Mortgage Crisis." *Journal of Post Keynesian Economics* 35 (3): 443–455.

7. This pressure came from a belief that certain segments of the population were discriminated against in a process known as redlining. However, within the economics and finance literature, it is not clear that much evidence exists confirming this practice. See, for example, Tootell, Geoffrey M. B. 1996. "Redlining in Boston: Do Mortgage Lenders Discriminate Against Neighborhoods?" *Quarterly Journal of Economics* 111 (4): 1049–1079. Also see Holmes, Andrew and Paul Horvitz. 1994. "Mortgage Redlining: Race, Risk, and Demand." *Journal of Finance* 49 (1): 81–99.

8. See, for example, Emmons, William R. and Bryan J. Noeth. 2013. "Why Did Young Families Lose So Much Wealth During the Crisis? The Role of Homeownership." *Federal Reserve Bank of St.Louis Review* 95 (1): 1–26.

9. The Obama Administration has been a strong supporter of higher education. It has doubled the investment in Pell Grants, helped students better manage student loan debt, expanded education tax credits, and kept student loan interest rates low. For a discussion of the Administration's higher education policies, see: "Higher Education." The White House. Accessed January 3, 2014, http://www.whitehouse .gov/issues/education/higher-education

10. Some introductory articles explaining Behavioral Finance are: Hirshleifer, David. 2001. "Investor Psychology and Asset Pricing." *Journal of Finance* 56 (4): 1533–1597; Malkiel, Burton G. 2003. "The Efficient Market Hypothesis and Its Critics." *Journal of Economic Perspectives* 17 (1): 59–82; and Shiller, Robert J. 2003. "From Efficient Markets Theory to Behavioral Finance." *Journal of Economic Perspectives* 17 (1): 83–104.

11. For a discussion of the role of that the three large credit rating agencies played in the financial crisis, see White, Lawrence J. 2010. "Markets: The Credit Rating Agencies." *Journal of Economic Perspectives* 24 (2): 211–226.

12. For insights from the academic literature on student debt, see Avery, Christopher and Sarah Turner. 2012. "Student Loans: Do College Students Borrow Too Much – Or Not enough?" *Journal of Economic Perspectives* 26 (1): 165–192. The earnings premium associated with higher education is documented in Carnevale, Anthony P., Jeff Strohl, and Michelle Melton. 2011. *What's It Worth? The Economic Value of College Majors.* Washington, DC: Georgetown University Center on Education and the Workforce. For a discussion of the nonpecuniary benefits, see Oreopoulos and Salvanes. "Priceless," 159–184.

13. "Parents and students covered 46 percent of total charges from funds other than grants and loans in 2002–2003 and 43 percent in 2007–2008;

in 2012–2013, they covered 38 percent. This decline occurred as grants and tax benefits received by the average full-time postsecondary student have increased by 56 percent over the decade and borrowing increased by 36 percent, but funds from other sources rose by only 6 percent in inflation-adjusted dollars." Payea, Kathleen, Sandy Baum, and Charles Kurose. 2013. *How Students and Parents Pay for College*. New York: College Board.

14. The impact on state economic growth is discussed in Baldwin, J. Norman and McCracken, William A. 2013. "Justifying the Ivory Tower: Higher Education and State Economic Growth." *Journal of Education Finance* 38 (3): 181–209. Civic returns are noted by Dee, Thomas S. 2004. "Are There Civic Returns to Education?" *Journal of Public Economics* 88 (9–10): 1697–1720. Social returns are estimated by Moretti, Enrico. 2004. "Estimating the Social Return to Higher Education: Evidence from Longitudinal and Repeated Cross-Sectional Data." *Journal of Econometrics* 121 (1–2): 175–212.

15. According to the College Board, full-time enrollments between fall 2000 and fall 2009 in degree granting for-profit institutions increased from 366,000 to 1.5 million. In just nine years, the sector went from enrolling 4 percent of all full-time students to 11 percent of the total. Baum, Sandy and Kathleen Payea. 2011. *Trends in for-Profit Postsecondary Education: Enrollment, Prices, Student Aid and Outcomes*. New York: College Board.

16. Two good resources for learning about MOOCs and tracking their progress can be found at the Chronicle of Higher Education (http://chronicle.com /article/What-You-Need-to-Know-About/133475/) and the New York Times (http://www.nytimes.com/2012/11/04/education/edlife/massive-open -online-courses-are-multiplying-at-a-rapid-pace.html?pagewanted=all). The lack of a revenue model for MOOCs is apparent in the contracts Coursera has signed with some major universities. For a discussion of the challenges, see Young, Jeffrey R. "Inside the Coursera Contract: How an Upstart Company Might Profit from Free Courses." *The Chronicle of Higher Education*. July 19, 2012. Accessed January 5, 2014, http://chronicle.com /article/How-an-Upstart-Company-Might/133065/.

17. Fifty three percent of freshman live within on hundred miles of home and this preference hasn't changed much over the course of the past 40 years. Sander, Libby. "Ties to Home." *The Chronicle of Higher Education*. January 24, 2013. Accessed on January 5, 2014, http://chronicle.com /article/Ties-to-Home/136789/. For a discussion of spatial competition, see McMillen, Daniel P., Larry D. Singell, and Glen R. Waddell. 2007. "Spatial Competition and the Price of College." *Economic Inquiry* 45 (4): 817–833.

18. The mismatch between the supply and demand for higher education is discussed in Bound, John, Brad Hershbein, and Bridget Terry Long. 2009. "Playing the Admissions Game: Student Reactions to Increasing College Competition." *Journal of Economic Perspectives* 23 (4): 119–146.

19. With the exception of the elite institutions, at least half of all colleges are less selective than they were in 1962. Hoxby, Caroline M. 2009. "The Changing Selectivity of American Colleges." *Journal of Economic Perspectives* 23 (4): 95–118.

20. The College Board's 2013 SAT Report reveals that only 43 percent of SAT takers in the class of 2013 met the SAT College and Career Readiness Benchmark. *2013 SAT Report on College & Career Readiness*. New York: College Board.

21. See, for example, Lang, Kevin and Russell Weinstein. 2012. "Evaluating Student Outcomes at for-Profit Colleges." National Bureau of Economic Research, Inc, NBER Working Papers: 18201.

22. Concerns over the number of stories questioning the value of higher education might have prompted the College Board to commission the report: Baum, Sandy, Charles Kurose, and Jennifer Ma. 2013. *How College Shapes Lives: Understanding the Issues*. New York: College Board.

23. Two-thirds of seniors graduating from four-year colleges in 2011 graduated with average debt of $26,600. "The American Dream 2.0." Accessed January 3, 2014, http://www.hcmstrategists.com/americandream2–0 /report/HCM_Gates_Report_1_17_web.pdf

24. The Obama Administration would like to hold colleges "accountable for cost, value and quality." It would accomplish this by reallocating student aid toward those institutions that score favorable on a set of criteria as determined by the Administration. *The President's Plan for a Strong Middle Class & a Strong America*. 2013. Washington, DC: The White House, 5. Accessed December 21, 2013, http://www.whitehouse.gov/sites/default /files/uploads/sotu_2013_blueprint_embargo.pdf

25. Vedder, Richard, Christopher Denhart, and Jonathan Robe. 2013. *Why Are Recent College Graduates Underemployed?* Washington, DC: Center for College Affordability and Productivity.

26. Between 2002–2003 and 2012–2013, tuition, fees, room, and board increased from $12,300 to $17,860 in inflation-adjusted dollars at public four-year universities. At the same time, financial aid at those same institutions increased from $3,730 to $5,750 in inflation-adjusted dollars. This represents a widening of the gap from $8,570 to $12,111. Payea, Baum, and Kurose. *How Students and Parents Pay for College.*

27. According to David Feldman, in 1975, the states picked up 60 percent of the cost of higher education. Today, states pay only 34 percent. Feldman, David H. "Myths and Realities about Rising College Tuition." National Association of Student Financial Aid Administrators. National Association of Student Financial Aid Administrators. Accessed December 1, 2013, http://www.nasfaa.org/advocacy/perspectives/articles/Myths_and _Realities_about_Rising_College_Tuition.aspx

In a report commissioned by the Center on Budget and Policy Priorities, between the academic years 2007–2008 and 2012–2013, average state support per enrolled student fell 27.7 percent. Oliff, Phil, Vincent Palacios, Ingrid Johnson, and Michael Leachman. 2013. *Recent Deep State Higher Education Cuts May Harm Students and the Economy for Years to Come.* Washington, DC: Center on Budget and Policy Priorities.

28. According to the College Board, in 2002, of those students studying for a bachelor's degree at four-year institutions, 57 percent earned their degree within six years. Completion rates averaged 65 percent at private nonprofit, 55 percent at public four-year and 22 percent at private for-profit institutions. Baumand Payea. *Trends in for-Profit Postsecondary Education.*

29. T Schwarz, Fred. 2009. "20 Reasons Why Campus Learning Is Better Than Online." *National Review Online*, September 28. Accessed October 28, 2013, http://www.nationalreview.com/phi-beta-cons/40288/20-reasons-why-campus-learning-better-online

30. STEMS stands for science, technology, engineering, and math. It also includes fields like economics. In the 2003–2004 academic year, about 28 percent of the bachelor's degree and 20 percent of the associate's degree students chose a STEM major. See Chen, Xianglei and Matthew Soldner. 2013. *STEM Attrition: College Students' Paths into and Out of STEM Fields.* US Department of Education.

31. See Bardhan, Ashok, Daniel L. Hicks, and Dwight Jaffee. 2013. "How Responsive Is Higher Education? The Linkages between Higher Education and the Labour Market." *Applied Economics* 45 (10–12): 1239–1256.

32. For a complete discussion of the crisis, see Barth, James R. 1991. *The Great Savings and Loan Debacle.* Washington, DC: AEI Press.

33. They were lending dollars that were worth more than the ones that they were being paid back.

34. See, for example, Humphrey, David B. and Lawrence B. Pulley. 1997. "Banks' Responses to Deregulation: Profits, Technology, and Efficiency." *Journal of Money, Credit & Banking* 29 (1): 73–93.

35. According to the College Board, between 2000–2001 and 2007–2008, the total discount has been relatively stable in the public sector, but continues to rise in the private sector. Looking at the difference between the published price the institution charges and the amount of tuition and fees it actually collects, the total discount rate increased from 28.6 percent in 2000–2001 to 31.5 percent in 2007–2008. Baum, Sandy and Jennifer Ma. 2010. *Tuition Discounting: Institutional Aid Patterns at Public and Private Colleges and Universities.* New York: College Board.

36. Moreover, as an industry, they adopted a unique strategy through their trade association (RIAA) to sue its customers. See Cavazos, David E. and

Dara Szyliowicz. 2011. "How Industry Associations Suppress Threatening Innovation: The Case of the US Recording Industry." *Technology Analysis and Strategic Management* 23 (5): 473–487.

37. How new artists are selected by the major recording labels is discussed in Ordanini, Andrea. 2006. "Selection Models in the Music Industry: How a Prior Independent Experience May Affect Chart Success." *Journal of Cultural Economics* 30 (3): 183–200.

38. The strategic advantages of bundling is discussed in Carbajo, Jose, David de Meza, and Daniel J. Seidmann. 1990. "A Strategic Motivation for Commodity Bundling." *Journal of Industrial Economics* 38 (3): 283–298.

39. Alexander, Peter J. 2002. "Peer-to-Peer File Sharing: The Case of the Music Recording Industry." *Review of Industrial Organization* 20 (2): 151–161.

40. For the first time, in 2012 digital revenue accounted for 54 percent of the total in the recording industry. Christman, Ed. 2013. "Digital's Tipping Point." *Billboard* 125 (21): 6.

41. The use of bundling in higher education is discussed in Spiegel, Uriel and Joseph Templeman. 1996. "'Bundling' in Learning." *Education Economics* 4 (1): 65–81.

42. The challenge of MOOCs is that they are still in search of a business model. Korn, Melissa and Jennifer Levitz. 2013. "Online Courses Look for a Business Model." *The Wall Street Journal*, January 1.

43. Clay Christensen has made a career over disruption. More recently, his ideas have been applied to higher education. See, Christensen, Clayton M. and Henry J. Eyring. 2011. *The Innovative University: Changing the DNA of Higher Education from the Inside Out.* San Francisco: Jossey-Bass.

44. For a discussion of economies of scale and scope, see Chandler, Alfred D. 1990. *Scale and Scope: The Dynamics of Industrial Capitalism.* Cambridge: Belknap Press.

45. Global PC shipments have fallen for six straight quarters hitting a five-year low of 80.3 million units as of the third quarter in 2013. "Global PC Shipments Drop to a Five-Year Low." *BBC News*, October 9, 2013. Accessed December 27, 2013, http://www.bbc.co.uk/news/business-24470639. Meanwhile Android shipments grew 73.5 percent between the second quarter 2012 and 2013. Android now represents 79.3 percent of smartphones shipped. Etherington, Darrell. 2013. "Android Nears 80% Market Share in Global Smartphone Shipments, as iOS and BlackBerry Share Slides, Per IDC." *TechCrunch*, August 7. Accessed December 27, 2013, http://techcrunch.com/2013/08/07/android-nears-80-market-share-in-global-smartphone-shipments-as-ios-and-blackberry-share-slides-per-idc/

46. This is the main point discussed in DeMillo, Richard A. 2011. *Abelard to Apple: The Fate of American Colleges and Universities.* 1st ed. Cambridge: MIT Press.

47. The American Association of University Professors (AAUP) promotes as part of its mission the principles of shared governance. See the *1966 Statement on Government of Colleges and Universities*. 1966. Accessed November 22, 2013, http://aaup.org/report/1966-statement-government -colleges-and-universities

48. This is particularly challenging given that governance resides in many institutions in the hands of the faculty. For a discussion of governance issues, see Cunningham, Brendan M. 2009. "Faculty: Thy Administrator's Keeper? Some Evidence." *Economics of Education Review* 28 (4): 444–453.

49. See the 1940 AAUP statement on tenure and academic freedom: *1940 Statement of Principles on Academic Freedom and Tenure*. 1940. Accessed November 22, 2013, http://aaup.org/report/1940-statement-principles -academic-freedom-and-tenure

50. In the absence of a large and vibrant market for senior faculty members, institutions have been able to pay lower salaries because they only run the risk of losing a small minority of their faculty. Thus the cost of a lifetime appointment is the inability of many to move from one institution to another and hence must accept a lower salary. A general discussion of tenure issues can be found in McPherson, Michael S. and Morton Owen Schapiro. 1999. "Tenure Issues in Higher Education." *Journal of Economic Perspectives* 13 (1): 85–98.

51. Presumably this creates benefits for the institution as a whole as it leads to a rise in reputation that translates in additional dollars either through increased enrollments, alumni contributions, or additional funded research.

52. This takes the form of a traditional principle agent problem. See Sappington (1991) for an extended discussion of principle-agent problems. Sappington, David E. M. 1991. "Incentives in Principal-Agent Relationships." *Journal of Economic Perspectives* 5 (2): 45–66.

53. As reported by Alexa. "Alexa Top 500 Global Sites." Alexa – The Web Information Company. Alexa Internet, Inc. Accessed January 2, 2014, http://www.alexa.com/topsites

54. In September 2013, comScore reported that Google was number one with 67 percent of all search traffic in the US market. "comScore Releases September 2013 U.S. Search Engine Ratings." comScore, Inc. Last modified October 16, 2013, http://www.comscore.com/Insights/Press_Releases/2013 /10/comScore_Releases_September_2013_US_Search_Engine_Rankings

55. According to Sarah Kessler, Yahoo's strategy is in plain sight: "The company wants to create a complete profile of everything you love, which in part explains the company's one billion dollar acquisition of Tumblr." Kessler, Sarah. 2013. "Exposing Yahoo's Strategy through Flickr and Startup Acquisitions." *Fast Company* (174): 40–45.

56. The Gartner group has forecasted that in 2014, PC device shipments will total 282 million units while tablets will total 263 million devices shipped. *Gartner Says Worldwide PC, Tablet and Mobile Phone Shipments to Grow 4.5 Percent in 2013 as Lower-Priced Devices Drive Growth.* Last modified October 21, 2013, http://www.gartner.com/newsroom/id/2610015

57. The Census Bureau as part of its American Community Survey reported that 72 percent of undergraduate students worked in 2011. Twenty percent worked full time all year round. Of those that work the length of a full academic year, roughly 50 percent worked over 20 hours a week. The results can be found in the report: Student Enrollment and Work Status: 2011 and downloaded at: http://nces.ed.gov/pubs2014/2014001rev.pdf

2 Insights from the Game Industry

1. See the Electronic Software Association's Fast Facts. "Industry Facts." The Entertainment Software Association. Accessed November, 25, 2013, http://theesa.com/facts/.

2. Plunkett Research, Ltd. 2013. "Sports Industry Overview." Accessed November 25, 2013, http://www.plunkettresearch.com/sports-recreation-leisure-market-research/industry-statistics

3. The Red Queen Effect, borrowed from the biological theory of evolution describes a corresponding "arms race" within economies. See, for example, Baumol, William J. 2004. "Red-Queen Games: Arms Races, Rule of Law and Market Economies." *Journal of Evolutionary Economics* 14 (2): 237–247; and Robson, Arthur J. 2005. "Complex Evolutionary Systems and the Red Queen." *The Economic Journal* 115 (505): F211–F224.

4. A discussion of baseball's immunity to antitrust can be found in Roberts, Gary R. 2003. "The Case for Baseball's Special Antitrust Immunity." *Journal of Sports Economics* 4 (4): 302–317.

5. The concept of competitive balance is discussed as part of a broader survey of the economics of sports in Szymanski, Stefan. 2003. "The Economic Design of Sporting Contests." *Journal of Economic Literature* 41 (4): 1137–1187.

6. See, for example, Zemsky, Robert. 2008. "The Rain Man Cometh – Again." *Academy of Management Perspectives* 22 (1): 5–14.

7. The influence of rankings on student applications is discussed in Luca, Michael and Jonathan Smith. 2013. "Salience in Quality Disclosure: Evidence from the U.S. News College Rankings." *Journal of Economics and Management Strategy* 22 (1): 58–77.

8. That is not to say that universities do not also compete on the basis of price. See, for example, McMillen, Daniel P., Larry D. Singell, and Glen R. Waddell. 2007. "Spatial Competition and the Price of College." *Economic Inquiry* 45 (4): 817–833.

9. See Robert Frank's insightful article asking whether arms races in higher education are a problem. Frank, Robert. 2004. "Are Arms Races in Higher Education a Problem?" *Forum for the Future of Higher Education.* Accessed December 1, 2013, https://net.educause.edu/ir/library/pdf/FFP0412S.pdf

10. Karmali, Luke. 2013. "Minecraft PC Sales at 12 Million; Franchise at 33 Million." *IGN.* Accessed November 26, 2013, http://www.ign.com/articles/2013/09/03/minecraft-pc-sales-at-12-million-franchise-at-33-million

11. See Ward, Marc. 2013. "Why Minecraft is More than just another Video Game." *BBC News,* September 6. Accessed November 26, 2013, http://www.bbc.co.uk/news/magazine-23572742

12. One explanation for why games are so attractive is the Self Determination Theory built on the principles of competence, autonomy, and relatedness. Encompassing feelings of being capable and effective, freedom in choice, and a connection with others, these same attributes could also be used to explain a positive student experience. Deci, Edward L. and Richard M. Ryan. 1985. *Intrinsic Motivation and Self-Determination in Human Behavior.* New York: Plenum Publishing Co.

13. The role of games in developing self-esteem is discussed in Niman, Neil B. 2013. "The Allure of Games: Toward an Updated Theory of the Leisure Class." *Games and Culture* 8 (1): 26–42.

14. An interesting discussion of the competitive dynamics found in the computer industry is contained in Bresnahan, Timothy F. and Shane Greenstein. 1999. "Technological Competition and the Structure of the Computer Industry." *Journal of Industrial Economics* 47 (1): 1–40.

15. Niman, Neil B. 2002. "Platform Externalities and the Antitrust Case Against Microsoft." *Antitrust Bulletin* 47 (4): 641–660.

16. As noted by Brad Stone, "the Kindle Fire isn't just a product but a philosophy." Quoting Jeff Bezos, he observes that Amazon makes "money when people use our products, not when they buy them." Stone, Brad. 2013. "Grading the Kindle Fire as Amazon's Tablet Turns Two." *Bloomberg Businessweek,* September 27. Accessed December 2, 2013, http://www.businessweek.com/articles/2013-09-27/grading-the-kindle-fire-as-amazons-tablet-turns-two

17. Consumer Intelligent Research Partners estimates that owning a Kindle boosts spending on Amazon by $443 dollars. Elmer-DeWitt, Philip. 2013. "Owning a Kindle Boosts Spending on Amazon by $433." *CNN Money,* December 13. Accessed December 27, 2013, http://tech.fortune.cnn.com/2013/12/13/apple-amazon-kindle-ipad/?iid=HP_River

18. Identified as "outlaw innovation," Stephen Flowers discusses the value created by users. Flowers, Stephen. 2008. "Harnessing the Hackers: The Emergence and Exploitation of Outlaw Innovation." *Research Policy* 37 (2): 177–193.

19. The emergence of user communities that contribute to the creation of a software product is discussed by Burger-Helmchen, Thierry and Patrick Cohendet. 2011. "User Communities and Social Software in the Video Game Industry." *Long Range Planning* 44 (5–6): 317–343.

20. The concept of network externalities is discussed in Shapiro, Carl and Hal R. Varian. 1999. *Information Rules: A Strategic Guide to the Network Economy.* Boston: Harvard Business School Press.

21. A history of the development of the modern curriculum can be found in Lucas, Christopher J. 1994. *American Higher Education: A History.* New York: St. Martins.

22. In 1971, as part of its annual survey of freshman, 37 percent of students at UCLA responded that it was essential or very important to be "very well-off financially," while 73 percent said the same about "developing a meaningful philosophy of life." In 2009, the values were reversed as 78 percent identified values as a goal and only 48 percent were after a meaningful philosophy. This has been one of the factors leading to a massive shift in the curriculum at many colleges and universities. Zernike, Kate. 2009. "Making College 'Relevant.'" *The New York Times*, December 29. Accessed December 15, 2013, http://www.nytimes.com/2010/01/03/education/edlife/03careerism-t.html?pagewanted=all&_r=2&

23. For a description of collaborative learning see Bruffee, Kenneth A. 1993. *Collaborative Learning: Higher Education, Interdependence, and the Authority of Knowledge.* Baltimore: Johns Hopkins University Press.

24. For a discussion of strategies surrounding physical branches, see Manhas, Parikshat S. 2012. "Role of Online Education in Building Brand Image of Educational Institutions." *Journal of Economics, Finance and Administrative Science* 17 (32): 75–85 and Kiley, Kevin. 2012. "Pruning the Branches." *Inside Higher Ed*, May 31. Accessed December 15, 2013, http://www.insidehighered.com/news/2012/05/31/shift-branch-campuses-reflects-changes-educational-delivery-and-demand

25. Sales data was obtained from the Video Game Sales Wiki. "Video Game Sales Wiki." Accessed November 25, 2013, http://vgsales.wikia.com/wiki/Halo

26. An experience good is one where it is difficult to observe in advance of consumption. In other words, you really don't know what you are getting until you actually consume it. Nelson, Philip. 1970. "Information and Consumer Behavior." *Journal of Political Economy* 78 (2): 311–329.

27. Shapiro, Carl and Hal R. Varian. 1998. "Versioning: The Smart Way to Sell Information." *Harvard Business Review* 76 (6): 106–114.

28. Katz, Michael L. and Carl Shapiro. 1994. "Systems Competition and Network Effects." *Journal of Economic Perspectives* 8 (2): 93–115.

29. Market power in the past came primarily through control of a proprietary gaming platform such as Xbox, PlayStation, Wii, and others.

30. This creates an interesting marketing and price discrimination model. See Belloni, Alexandre, Mitchell J. Lovett, William Boulding, and Richard Staelin. 2012. "Optimal Admission and Scholarship Decisions: Choosing Customized Marketing Offers to Attract a Desirable Mix of Customers." *Marketing Science* 31 (4): 621–636.

3 Gamification as a Business Strategy

1. See Chandler, Alfred D. 1977. *The Visible Hand: The Managerial Revolution in American Business*. Cambridge: Belknap Press.
2. Smith, Adam. 1976. *An Inquiry into the Nature and Causes of the Wealth of Nations*. Chicago: University of Chicago Press.
3. The transactions cost approach was pioneered by Oliver Williamson. See for example, Williamson, Oliver E. 1981. "The Modern Corporation: Origins, Evolution, Attributes." *Journal of Economic Literature* 19 (4): 1537–1568.
4. The make/buy decision depends on whether it is cheaper to produce something internally or can be purchased at a lower price through the market. Often this decision is influenced by the magnitude of transaction costs. An interesting discussion of the decision is found in Glimstedt, Henrik, Donald Bratt, and Magnus P. Karlsson. 2010. "The Decision to Make Or Buy a Critical Technology: Semiconductors at Ericsson, 1980–2010." *Industrial and Corporate Change* 19 (2): 431–464.
5. The definitive work on Human Capital has been done by Gary Becker. See, for example, Becker, Gary. 1993. *Human Capital: A Theoretical and Empirical Analysis, with Special Reference to Education*. 3rd ed. Chicago: University of Chicago Press.
6. An interesting historical study on how standards emerged in the wire industry can be found in Velkar, Aashish. 2009. "Transactions, Standardisation and Competition: Establishing Uniform Sizes in the British Wire Industry C. 1880." *Business History* 51 (2): 222–247. For a discussion of standards-based competitive strategies, see Besen, Stanley M. and Joseph Farrell. 1994. "Choosing How to Compete: Strategies and Tactics in Standardization." *Journal of Economic Perspectives* 8 (2): 117–131.
7. Windows, the operating system developed by Microsoft is perhaps the best example of how a product can serve as a product platform.
8. Tuttle, Brad. 2013. "Auto Navigation Systems: Too Complicated, Too Pricey, Just Plain Unnecessary?" *Time*, January 25. Accessed December 10, 2013, http://business.time.com/2013/01/25/auto-navigation-systems-too -complicated-too-pricey-just-plain-unnecessary/
9. An introduction to the economics of licensing can be found in Gallini, Nancy T. and Ralph A. Winter. 1985. "Licensing in the Theory of Innovation." *The Rand Journal of Economics* 16 (2): 237–252.

10. See, for example, Keil, Thomas (2002) for how Bluetooth became open source. "De-Facto Standardization through Alliances – Lessons from Bluetooth." *Telecommunications Policy* 26 (3–4): 205–213.

11. Android and IOS represent competing product platforms.

12. An early discussion of the intrusion of business principles into higher education can be found in Veblen, Thorstein. 1935. *The Higher Learning in America: A Memorandum on the Conduct of Universities by Business Men.* New York: Viking Press.

13. For a discussion of the social and economic benefits of higher education, see Baum, Sandy, Jennifer Ma, and Kathleen Payea. 2013. *Education Pays: The Benefits of Higher Education for Individuals and Society.* New York: College Board.

14. Marshall, Alfred. 1874. *Where to House the London Poor*, reprinted in Pigou, A.C., 1966, *Memoirs of Alfred Marshall.* New York: Kelley.

15. For example, between 1819 and 1851, real wages doubled in Great Britain as a result of the industrial revolution. Lindert, Peter H. and Jeffrey G. Williamson. 1983. "English Workers Living Standard during the Industrial Revolution: A New Look." *Economic History Review* 36: 1–25.

16. The case for state support of higher education can be found in Akai, Nobuo and Masayo Sakata. 2002. "Fiscal Decentralization Contributes to Economic Growth: Evidence from State-Level Cross Section Data for the United States." *Journal of Urban Economics* 52: 93–108. Also look at Feller, Irwin. 2004. "Virtuous and Vicous Cycles in the Contributions of Public Research Universities to State Economic Development Objectives." *Economic Development Quarterly* 18 (2): 138–150.

17. The role of the public university was laid out in the Morrill Act of 1862 where the concept of a land-grant institution was created.

18. Cohn, Elchanan, Sherrie L. W. Rhine, and Maria C. Santos. 1989. "Institutions of Higher Education as Multi-Product Firms: Economies of Scale and Scope." *Review of Economics & Statistics* 71 (2): 284. Also see Laband, David N. and Bernard F. Lentz. 2003. "New Estimates of Economies of Scale and Scope in Higher Education." *Southern Economic Journal* 70 (1): 172.

19. Lucas, Christopher J. 1994. *American Higher Education: A History.* New York: St. Martins.

20. For a different perspective, David Morris finds economies of scale but not of scope. Morris, David. 2008. "Economies of Scale and Scope in E-Learning." *Studies in Higher Education* 33 (3): 331–343. On the other hand, economies of scope but not of scale are found in Smith, David E. and Darryl J. Mitry. 2008. "Investigation of Higher Education: The Real Costs and Quality of Online Programs." *Journal of Education for Business* 83 (3): 147–152. Both analyses precede the emergence of MOOCs. It is not just faculty time, but physical infrastructure that is the important point

ignored by both papers. It is the same reason the Internet has displaced many industries that had previously relied on physical spaces.

21. A discussion of crowdsourcing can be found in Bloodgood, James. 2013. "Crowdsourcing: Useful for Problem Solving, But What about Value Capture." *Academy of Management Review* 38 (3): 455–465; Chandler, Dana and Adam Kapelner. 2013. "Breaking Monotony with Meaning: Motivation in Crowdsourcing Markets." *Journal of Economic Behavior and Organization* 90: 123–133; and Busarovs, Aleksejs. 2011. "Crowdsourcing as User-Driven Innovation, New Business Philosophy's Model." *Journal of Business Management* (4): 53–60.

22. The classic article that is often cited to demonstrate how markets emerge is Radford, Richard A. 1945. "The Economic Organisation of a P.O.W. Camp." *Economica, N.S.* 12: 189–201.

23. This is the essence of Austrian economics. See, for example, the classic article Hayek, Friedrich A. 1945. "The Use of Knowledge in Society." *American Economic Review* 35: 519–530.

24. Howe, Jeff. 2012. "The Crowdsourcing of Talent." *Slate*, February 27. Accessed September 14, 2013, http://www.slate.com/articles/technology/future_tense/2012/02/foldit_crowdsourcing_and_labor_.html

25. "*Meaningful play* occurs when the relationships between actions and outcomes in a game are both *discernible* and *integrated* into the larger context of the game." Salen, Katie and Eric Zimmerman. 2004. *Rules of Play: Game Design Fundamentals*. Cambridge: MIT Press, 34.

26. The Buckley Amendment is also known as the Family Educational and Privacy Rights Act. It can be downloaded from http://epic.org/privacy/education/ferpa.html

27. Analysts place the value of Valve somewhere between $2 and $4 billion dollars. Chiang, Oliver. 2011. "Valve and Stream Worth Billions." *Forbes*, February 15. Accessed December 21, 2013, http://www.forbes.com/sites/oliverchiang/2011/02/15/valve-and-steam-worth-billions/

4 The Allure of Games

1. The average freshman spends 14 hours studying each week see National Survey of Student Engagement. *A Fresh Look at Student Engagement: Annual Results 2013*. In contrast, the typical MMORPG gamer spends on average 21 hours each week playing the game Yee, Nick. "Hours of Play Per Week." Last modified February 24, 2004, http://www.nickyee.com/daedalus/archives/000758.php

2. The importance of the origin story is described in the following manner: "In comic books, the origin story reveals how a character became a superhero – where their powers came from, who inspired them, and what events set them on a path to change the world. Before YOU can change

the world, you need to figure out your superhero origins." "Quest List." Urgent Evoke. http://www.urgentevoke.com/page/quest-list

3. For a discussion of life stories, see McAdams, Dan P. 1993, 1997. *The Stories We Live by: Personal Myths and the Making of the Self.* New York: Guilford Press.

4. Some of the reasons why people like to play World of Warcraft is discussed in Billieux, Joel, Martial Van der Linden, Sophia Achab, Yasser Khazaal, Laura Paraskevopoulos, Daniele Zullino, and Gabriel Thorens. 2013. "Why Do You Play World of Warcraft? An In-Depth Exploration of Self-Reported Motivations to Play Online and In-Game Behaviours in the Virtual World of Azeroth." *Computers in Human Behavior* 29: 103–109. A general review of the literature about engagement in games can be found in Boyle, Elizabeth A., Thomas M. Connolly, Thomas Hainey, and James M. Boyle. 2012. "Engagement in Digital Entertainment Games: A Systematic Review." *Computers in Human Behavior* 28: 771–780.

5. A sense of belonging and the importance for student retention is discussed in Morrow, Jennifer Ann and Margot E. Ackermann. 2012. "Intention to Persist and Retention of First-Year Students: The Importance of Motivation and Sense of Belonging." *College Student Journal* 46 (3): 483–491 and Freeman, Tierra M., Lynley H. Anderman, and Jane M. Jensen. 2007. "Sense of Belonging in College Freshmen at the Classroom and Campus Levels." *Journal of Experimental Education* 75 (3): 203–220.

6. For an example using World of Warcraft, see Bessiere, Katherine, A. Fleming Seay, and Sara Kiesler. 2007. "The Ideal Elf: Identity Exploration in World of Warcraft." *CyberPsychology & Behavior* 10 (4): 530–535.

7. See Przybylski, Andrew K., Netta Weinstein, Kou Murayama, Martin F. Lynch, and Richard M. Ryan. 2012. "The Ideal Self at Play: The Appeal of Video Games That Let You Be All You Can Be." *Psychological Science* 23 (1): 69–76.

8. See, for example, Kim, Changsoo, Sang-Gun Lee, and Minchoel Kang. 2012. "I Became an Attractive Person in the Virtual World: Users' Identification with Virtual Communities and Avatars." *Computers in Human Behavior* 28: 1663–1669.

9. Blascovich, Jim and Jeremy Bailenson. 2011. *Infinite Reality: Avatars, Eternal Life, New Worlds and the Dawn of the Virtual Revolution.* New York: HaperCollins.

10. Yee, Nick, Jeremy N. Bailenson, and Nicolas Ducheneaut. 2009. "The Proteus Effect." *Communication Research* 36 (2): 285–312.

11. Blascovich and Bailenson. *Infinite Reality.*

12. The importance of meaning is discussed in Baumeister, Roy F. 1991. *Meanings of Life.* New York: The Guilford Press. When surveying academics, graduate

students, and administrators, Linda Hagedorn identified the following as the most important source of meaning: "I live to contribute something that is greater than myself." Hagedorn, Linda Serra. 2012. "The Meaning of Academic Life." *The Review of Higher Education* 35 (3): 485–512.

13. For another perspective on the importance of story, see Sachs, Jonah. 2012. *Winning the Story Wars: Why Those Who Tell (and Live) the Best Stories Will Rule the Future.* Cambridge: Harvard Business School Press.

14. Kahneman, Daniel. 2011. "Thinking, Fast and Slow." Chap. 11. New York: Farrar, Straus, and Giroux.

15. In the Undergraduate Teaching Faculty 2010–2011 HERI survey conducted at UCLA, 62.7 percent of faculty characterized themselves as "far left" or liberal while only 11.9 percent described themselves as conservative or "far right." Hurtado, Sylvia, Kevin Eagan, John H. Pryor, Hannah Whang, and Serge Tran. *Undergraduate Teaching Faculty: The 2010–2011 HERI Faculty Survey.* Los Angeles: Higher Education Research Institute.

16. The role of morality in experimental outcomes and what it says about the real world is explored in Levitt, Steven D. and John A. List. 2007. "What Do Laboratory Experiments Measuring Social Preferences Reveal about the Real World?" *Journal of Economic Perspectives* 21 (2): 153–174.

17. For a discussion of status quo bias, see Kahneman, Daniel, Jack L. Knetsch, and Richard H. Thaler. 1991. "The Endowment Effect, Loss Aversion, and Status Quo Bias: Anomalies." *Journal of Economic Perspectives* 5 (1): 193–206.

18. Perhaps the clearest statement of the role of freedom in economics was made by Milton Friedman in Friedman, Milton. 1962. Capitalism and Freedom. Chicago: University of Chicago Press.

19. Loewenstein, George F. and Elizabeth A. Mannix. 1994. "The Effects of Interfirm Mobility and Individual Versus Group Decision Making on Managerial Time Horizons." *Organizational Behavior and Human Decision Processes* 59: 371–390.

20. Thaler, Richard H. and Cass R. Sunstein. 2008. *Nudge: Improving Decisions about Health, Wealth and Happiness.* New Haven: Yale University Press.

21. The concept of bounded rationality was introduced in Simon, Herbert A. 1955. "A Behavioral Model of Rational Choice." *Quarterly Journal of Economics* 69: 99–118.

22. See Scitovsky, Tibor. 1992. *The Joyless Economy: The Psychology of Human Satisfaction.* Revised Edition ed. New York: Oxford University Press.

23. In a later article that discusses the issue of school violence, Scitovsky argues that in contrast to calls for schools to focus more of their attention on reading, writing, and arithmetic, they should instead increase the teaching of leisure skills. Increases in worker productivity has increased the amount of leisure time, which has expanded the need for an increase

in peaceful leisure activities to alleviate boredom and the violence that it generates. Scitovsky, Tibor. 1999. "Boredom – an Overlooked Disease?" *Challenge* 42 (5): 5–15.

24. Instead we just assign homework problems. This is all changing as electronic learning platforms become more prevalent and they incorporate more gaming features.

25. Although materialism was also related to several meanings of education, the current study suggests that in terms of aspirations, what matters most in predicting such students' meanings of education is the degree to which their values are grounded in an interest in their own psychological development, their relationships with others, and their wider community. Henderson-King, Donna and Amanda M. Mitchell. 2011. "Do Materialism, Intrinsic Aspirations, and Meaning in Life Predict Students' Meanings of Education?" *Social Psychology of Education* 14: 130.

26. Flow is an idea developed by Csikszenthmihalyi, one of the founders of positive psychology, in Csikszenthmihalyi, Mihaly. 1975. *Beyond Boredom and Anxiety.* San Francisco: Jossey-Bass.

27. The concept of flow in collaborative game-based learning is discussed in Admiraal, Wilfried, Jantina Huizenga, Sanne Akkerman, and Geert ten Dam. 2011. "The Concept of Flow in Collaborative Game-Based Learning." *Computers in Human Behavior* 27: 1185–1194. An attempt to measure the flow experience for gamers can be found in Procci, Katelyn, Allysa R. Singer, Katherine R. Levy, and Clint Bowers. 2012. "Measuring the Flow Experience of Gamers: An Evaluation of the DFS-2." *Computers in Human Behavior* 28: 2306–2312.

28. See Baum, Sandy, Jennifer Ma, and Kathleen Payea. 2013. *Education Pays: The Benefits of Higher Education for Individuals and Society.* New York: College Board.

29. Wong, David. 2010. "5 Creepy Ways Video Games Are Trying to Get You Addicted." *Cracked* March 19, 2013, http://www.cracked.com/article _18461_5-creepy-ways-video-games-are-trying-to-get-you-addicted.html.

30. Skinner, Burrhus F. 1971. *Beyond Freedom and Dignity.* New York: Knopf.

31. Seligman, Martin E. P. and Mihaly Csikszenthmihalyi. 2000. "Positive Psychology: An Introduction." *American Psychologist* 55 (1): 5–14.

32. Niman, Neil B. 2013. "The Allure of Games: Toward an Updated Theory of the Leisure Class." *Games and Culture* 8 (1): 26–42.

33. Pingle, Mark and Mark Mitchell. 2002. "What Motivates Positional Concerns for Income?" *Journal of Economic Psychology* 23 (1): 127–148. See also: Solnick, Sara J. and David Hemenway. 1998. "Is More always Better? A Survey on Positional Concerns." *Journal of Economics Behavior and Organization* 37 (3): 373–383.

34. That is presumably the reason why Moses is never allowed into the promised land.

35. "In order to gain and to hold the esteem of men it is not sufficient merely to possess wealth or power. The wealth or power must be put in evidence, for esteem is awarded only on evidence." Veblen, Thorstein. 1899. *The Theory of the Leisure Class*. New York: Macmillan, p. 36.

36. While conspicuous consumption provides one avenue for determining relative position, it is most certainly not the only way. Materialism could be rejected entirely and yet comparisons will still be made. It is just that the basis for making those comparisons will change. Niman. "The Allure of Games," 26–42.

37. Frank, Robert H. 1999. *Luxury Fever: Money and Happiness in an Era of Excess*. Princeton: Princeton University Press.

38. Frederick, Shane and George Loewenstein. 1999. "Hedonic Adaptation." In *Well-being: The Foundations of Hedonic Psychology*, edited by Daniel Kahneman, Ed Diener, and Norbert Schwarz, 302–329. New York: Russel Sage Foundation.

39. If conspicuous consumption is the visual display of one's relative economic success, then an even higher measure of success would be to not work at all. If work is the embodiment of all that is productive, then the antithesis of work is leisure; an activity that becomes the embodiment of waste. As such, the luxury of wasting time becomes the highest measure of economic success. "...a life of leisure is the readiest and most conclusive evidence of pecuniary strength, and therefore of superior force; provided always that the gentleman of leisure can live in manifest ease and comfort." Veblen. *The Theory of the Leisure Class*, 38.

40. Niman"The Allure of Games," 26–42.

41. In the most recent American College Health Association/National College Health Assessment II survey, 31.3 percent of students reported that within the last 12 months, they felt so depressed that it was difficult to function.

42. Kahneman, Daniel and Amos Tversky. 1979. "Prospect Theory: An Analysis of Decisions Under Risk." *Econometrica* 47 (2): 263–291.

43. Loss aversion and housing is discussed in Bokhari, Sheharyar and David Geltner. 2011. "Loss Aversion and Anchoring in Commercial Real Estate Pricing: Empirical Evidence and Price Index Implications." *Real Estate Economics* 39 (4): 635–670.

44. Nalley, Lanier and Andrew McKenzie. 2011. "How Much Is That Exam Grade Really Worth? An Estimation of Student Risk Aversion to Their Unknown Final College Course Grades." *Journal of Economic Education* 42 (4): 338–353.

5 Design Elements

1. A good introduction to the principles underlying game design can be found in Schell, Jessie. 2008. *The Art of Game Design: A Book of Lenses.* Burlington: Morgan Kaufman.

2. Looking at longitudinal data covering 2,322 students at a diverse selection of colleges and universities, the Collegiate Learning Assessment Survey was given to entering freshman in 2005. The students were tracked over three semesters until the end of their sophomore year in 2007. The survey assessed core competencies that included: critical thinking, analytical reasoning, problem solving, and writing. The average improvement was almost imperceptible over the three semesters with average gains of only 7 percent. Arum, Richard and Josipa Roksa. 2011. *Academically Adrift: Limited Learning on College Campuses.* Chicago: University of Chicago Press.

3. Having too many choices can lead to anxiety. Schwartz, Barry. 2009. *The Paradox of Choice: Why More Is Less.* New York: HarperCollins.

4. Sunstein, Cass R. 2013. "The Storrs Lectures: Behavioral Economics and Paternalism." *Yale Law Journal* 122 (7): 1826–1899.

5. Another example of the effectiveness of choice architectures can be found in Dolan, Paul, Antony Elliott, Robert Metcalfe, and Ivo Vlaev. 2012. "Influencing Financial Behavior: From Changing Minds to Changing Contexts." *Journal of Behavioral Finance* 13 (2): 126–142.

6. See, for example, Azariadis, Costas. 1975. "Implicit Contracts and Underemployment Equilibria." *Journal of Political Economy* 83 (6): 1183–1202.

7. For a discussion of the misallocation of resources issues created by tenure, see Johnson, William R. and Sarah Turner. 2009. "Faculty without Students: Resource Allocation in Higher Education." *Journal of Economic Perspectives* 23 (2): 169–189.

8. Lanier, Nalley and Andrew McKenzie. 2011. "How Much Is That Exam Grade Really Worth? An Estimation of Student Risk Aversion to Their Unknown Final College Course Grades." *Journal of Economic Education* 42 (4): 338–353.

9. Lopez-Perez, Raul. 2009. "Followers and Leaders: Reciprocity, Social Norms and Group Behavior." *Journal of Socio-Economics* 38 (4): 137–158. See also Ostrom, Elinor. 2000. "Collective Action and the Evolution of Social Norms." *Journal of Economic Perspectives* 14 (3): 137–158.

10. See, for example, Park, Andreas and Hamid Sabourian. 2011. "Herding and Contrarian Behavior in Financial Markets." *Econometrica* 79 (4): 973–1026.

11. For a review of the literature, see Borsari, Brian and Kate B. Carey. 2001. "Peer Influences on College Drinking: A Review of the Research." *Journal of Substance Abuse* 13: 391–424.

12. Based on the number of hours played, League of Legends is the most played video game in the world. Evangelho, Jason. 2012. "'League of Legends' Bigger than 'WoW,' More Daily Players than 'Call of Duty.'" *Forbes*, October 12. Accessed January 5, 2014, http://www.forbes.com /sites/jasonevangelho/2012/10/12/league-of-legends-bigger-than-wow -more-daily-players-than-call-of-duty/

13. The game has such a bad reputation, that Riot Games felt compelled to discuss the issue at a panel held at PaxEast 2013. For a description of the event, see Sarkar, Samit. 2013. "Riot Games Believes in the Goodness of League of Legends Players." March 24. Accessed January 5, 2014, http:// www.polygon.com/2013/3/24/4140968/league-of-legends-riot-games -player-behavior-pax-east-2013

14. The concept of Service Dominant Logic can be found in Vargo, Stephen L. and Robert F. Lusch. 2004. "Evolving to a New Dominant Logic for Marketing." *Journal of Marketing* 68: 1–17. The idea of Value Co-Creation is discussed in Prahalad, Coimbatore K. and Venkat Ramaswamy. 2004. "Co-Creation Experiences: The Next Practice in Value Creation." *Journal of Interactive Marketing* 18 (3): 5–14.

15. Marandi, Ebi, Ed Little, and Tim Hughes. 2010. "Innovation and the Children of the Revolution: Facebook and Value Co-Creation." *The Marketing Review* 10 (2): 169–183. See also Pongsakornrungsilp, Siwarit and Jonathan E. Schroeder. 2011. "Understanding Value Co-Creation in a Co-Consuming Brand Community." *Marketing Theory* 11 (3): 303–324.

16. Prahalad and Ramaswamy. "Co-Creation Experiences," 5–14.

17. In one of the few empirical tests of the co-creation hypothesis, it was observed that when knives where constructed from kits as part of a co-created process, consumers had a greater sense of accomplishment, connection to the self and social recognition. Peters, Cara, Charles D. Bodkin, and Scott Fitzgerald. 2012. "Toward an Understanding of Meaning Creation via the Collective Co-Production Process." *Journal of Consumer Behavior* 11 (2): 124–135. In their study of community-sponsored agriculture, similar benefits were observed by Hunt, David M., Stephanie Geiger-Oneto, and Philip E. Varca. 2012. "Satisfaction in the Context of Customer Co-Production: A Behavioral Involvement Perspective." *Journal of Consumer Behavior* 11 (5): 347–356.

18. NG, Irene C. L. and Jeannie Forbes. 2009. "Education as Service: The Understanding of University Experience through the Service Logic." *Journal of Marketing for Higher Education* 19: 38–64.

19. Game development as a co-created experience is discussed in Davidovici-Nora, Myriam. 2009. "The Dynamics of Co-Creation in the Video Game Industry: The Case of World of Warcraft." *Communications and Strategies* (73): 43–66.

20. This occurs because of network effects.

21. The benefit of attending an elite university is discussed by Brewer, Dominic J., Eric R. Eide, and Ronald G. Ehrenberg. 1999. "Does It Pay to Attend an Elite Private College? Cross-Cohort Evidence on the Effects of College Type on Earnings." *Journal of Human Resources* 34 (1): 104–123. It is also discussed in Dale, Stacy Berg and Alan B. Krueger. 2002. "Estimating the Payoff to Attending a More Selective College: An Application of Selection on Observables and Unobservables." *Quarterly Journal of Economics* 117 (4): 1491–1527.

22. For an extensive look at this, see Liu, Liqun and William S. Neilson. 2011. "High Scores But Low Skills." *Economics of Education Review* 30 (3): 507–516.

23. While standardized tests are not often used in higher education, professor quality was examined when students were randomly assigned to core courses at the Air Force Academy and then track performance in follow-on courses. What was discovered was that students who rated their instructors highly in the core courses, tended to perform poorly in the follow-on courses. This suggests that students reward professors who give high grades in the core courses and punish those who increase deep learning. Carrell, Scott E. and James E. West. 2010. "Does Professor Quality Matter? Evidence from Random Assignment of Students to Professors." *Journal of Political Economy* 118 (3): 409–432.

24. In a national survey of 192,912 first-time, full-time students, entering 283 four-year colleges and universities in the United States, Pryor et.al. (2012) report that the most prevalent reason for going to college as reported by 87.9 percent of the respondents was to get a better job. This was considerably higher than the 67.8 percent who responded the same in 1976. Pryor, John H., Kevin Eagan, Laura Paluki Blake, Sylvia Hurtado, Jennifer Berdan, and Matthew H. Case. 2012. *The American Freshman: National Norms Fall 2012*. Los Angeles: Higher Education Research Institute.

25. A discussion of learning by doing can be found in Callander, Steven. 2011. "Searching and Learning by Trial and Error." *American Economic Review* 101 (6): 2277–2308.

26. Taylorism was also known as Scientific Management at the end of the twentieth century. For a discussion of his principles of scientific management see Taylor, Fredrick W. 1967. *The Principles of Scientific Management*. New York: Norton.

27. An often cited study demonstrates that there is only a marginal difference in retention between a student that has taken an economics course and one that has not. College seniors who had taken a class in economics scored on average just 14 points higher on a 15-question test than those that had no background in economics. Although economic students did score higher, the median grade was only in the sixties, thus confirming that they had remembered only a very limited amount. Walstad, William and

Sam Allgood. 1999. "What Do College Seniors Know about Economics?" *American Economic Review* 89 (2): 350–354.

28. A survey of the feedback literature can be found in Evans, Carol. 2013. "Making Sense of Assessment Feedback in Higher Education." *Review of Educational Research* 83 (1): 70–120.

29. The concept of keeping up with the Jones can be traced back to the work of Thorstein Veblen. Modern uses of the concept include Miles, Daniel and Maximo Rossi. 2007. "Learning about One's Relative Position and Subjective Well-Being." *Applied Economics* 39 (13–15): 1711–1718; Luttmer, Erzo F. P. 2005. "Neighbors as Negatives: Relative Earnings and Well-Being." *Quarterly Journal of Economics* 120 (3): 963–1002; and Leibenstein, Harvey. 1950. "Bandwagon, Snob and Veblen Effects in the Theory of Consumers' Demand." *Quarterly Journal of Economics* 64: 183–207.

30. For a more extensive of the principles underlying the Weight Watchers Model, see Moisio, Risto and Mariam Beruchashvili. 2010. "Questing for Well-being at Weight Watchers: The Role of the Spiritual-Therapeutic Model in a Support Group." *Journal of Consumer Research* 36 (5): 857–875.

31. The hat page on the official Team Fortress 2 Wiki begins with the following: "Throughout history, men have worn hats as a way of showing how much better they are than other men. 'I buy hats,' a behatted man seems to say. 'I am better than you.'" Accessed January 5, 2014, http://wiki .teamfortress.com/wiki/Hat

32. A description of the hat economy in Team Fortress 2 can be found at: "Team Fortress 2: An Economy of Hats." The Scientific Gamer. Last modified August 15, 2012, http://scientificgamer.com/an-economy-of-hats/

6 Structural Design

1. Bioshock is a game where each element is designed to further the narrative. The narrative plays an integral role that encompasses every element in the game.

2. In the game Bastion, after a player unlocks their weapons, they are given an opportunity to perform in a special challenge area and gain additional bonuses based on their display of skill.

3. Puzzle games like Angry Birds or Cut the Rope contain a system that assesses player performance based on metrics such as time and efficiency.

4. Arcade games generally have the player earn points. After a certain number of points are reached, the player may win a free game.

5. Nintendo's Pokemon franchise is heavily focused on levels. Moving from level to level, Pokemon grows stronger and new moves are learned and abilities are developed.

6. Game services like Steam use an achievement system to encourage players to increase the amount of time they spend playing games. Achievements based on milestones, time played, and specific actions are provided with each game.

7. In Alan Wake, a torch is used as a symbol to identify safe areas and stashes of items. When the player shines the flashlight on a torch, secrets are revealed.

8. Guild Wars 2 is one example of a game that includes a leader board.

9. It is the equivalent of the blood ties that bonded individuals in the old days.

10. First person shooters, such as Activisions's Call of Duty series, use the concept of a clan to organize competitions, identify members of a team, and host events to support community.

11. In games such as Halo or Call of Duty, there are team chat areas that are separate from the game or lobby chat. Private team chat areas are used exclusively to coordinate actions within a team. Games like League of Legends place players in different tiers based on their skill level. This is designed to exclude lower level players from competing with those with a demonstrated higher level of skill. Players may gain admission to higher levels once they have defeated certain teams or individuals.

12. In the game of Runescape, when a player levels up or achieves something important, fireworks are displayed and a chat message is sent to players in the surrounding area. Often players attempting to do the same thing will congratulate each other on the achievement. In games like Halo 4, each member of a clan will wear the same emblem on their armor to display their affiliation. In the game, Asheron's Call, members of the development team will sometimes enter the game and act as characters or monsters. Players often flow to the area in order to see and participate in the events. World of Warcraft and other games like it use a system of raids and cooperative missions to complete an objective through combat.

13. Team Fortress 2 utilizes teams as the foundation for the competitive struggles in the game. Teammates assume a number of different roles as they cooperatively work together in order to defeat the other team.

14. World of Warcraft includes a system of guilds. Guilds facilitate collaboration to achieve common goals, host events, and manage finances for the benefits of members.

15. Conventions exist for measuring the performance of athletes. A baseball player's batting average, the number of touchdowns scored per game by a football, the goals against average by a goalkeeper in hockey or soccer, are all examples of how performance measures are turned into conventions designed to assess player performance.

16. Cooperative games like Left 4 Dead have players working toward a common goal. Players cooperate to reach a safe house at the end of a level in

order to survive. Each level completed brings the player closer to the goal of being rescued.

17. League of Legends is a highly competitive game with a vocal fan base. There are many dedicated forums for discussing strategy about the game. Dota 2 is an example of a game with a large trading community. Specialty websites have been created to allow players to easily trade with one another.

18. Scarcity forms the central premise of the game Eve Online. With most of the Earth's resources exhausted, players need to search the universe to mine, trade, or conquer in the pursuit of the basics needed to sustain life.

19. Gearbox Software's Borderlands is built on a system of quests that promises players experience points and other rewards in exchange for completing a set of objectives assigned to a particular quest. Progress in the game is achieved by completing a series of quests.

20. In many board games like Monopoly, the player roles a pair of dice and moves the number of spaces indicated by the role. The path is cyclical and different actions are taken depending on where the player lands on the board.

21. In Fallout New Vegas, a player progresses through different stages in a variety of ways. They can gain different titles and advance through a system of levels as the result of strength, experience, karma, or through reputations earned. In Metal Gear Solid: Peace Walker, the game was designed to be played on mobile platforms. Hence it was broken down into small chunks in order to all a mission to be played with a clear breaking point.

22. The game LA Noir uses pacing to ensure that the difficulty of play does not progress at a faster rate than the player's ability to solve the clues required for success.

23. Blizzard's extremely successful Diablo series relies on randomly generated areas to advance play. These areas known as "dungeons" are not the same for each player or groups of players.

24. Strategy games like chess allow for multiple paths in order to achieve victory (checkmate).

25. At the end of Fallout 3, the player can destroy the oppressive forces of the Enclave and bring clean water to an irradiated wasteland. The effects are shown around the game world and a player becomes something of a legend among nonplaying characters.

26. MMORPGs such as Dungeons and Dragons Online by Turbine train players in basic skills early in the game. Generally this takes place in the form of an introductory mission under the guidance of a nonplayer.

27. Just Cause 2 is a game that is notable for its sandbox style of play. The game world can be roamed about freely and various secrets or minor objectives exist for the player to complete at their leisure.

28. Fallout is an isometric role-playing game developed by Interplay. As the player progresses they earn points that can be used to acquire select skills

(e.g., speech, lock picking, medicine, and firearms). Which skills the player selects and how many points they put into each skill will greatly change what opportunities they have throughout the game.

7 The Classroom as a Game Space

1. A more general discussion can be found in Gee, James Paul. 2007. *What Video Games Have to Teach Us about Learning and Literacy.* Second edition. New York: Macmillan.
2. See, for example, Przybylski, Andrew K., Netta Weinstein, Kou Murayama, Martin F. Lynch, and Richard M. Ryan. 2012. "The Ideal Self at Play: The Appeal of Video Games That Let You Be All You Can Be." *Psychological Science* 23 (1): 69–76 and Blascovich, Jim and Jeremy Bailenson. 2011. *Infinite Reality: Avatars, Eternal Life, New Worlds and the Dawn of the Virtual Revolution.* New York: HaperCollins.
3. Niman, Neil B. 2013. "The Allure of Games: Toward an Updated Theory of the Leisure Class." *Games and Culture* 8(1): 26–42.
4. Bessiere, Katherine, A. Fleming Seay, and Sara Kiesler. 2007. "The Ideal Elf: Identity Exploration in World of Warcraft." *CyberPsychology & Behavior* 10 (4): 530–535 and Crowe, Nic and Simon Bradford. 2006. "'Hanging Out in Runescape': Identity, Work and Leisure in the Virtual Playground." *Children's Geographies* 4 (3): 331–346.
5. In conjunction with massively multiplayer online games, this concept of learning is discussed by Thomas, Douglas and John Seely Brown. 2009. "Why Virtual Worlds Can Matter." *International Journal of Media and Learning* 1 (1): 37–49.
6. How fun can motivate play and what is required for a player to enjoy a game has been discussed in Malone, Thomas W. 1981. "Toward a Theory of Intrinsically Motivating Instruction." *Cognitive Science* 4: 333–369 and Malone, Thomas W. and Mark R. Lepper. 1987. "Making Learning Fun: A Taxonomy of Intrinsic Motivations for Learning." *Aptitude, Learning, and Instruction* 3: 223–253.
7. See, for example, Nalley, Lanier and Andrew McKenzie. 2011. "How Much Is That Exam Grade Really Worth? An Estimation of Student Risk Aversion to Their Unknown Final College Course Grades." *Journal of Economic Education* 42 (4): 338–353.
8. See Kahneman, Daniel and Amos Tversky. 1979. "Prospect Theory: An Analysis of Decisions Under Risk." *Econometrica* 47 (2): 263–291.
9. "If you read between the lines, you'll discover that the entire *Facebook* platform is organized around the generation and amplification of stories." Savitz, Edward and Jamie Tedford. 2012. "Facebook Timeline for Brands: It's about Storytelling." *Forbes* February 29. Accessed December 14, 2013,

http://www.forbes.com/sites/ciocentral/2012/02/29/facebook-timeline-for-brands-its-about-storytelling/

10. The appeal of stories might stem from the belief that human beings do not naturally reason deductively Schank, David. 1990. *Tell Me a Story: A New Look at Real and Artificial Memory.* New York: Charles Scribner's Sons; they are more entertaining and believable Neuhauser, Peg C. 1993. *Corporate Legends and Lore: The Power of Storytelling as a Management Tool.* New York: McGraw Hill; or are a more efficient way of dealing with complexity Yearwood, John and Andrew Stranieri. 2007. "Narrative-Based Interactive Learning Environments from Modeling Reasoning." *Educational Technology & Society* 10 (3): 192–208. Recent research utilizing the power of storytelling in an online environment demonstrated that it led to significantly greater levels of attention, relevance, confidence, satisfaction, and overall motivation when compared to the exactly same course taught using a more standard instructional approach. Hirumi, Atsusi, Stephen Sivo, and Kelly Pounds. 2012. "Telling Stories to Enhance Teaching and Learning: The Systematic Design, Development and Testing of Two Online Courses." *International Journal of E-Learning* 11 (2): 125–151.

11. For many students, the result is that their online identity has become potentially richer and more complete than their offline one Townsend, Allie. 2012. "This Is Your Life (According to Your New Timeline)." *Time* February 13. Accessed November 20, 2013, http://content.time.com/time/magazine/article/0,9171,2105972,00.html

12. This could occur in a manner similar to how story is currently being used to engage gamers in learning and skill development that is useful in both the real world and virtual game environment. See for example, Yearwood and Stranieri. "Narrative-Based Interactive Learning," 192–20; Conle, Carola and Michelle Boone. 2008. "Local Heroes, Narrative Worlds and the Imagination: The Making of a Moral Curriculum through Experiential Narratives." *Curriculum Inquiry* 38 (1): 7–37 and Dickie, Michelle D. 2011. "Murder on Grimm Isle: The Impact of Game Narrative Design in an Educational Game-Based Learning Environment." *British Journal of Educational Technology* 42 (3): 456–469.

13. As noted by Sara Worth: "When we begin to learn to reason, it is not entirely discursive or empirical. We learn through the structure of stories. That is, we learn to reason through the reasoning provided to us through hearing and telling stories. By engaging with narratives, we practice using our narrative reason. The structure found within narratives helps us to imagine more broadly than we are called to do with discursive thinking…The way we construct our narratives (fictional and nonfictional) is importantly tied to the way we understand, order, and construct our own reality and our own personal identity." Worth, Sarah. 2008. "Storytelling

and Narrative Knowing: An Examination of the Epistemic Benefits of Well-Told Stories." *Journal of Aesthetic Education* 42 (3): 54.

14. The importance of creating a learning environment has been developed by Winn, William. 2003. "Learning in Artificial Environments: Embodiment, Embeddedness and Dynamic Adaptation." *Tech., Inst., Cognition and Learning* 1: 87–114.

15. The concept of transformational play is discussed extensively by Barab, Sasha, Patrick Pettyjohn, Melissa Gresalfi, Charlene Volk, and Maria Solomou. 2012. "Game-Based Curriculum and Transformational Play: Designing to Meaningfully Positioning Person, Content, and Context." *Computers & Education* 58: 518–533.

16. It is perhaps worthwhile to point out that this is not a new idea. See for example Keller, Fred S. 1968. "'Good-Bye Teacher...'" *Journal of Applied Behavior Analysis* (1): 79.

17. A survey looking at the relationship between game attributes and learning outcomes is provided by Wilson, Katherine A., Wendy L. Bedwell, Elizabeth H. Lazzara, Eduardo Salas, C. Shawn Burke, Jamie L. Estock, Kara L. Orvis, and Curtis Conkey. 2009. "Relationships between Game Attributes and Learning Outcomes." *Simulation & Gaming* 40 (2): 217–266.

18. The importance of context is discussed in Rieber, Lloyd P. and David Noah. 2008. "Games, Simulations, and Visual Metaphors in Education: Antagonism between Enjoyment and Learning." *Educational Media International* 45 (2): 77–92.

19. For a discussion of the importance of meaning, see Bruner, Jerome S. 1990. *Acts of Meaning*. Cambridge: Harvard University Press.

20. The importance of narrative for achieving learning objectives is discussed extensively in Dickey, Michele D. 2006. "Game Design Narrative for Learning: Appropriating Adventure Game Design Narrative Devices and Techniques for the Design of Interactive Learning Environments." *Educational Technology Research & Development* 54 (3): 245–263 and Dickey, Michele D. 2007. "Game Design and Learning: A Conjectural Analysis of how Massively Multiple Online Role-Playing Games (MMORPGs) Foster Intrinsic Motivation." *Educational Technology Research & Development* 55: 253–273.

21. An Epic Win is defined in the following way by Jane McGonigal "' Epic win' is a gamer term. It's used to describe a big, and usually surprising, success; a come-from-behind victory, an unorthodox strategy that works out spectacularly well, a team effort that goes much better than planned, a heroic effort from the most unlikely player." McGonigal, Jane. 2011. *Reality is Broken: Why Games Make Us Better and How They Can Change the World*. New York: Penguin, 247.

22. The definitive work is Campbell, Joseph. 1968. *The Hero with a Thousand Faces*, 2nd Ed. Princeton: Princeton University Press.

23. This is an adaptation of Christopher Vogler's condensed version of Joseph Campbell's original Monomyth.

24. For Dan McAdams, identity is a life story that takes the form of a personal myth. This myth provides a sense of unity or purpose capable of fashioning a meaningful niche in the psychosocial world. Exploring the psychology of life stories provides a series of guideposts that reveal the important elements that are contained in personal stories about the self. McAdams, Dan P. 1993, 1997. *The Stories We Live by: Personal Myths and the Making of the Self.* New York: Guilford Press.

8 Creating a Game-Based Student Experience

1. A flipped classroom is one where the lectures take place outside the classroom and learning activities take place inside.

2. For a discussion of how technology is affecting the concept of Friendship, see Amichai-Hamburger, Yair, Mila Kingsbury, and Barry H. Schneider. 2013. "Friendship: An Old Concept with a New Meaning?" *Computers in Human Behavior* 29: 33–39.

3. Smartphone usage has now exceeded 50 percent of the population. How college students use their smartphones can be found at: Laird, Sam. "In a Relationship: College Students and their Smartphones." Mashable. Last modified June 30, 2012, http://mashable.com/2012/06/30 /smartphones-college-students-infographic/.

4. See Antheunis, Marjolijn L., Patti M. Valkenburg, and Jochen Peter. 2010. "Getting Acquainted through Social Network Sites: Testing a Model of Online Uncertainty Reduction and Social Attraction." *Computers in Human Behavior* 26: 100–109.

5. Individuals generally have a harder time having meaningful conversations when a mobile phone is present. Przybylski, Andrew K. and Netta Weinstein. 2013. "Can You Connect with Me Now? How the Presence of Mobile Communication Technology Influences Face-to-Face Conversation Quality." *Journal of Social and Personal Relationships* 30 (3): 237–246.

6. The problem is exacerbated with the use of technologies such as Snapchat where the pictures self-destruct. Gillette, Felix. 2013. "Snapchat and the Erasable Future of Social Media." *Bloomberg Businessweek* February 7. Accessed January 5, 2014, http://www.businessweek .com/articles/2013–02–07/snapchat-and-the-erasable-future-of-social-media.

7. For a discussion of the importance of context in the construction of life stories, see Gregg, Gary S. 1991. *Self-Representation: Life Narrative Studies in Identity and Ideology.* New York: Greenwood Press.

8. In a perceptive article about the future of ESPN (the sports network), Douglas Warshaw observed that "most of us are far more interested in capturing the moment than truly experiencing it. It's no longer about being at the event, as much as it's about showing the world that you were at the event." Warshaw, Douglas A. 2013. "Nate Silver, Data, and Storytelling." *CNN Money* July 24. Accessed on September 10, 2013, http://features.blogs.fortune.cnn.com/2013/07/24/nate-silver-data -and-storytelling/.

9. The role of Facebook in building social capital is explored in Steinfield, Charles, Nicole B. Ellison, and Cliff Lampe. 2008. "Social Capital, Self-Esteem, and Use of Online Social Network Sites: A Longitudinal Analysis." *Journal of Applied Developmental Psychology* 29 (6): 434–445. Facebook as a means for improving self-esteem is developed in Gonzales, Amy L. and Jeffrey T. Hancock. 2011. "Mirror, Mirror on My Facebook Wall: Effects of Exposure to Facebook on Self-Esteem." *Cyberpsychology, Behavior, and Social Networking* 14 (1–2): 79–83.

10. The potential impact of information technology on identity is discussed by Nach, Hamid and Albert Lejeune. 2010. "Coping with Information Technology Challenges to Identity: A Theoretical Framework." *Computers in Human Behavior* 26: 618–629.

11. At UNH we teach approximately 2,400 students in Principles of Economics during the course of an academic year.

12. It may be because 69 percent of freshman believe that they are in the top 10 percent or above average and hence there is little need to study very much. Pryor, John H., Kevin Eagan, Laura Paluki Blake, Sylvia Hurtado, Jennifer Berdan, and Matthew H. Case. 2012. *The American Freshman: National Norms Fall 2012*. Los Angeles: Higher Education Research Institute, 42.

13. Kahneman, Daniel. 2011. *Thinking, Fast and Slow*. New York: Farrar, Straus and Giroux.

14. A general introduction to time discounting and time preference can be found in Frederick, Shane, George Loewenstein, and Ted O'Donoghue. 2002. "Time Discounting and Time Preference: A Critical Review." *Journal of Economic Literature* 40 (2): 351–401. For an accessible introduction to some of the anomalies that exist when making intertemporal choices, see Loewenstein, George and Richard H. Thaler. 1989. "Intertemporal Choice." *Journal of Economic Perspectives* 3 (4): 181–193.

15. For an extended discussion of how students "game" the system, see Johnson, Valen E. 2003. *Grade Inflation: A Crisis in College Education*. New York: Springer-Verlag.

16. Walstad, William and Sam Allgood. 1999. "What Do College Seniors Know about Economics?" *American Economic Review* 89 (2): 350–354.

17. One student's experience at Harvard is detailed in "The Truth about Harvard." Of particular note is one professor's system of dual grades: a

grade that reflects a student's actual performance and the other grade that appears on their transcript. Douthat, Ross. 2005. "The Truth about Harvard." *The Atlantic* March. Accessed on December 22, 2013, http://www.theatlantic.com/magazine/archive/2005/03/the-truth-about -harvard/303726/.

18. It is perhaps worthwhile to point out that commercial products currently exist that perform some of the tasks. For example, the Jawbone Up or the Fitbit One are just two examples.

19. This is no different than what companies like Google currently do in order to track a person's browsing behavior and serve up customized ads to maximize the effectiveness of its online marketing efforts. The Google Adwords program is described at: "Google AdWords – Online Advertising by Google," http://www.google.com/adwords/?sourceid=awo&subid=ww -et-awhp_nelsontest3_nel_p&clickid.

20. Two of the more prominent electronic learning platforms is the MyLab series by Pearson and Connect by McGraw Hill.

21. The use of benchmarks to develop best practices is a common practice in business. The strategic use of benchmarks is discussed in Boxwell, Robert J. 1994. *Benchmarking for Competitive Advantage.* New York: McGraw Hill.

22. The danger is that by slicing and dicing the data in various ways, everyone finds themselves in a category where they are considered to be "special." Of course, if everyone is special, then no one really is and efforts to build self-esteem are for naught. Moreover, discovering that you are not at the top is discouraging if there is no way to realistically to get there. Thus the use of status indicators and benchmarks only make sense if they are coupled with the creation of new opportunities for personal growth and development.

9   The Future of Higher Education

1. Within the field of economics, the most recent national survey of teaching and assessment methods (2010) revealed that once again, lecturing was the preferred format of the vast majority of instructors. In fact, about 83 percent of class time is spent lecturing to students; a statistic that has not changed since 1995. Watts, Michael and Georg Schaur. 2011. "Teaching and Assessment Methods in Undergraduate Economics: A Fourth Quinquennial Survey." *Journal of Economic Education* 42 (3): 294–309. Even though there has not been much of a change in teaching styles, studies have shown that students taught in a traditional lecture format only retain 55 percent of information. Cherney, Isabelle D. 2008. "The Effects of Active Learning on Student's Memories for Course Content." *Active Learning in Higher Education* 9: 152–171.

2. For a recent account of an attempt to gamify the learning process see Dominguez, Adrian, Joseba Saenz-de-Navarrete, Luis de-Marcos,

Luis Fernandez-Sanz, Carmen Pages, and Jose Martinez-Herraiz. 2013. "Gamifying Learning Experiences: Practical Implications and Outcomes." *Computers & Education* 63: 380–392. For a review of the literature on computer games and learning, see Schrader, Claudia and Theo Bastiaens. 2012. "Computer Games and Learning: The Relationship between Design, Gameplay and Outcomes." *Journal of Interactive Learning Research* 23 (3): 251–271.

3. One prominent form of protest in the nineteenth century came from a group of British textile workers known as Luddites who feared the widespread adoption of labor saving machinery would do nothing more than displace workers and create unemployment.

4. In an opinion piece written for US News and World Report, Doug Guthrie describes the coming Big Data revolution in higher education. Offering the perspective that Big Data rather than MOOCs represents the future, he concludes by commenting: "Scaling online courses for the masses creates a crowd; it does not constitute a classroom or an online learning environment." Guthrie, Doug. 2013. "The Coming Big Data Education Revolution." *US News & World Report* August 15. Accessed August 21, 2013, http://www.usnews.com/opinion/articles/2013/08/15/why-big-data-not-moocs-will-revolutionize-education

5. The 2013 National Survey of Student Engagement revealed "Results confirmed previous research that first-year students and seniors who more frequently interacted with diverse peers also engaged in deeper, more complex learning activities, perceived a more supportive campus environment, and had more positive interactions with students, faculty, and staff." 2013. *National Survey of Student Engagement 2013*. Bloomington: National Survey of Student Engagement, 15.

6. This stands in stark contrast to approaches that want to "fix" the problem by making the grades themselves more meaningful. Levine, Arthur and Diane R. Dean. 2012. *Generation on a Tightrope: A Portrait of Today's College Student*. San Francisco: Jossey-Bass.

7. Goldin, Clauda D. and Lawrence F. Katz. 2008. *The Race between Education and Technology*. Cambridge: Belknap Press, 1.

8. Economies that promote the development of general skills grow faster than those whose educational systems focus on specific skills. Krueger, Dirk and Krishna B. Kumar. 2004. "Skill-Specific Rather Than General Education: A Reason for US-Europe Growth Differences?" *Journal of Economic Growth* 9: 167–207.

9. A recent survey of the returns to higher education can be found in an NBER working paper by Oreopoulos, Philip and Uros Petronijevic. "Making College Worth It: A Review of Research on the Returns to Higher Education." NBER Working Paper No. 19053, National Bureau of Economic Research.

10. A review of the literature can be found in Krueger, Alan B. and Mikael Lindahl. 2001. "Education for Growth: Why and for Whom?" *Journal of Economic Literature* 39: 1101–1136.

11. Goldin and Katz. *The Race between Education and Technology*, 8.

12. For a modern discussion of the concept of alienation from an economics perspective, see Dolan, Edwin G. 1971. "Alienation, Freedom, and Economic Organization." *Journal of Political Economy* 79 (5): 1084–1094.

13. The desirability of general versus specific skills has been discussed in Krueger and Kumar. "Skill-Specific rather than General Education," 167–207 and Berman, Eli, John Bound, and Zvi Griliches. 1994. "Changes in the Demand for Skilled Labor within U.S. Manufacturing Evidence from the Annual Survey of Manufactures." *The Quarterly Journal of Economics*: 367–397. Autor, David H., Frank Levy, and Richard J. Murnane. 2003. "The Skill Content of Recent Technological Change: An Empirical Exploration." *The Quarterly Journal of Economics* 118 (4): 1279–1333.

14. The shift from students as members of a community to that of a client as part of a contractual relationship is discussed in Rochford, Francine. 2008. "The Contested Product of a University Education." *Journal of Higher Education Policy and Management* 30 (1): 41–52.

15. In 2007, the unemployment rate for college graduates was 5.7 percent. In 2010, that had risen to a high of 10.4 percent. While the rate has moderated somewhat, the Economic Policy Institute still believes that the prospect for graduates remains dim. Shierholz, Heidi, Natalie Sabadish, and Nicholas Finio. 2013. "The Class of 2013: Young Graduates Still Face Dim Job Prospects." *Economic Policy Institute* April 10. Accessed January 5, 2013, http://www.epi.org/publication/class-of-2013-graduates-job-prospects/

16. Concerns about the quantity of science, technology, engineering, and mathematics graduates in the United States is outlined in a 2008 report by the Congressional Research Service. Kuenzi, Jeffrey J. 2008. *Science, Technology, Engineering, and Mathematics (STEM) Education: Background, Federal Policy, and Legislative Action*: Congressional Research Service.

17. Our love/hate affair with Apple is described in Carr, Austin. 2013. "5 Truths That Explain Our Love-Hate Affair with Apple." *Fast Company*. Accessed December 26, 2013, http://www.fastcompany.com/3006698/most-innovative -companies-2013/5-truths-that-explain-our-love-hate-affair-with-apple

18. How computers affect job skill demands is discussed in Autor, Levy, and Murnane. 2003. "The Skill Content of Recent Technological Change," 1279–1333.

19. The financial challenges facing institutions of higher education today is discussed by Selingo, Jeffrey J. 2013. "A Matter of Ballast." *The New York Times* April 12. Accessed January 5, 2014, http://www.nytimes .com/2013/04/14/education/edlife/many-colleges-and-universities-face -financial-problems.html. Most disconcerting is the number of institutions

that have had their credit ratings downgraded and the negative outlook placed on the entire sector by Moody's Investor Service.

20. The need for workers with a new skill set created by advances in information technology is discussed in Bresnahan, Timothy F., Erik Brynjolfsson, and Lorin M. Hitt. 2002. "Information Technology, Workplace Organization, and the Demand for Skilled Labor: Firm-Level Evidence." *The Quarterly Journal of Economics*: 339–376.

21. Credit card debt statistics were obtained from: Ray, Daniel P. and Ghahremani, Yasmin. "Credit Card Statistics, Industry Facts, Debt Statistics." Last modified December 26, 2013, http://www.creditcards. com/credit-card-news/credit-card-industry-facts-personal-debt-statistics -1276.php

22. Of course the same argument could be made with respect to the size of the national debt which at the end of 2013 was just in excess of $17 trillion dollars.

23. See the Huffington Post Blog post: "Why Generation Y Yuppies are Unhappy," http://www.huffingtonpost.com/wait-but-why/generation-y -unhappy_b_3930620.html

24. The propensity for students to take the easy path is verified by the research contained in Johnson, Valen E. 2003. *Grade Inflation: A Crisis in College Education*. New York: Springer-Verlag.

25. A description of campus life that remains true for today is provided in Horowitz, Helen Lefkowitz. 1987. *Campus Life: Undergraduate Culture:From the End of the Eighteenth Century to the Present*. New York: Knopf.

26. The incentive structure of many universities is organized around a flow of funds based on the number of majors, enrollment figures in individual courses, or the ability to generate research dollars. Students and the dollars they represent can be the difference between an aging faculty declining in numbers and a growing department populated with rising "stars." Since the quality of a faculty members' life primarily revolves around the vibrancy of their department, strong incentives exist to ensure that student enrollments stay strong. Teaching courses that are harder than the norm, or establishing a reputation where students will pay a negative price in terms of their grade point average for selecting a particular course or major is not a recipe for success.

27. See, for example, efforts by organizations such as College Measures to create an Economic Success Metrics Program to evaluate the performance of colleges and universities at: "Economics Success Metrics (ESM) Program." College Measures, http://collegemeasures.org/esm/

28. Kim, Jeffrey, Lee, Elan, Thomas, Timothy and Dombrowski, Caroline. "Storytelling in New Media." Wikibruce. Last modified June 2, 2009, http://wikibruce.com/2009/06/kim-lee-thomas-dombrowski-storytelling

-in-new-media/. Kim, Jeffrey Y., Jonathan P. Allen, and Elan Lee. 2008. "Alternative Reality Gaming." *Communications of the ACM* 51 (2): 36–42.

29. They were initially developed to promote a movie in the case of *A.I.* (a Steven Spielberg production) or a particular product such as Halo 2. *The Beast* is generally recognized as one of the first ARGs and was used in 2001 to promote the movie *A.I.* Funded by Microsoft, the project was an attempt to introduce the audience to the science fiction world in which the movie takes place in order to heighten the experience when subsequently viewing the film. This medium was used again by Microsoft to promote the release of Halo 2, a first person shooter video game for the Xbox 360. Known as *I Love Bees*, this ARG in 2004 attempted to build a new fan base and reengage the existing base in order to build a buzz leading up to the release of the game.

30. The movement to infuse sustainability into higher education is reflected in organizations such as the Association for the Advancement of Sustainability in Higher Education located at: http://www.aashe.org/

31. They seek to employ the concept of collective intelligence. See, for example, Woolley, Anita., Chabris, Christopher, Pentland, Alex, Hasmi, Nada, and Malone, Thomas. 2010. "Evidence for a Collective Intelligence Factor in the Performance of Human Groups." *Science*. 330: 686–688 and Pentland, Alex. 2007. "On the Collective Nature of Human Intelligence." *Adaptive Behavior*. 15, 189–198.

32. An example of a game designed to change the world is EVOKE. It can be found at: "A Crash Course in Changing the World." The game can be accessed at: http://www.urgentevoke.com/.

33. For a description of the program at Florida State University, see Lumsden, Jill A. 2007. "Development and Implementation of an E-Portfolio as a University-Wide Program." *New Directions for Student Services* (119): 43–63.

34. A critical look at the portfolio "craze" is discussed in Ayala, Javier I. 2006. "Electronic Portfolios for Whom?" *Educause Quarterly* (1): 12–13.

35. See Bandura, Albert. 1986. *Social Foundations of Thought and Action: A Social Cognitive Theory*. Englewood Cliffs: Prentice Hall and Bandura, Albert and Carol J. Kupers. 1964. "Transmission of Patterns of Self-Reinforcement through Modeling." *The Journal of Abnormal and Social Psychology* 69 (1): 1–9. The important role that imitation plays in the process of natural selection is discussed by Sweller, John and Susan Sweller. 2006. "Natural Information Processing Systems." *Evolutionary Psychology* 4: 434–458.

36. For some of the problems this creates, see Johnson, William R. and Sarah Turner. 2009. "Faculty without Students: Resource Allocation in Higher Education." *Journal of Economic Perspectives* 23 (2): 169–189.

37. For some empirical evidence that supports this point, see Vedder, Richard. 2004. "Private Vs. Social Returns to Higher Education: Some New Cross-Sectional Evidence." *Journal of Labor Research* 25 (4): 677–686.

38. The changing mix between tenure and nontenure track faculty is discussed in Monk, David H., Michael J. Dooris, and Rodney A. Erickson. 2009. "In Search of a New Equilibrium: Economic Aspects of Higher Education's Changing Faculty Composition." *Education Finance and Policy* 4 (3): 300–318 and Ehrenberg, Ronald G. 2012. "American Higher Education in Transition." *Journal of Economic Perspectives* 26 (1): 193–216.

Bibliography

1940 Statement of Principles on Academic Freedom and Tenure. 1940. Washington, DC: American Association of University Professors.

1966 Statement on Government of Colleges and Universities. 1966. Washington, DC: American Association of University Professors.

2013 SAT Report on College & Career Readiness. 2013. New York: The College Board.

"Alexa Top 500 Global Sites" Alexa – The Web Information Company, accessed January 2, 2014, http://www.alexa.com/topsites

"The American Dream 2.0 Report," accessed January 3, 2014, http://www .hcmstrategists.com/americandream2–0/report/HCM_Gates_Report_1_17 _web.pdf

"ComScore Releases September 2013 U.S. Search Engine Ratings." ComScore, Inc., last modified on October 16, 2013, http://www.comscore .com/Insights/Press_Releases/2013/10/comScore_Releases_September_2013 _US_Search_Engine_Rankings

"Employment Status of the Civilian Population 25 Years and Over by Educational Attainment." U.S. Bureau of Labor Statistics. United States Bureau of Labor Statistics, last modified on December 6, 2013, http://www .bls.gov/news.release/empsit.t04.htm

Gartner Says Worldwide PC, Tablet and Mobile Phone Shipments to Grow 4.5 Percent in 2013 as Lower-Priced Devices Drive Growth. 2013. Stamford: Gartner, Inc., last modified on October 21, 2013, http://www.gartner.com /newsroom/id/2610015

"Global PC Shipments Drop to a Five-Year Low." *BBC News*, October 9, 2013. accessed December 27, 2013, http://www.bbc.co.uk/news/business-24470639

"Google AdWords – Online Advertising by Google." Google, accessed January 5, 2014, http://www.google.com/adwords/?sourceid=awo&subid=ww-et-awhp _nelsontest3_nel_p&clickid

"Higher Education." The White House, accessed January 3, 2014, http://www .whitehouse.gov/issues/education/higher-education

"Industry Facts." The Entertainment Software Association, accessed November 25, 2013, http://theesa.com/facts/

National Survey of Student Engagement. 2013. Bloomington: National Survey of Student Engagement.

The President's Plan for a Strong Middle Class & a Strong America. 2013. Washington, DC: The White House.

"Quest List." Urgent Evoke, accessed January 5, 2014, http://www.urgentevoke.com/page/quest-list

"Sports Industry Overview." Plunkett Research, Ltd., accessed November 25, 2013, http://www.plunkettresearch.com/sports-recreation-leisure-market-research/industry-statistics

"Team Fortress 2: An Economy of Hats." The Scientific Gamer, last modified August 15, 2012, http://scientificgamer.com/an-economy-of-hats/

"Video Game Sales Wiki." Wikia, accessed November 25, 2013, http://vgsales.wikia.com/wiki/Halo

"Why Generation Y Yuppies are Unhappy." 2013. Huffington Post, accessed January 5, 2014, http://www.huffingtonpost.com/wait-but-why/generation-y-unhappy_b_3930620.html

Admiraal, Wilfried, Jantina Huizenga, Sanne Akkerman, and Geert ten Dam. 2011. "The Concept of Flow in Collaborative Game-Based Learning." Computers in Human Behavior 27: 1185–1194.

Akai, Nobuo and Masayo Sakata. 2002. "Fiscal Decentralization Contributes to Economic Growth: Evidence from State-Level Cross Section Data for the United States." Journal of Urban Economics 52: 93–108.

Alexander, Peter J. 2002. "Peer-to-Peer File Sharing: The Case of the Music Recording Industry." Review of Industrial Organization 20 (2): 151–161.

Amichai-Hamburger, Yair, Mila Kingsbury, and Barry H. Schneider. 2013. "Friendship: An Old Concept with a New Meaning?" Computers in Human Behavior 29: 33–39.

Arum, Richard and Josipa Roksa. 2011. Academically Adrift: Limited Learning on College Campuses. Chicago: University of Chicago Press.

Autor, David H., Frank Levy, and Richard J. Murnane. 2003. "The Skill Content of Recent Technological Change: An Empirical Exploration." The Quarterly Journal of Economics 118(4): 1279–1333.

Avery, Christopher and Sarah Turner. 2012. "Student Loans: Do College Students Borrow Too Much – or Not enough?" Journal of Economic Perspectives 26 (1): 165–192.

Ayala, Javier I. 2006. "Electronic Portfolios for Whom?" Educause Quarterly 29(1): 12–13.

Azariadis, Costas. 1975. "Implicit Contracts and Underemployment Equilibria." Journal of Political Economy 83 (6): 1183–1202.

Baldwin, Norman J. andWilliam A. McCracken, III. 2013. "Justifying the Ivory Tower: Higher Education and State Economic Growth." Journal of Education Finance 38 (3): 181–209.

Bandura, Albert. 1986. *Social Foundations of Thought and Action: A Social Cognitive Theory*. Englewood Cliffs: Prentice Hall.

Barab, Sasha, Patrick Pettyjohn, Melissa Gresalfi, Charlene Volk, and Maria Solomou. 2012. "Game-Based Curriculum and Transformational Play: Designing to Meaningfully Positioning Person, Content, and Context." *Computers & Education* 58: 518–533.

Bardhan, Ashok, Daniel L. Hicks, and Dwight Jaffee. 2013. "How Responsive Is Higher Education? The Linkages between Higher Education and the Labour Market." *Applied Economics* 45 (10–12): 1239–1256.

Barth, James R. 1991. *The Great Savings and Loan Debacle*. Washington, DC: AEI Press.

Baum, Sandy, Charles Kurose, and Jennifer Ma. 2013. *How College Shapes Lives: Understanding the Issues*. New York: College Board.

Baum, Sandy and Jennifer Ma. 2010. *Tuition Discounting: Institutional Aid Patterns at Public and Private Colleges and Universities*. New York: College Board.

Baum, Sandy, Jennifer Ma, and Kathleen Payea. 2013. *Education Pays: The Benefits of Higher Education for Individuals and Society*. New York: College Board.

Baum, Sandy and Kathleen Payea. 2011. *Trends in for-Profit Postsecondary Education: Enrollment, Prices, Student Aid and Outcomes*. New York: College Board.

Baumeister, Roy F. 1991. *Meanings of Life*. New York: The Guilford Press.

Baumol, William J. 2004. "Red-Queen Games: Arms Races, Rule of Law and Market Economies." *Journal of Evolutionary Economics* 14 (2): 237–247.

Becker, Gary. 1993. *Human Capital: A Theoretical and Empirical Analysis, with Special Reference to Education*. 3rd ed. Chicago: University of Chicago Press.

Berman, Eli, John Bound, and Zvi Griliches. 1994. "Changes in the Demand for Skilled Labor within U.S. Manufacturing Evidence from the Annual Survey of Manufactures." *The Quarterly Journal of Economics*: 367–397.

Besen, Stanley M. and Joseph Farrell. 1994. "Choosing How to Compete: Strategies and Tactics in Standardization." *Journal of Economic Perspectives* 8 (2): 117–131.

Bessiere, Katherine, A. Fleming Seay, and Sara Kiesler. 2007. "The Ideal Elf: Identity Exploration in World of Warcraft." *CyberPsychology & Behavior* 10 (4): 530–535.

Billieux, Joel, Martial Van der Linden, Sophia Achab, Yasser Khazaal, Laura Paraskevopoulos, Daniele Zullino, and Gabriel Thorens. 2013. "Why Do You Play World of Warcraft? An in-Depth Exploration of Self-Reported Motivations to Play Online and in-Game Behaviours in the Virtual World of Azeroth." *Computers in Human Behavior* 29: 103–109.

Blascovich, Jim and Jeremy Bailenson. 2011. *Infinite Reality: Avatars, Eternal Life, New Worlds and the Dawn of the Virtual Revolution*. New York: HaperCollins.

Bloodgood, James. 2013. "Crowdsourcing: Useful for Problem Solving, But What about Value Capture." *Academy of Management Review* 38 (3): 455–465.

Bokhari, Sheharyar and David Geltner. 2011. "Loss Aversion and Anchoring in Commercial Real Estate Pricing: Empirical Evidence and Price Index Implications." *Real Estate Economics* 39 (4): 635–670.

Borsari, Brian and Kate B. Carey. 2001. "Peer Influences on College Drinking: A Review of the Research." *Journal of Substance Abuse* 13: 391–424.

Bound, John, Brad Hershbein, and Bridget Terry Long. 2009. "Playing the Admissions Game: Student Reactions to Increasing College Competition." *Journal of Economic Perspectives* 23 (4): 119–146.

Boxwell, Robert J. 1994. *Benchmarking for Competitive Advantage*. New York: McGraw Hill.

Boyle, Elizabeth A., Thomas M. Connolly, Thomas Hainey, and James M. Boyle. 2012. "Engagement in Digital Entertainment Games: A Systematic Review." *Computers in Human Behavior* 28: 771–780.

Bresnahan, Timothy F., Erik Brynjolfsson, and Lorin M. Hitt. 2002. "Information Technology, Workplace Organization, and the Demand for Skilled Labor: Firm-Level Evidence." *The Quarterly Journal of Economics*: 339–376.

Bresnahan, Timothy F. and Shane Greenstein. 1999. "Technological Competition and the Structure of the Computer Industry." *Journal of Industrial Economics* 47 (1): 1–40.

Brewer, Dominic J., Eric R. Eide, and Ronald G. Ehrenberg. 1999. "Does It Pay to Attend an Elite Private College? Cross-Cohort Evidence on the Effects of College Type on Earnings." *Journal of Human Resources* 34 (1): 104–123.

Bruffee, Kenneth A. 1993. *Collaborative Learning: Higher Education, Interdependence, and the Authority of Knowledge*. Baltimore: Johns Hopkins University Press.

Bruner, Jerome S. 1990. *Acts of Meaning*. Cambridge: Harvard University Press.

Burger-Helmchen, Thierry and Patrick Cohendet. 2011. "User Communities and Social Software in the Video Game Industry." *Long Range Planning* 44 (5–6): 317–343.

Busarovs, Aleksejs. 2011. "Crowdsourcing as User-Driven Innovation, New Business Philosophy's Model." *Journal of Business Management* (4): 53–60.

Callander, Steven. 2011. "Searching and Learning by Trial and Error." *American Economic Review* 101 (6): 2277–2308.

Campbell, Joseph. 1968. *The Hero with a Thousand Faces*. 2nd Ed. Princeton: Princeton University Press.

Carbajo, Jose, David de Meza, and Daniel J. Seidmann. 1990. "A Strategic Motivation for Commodity Bundling." *Journal of Industrial Economics* 38 (3): 283–298.

Carnevale, Anthony P., Jeff Strohl, and Michelle Melton. 2011. *What's It Worth? The Economic Value of College Majors.* Washington, DC: Georgetown University Center on Education and the Workforce.

Carr, Austin. 2013. "5 Truths That Explain Our Love-Hate Affair with Apple." Fast Company, accessed December 26, 2013, http://www.fastcompany.com/3006698/most-innovative-companies-2013/5-truths-that-explain-our-love-hate-affair-with-apple

Carrell, Scott E. and James E. West. 2010. "Does Professor Quality Matter? Evidence from Random Assignment of Students to Professors." *Journal of Political Economy* 118 (3): 409–432.

Cavazos, David E. and Dara Szyliowicz. 2011. "How Industry Associations Suppress Threatening Innovation: The Case of the US Recording Industry." *Technology Analysis and Strategic Management* 23 (5): 473–487.

Chandler, Alfred D. 1990. *Scale and Scope: The Dynamics of Industrial Capitalism.* Cambridge: Belknap Press.

———. 1977. *The Visible Hand: The Managerial Revolution in American Business.* Cambridge: Belknap Press.

Chandler, Dana and Adam Kapelner. 2013. "Breaking Monotony with Meaning: Motivation in Crowdsourcing Markets." *Journal of Economic Behavior and Organization* 90: 123–133.

Chen, Xianglei and Matthew Soldner. 2013. STEM Attrition: College Students' Paths into and Out of STEM Fields. U.S. Department of Education.

Cherney, Isabelle, D. 2008. "The Effects of Active Learning on Student's Memories for Course Content." *Active Learning in Higher Education* 9: 152–171.

Chiang, Oliver. 2011. "Valve and Steam Worth Billions." Forbes, accessed March 18, 2014 http://www.forbes.com/sites/oliverchiang/2011/02/15/valve-and-steam-worth-billions/

Christensen, Clayton M. and Henry J. Eyring. 2011. *The Innovative University: Changing the DNA of Higher Education from the Inside Out.* San Francisco: Jossey-Bass.

Christman, Ed. 2013. "Digital's Tipping Point." *Billboard* 125 (21): 6.

Cohn, Elchanan, Sherrie L. W. Rhine, and Maria C. Santos. 1989. "Institutions of Higher Education as Multi-Product Firms: Economies of Scale and Scope." *Review of Economics & Statistics* 71 (2): 284.

Crowe, Nic and Simon Bradford. 2006. "'Hanging Out in Runescape: Identity, Work and Leisure in the Virtual Playground." *Children's Geographies* 4 (3): 331–346.

Csikszenthmihalyi, Mihaly. 1975. *Beyond Boredom and Anxiety.* San Francisco: Jossey-Bass.

Cunningham, Brendan M. 2009. "Faculty: Thy Administrator's Keeper? Some Evidence." *Economics of Education Review* 28 (4): 444–453.

Dale, Stacy Berg and Alan B. Krueger. 2002. "Estimating the Payoff to Attending a More Selective College: An Application of Selection on Observables and Unobservables." *Quarterly Journal of Economics* 117 (4): 1491–1527.

Davidovici-Nora, Myriam. 2009. "The Dynamics of Co-Creation in the Video Game Industry: The Case of World of Warcraft." *Communications and Strategies* (73): 43–66.

Deci, Edward L. and Richard M. Ryan. 1985. *Intrinsic Motivation and Self-Determination in Human Behavior.* New York: Plenum Publishing Co.

Dee, Thomas S. 2004. "Are There Civic Returns to Education?" *Journal of Public Economics* 88 (9–10): 1697–1720.

DeMillo, Richard A. 2011. *Abelard to Apple: The Fate of American Colleges and Universities.* Cambridge: MIT Press.

Dickey, Michelle D. 2011. "Murder on Grimm Isle: The Impact of Game Narrative Design in an Educational Game-Based Learning Environment." *British Journal of Educational Technology* 42 (3): 456–469.

———. 2007. "Game Design and Learning: A Conjectural Analysis of How Massively Multiple Online Role-Playing Games (MMORPGs) Foster Intrinsic Motivation." *Educational Technology Research & Development* 55: 253–273.

———. 2006. "Game Design Narrative for Learning: Appropriating Adventure Game Design Narrative Devices and Techniques for the Design of Interactive Learning Environments." *Educational Technology Research & Development* 54 (3): 245–263.

Dolan, Edwin G. 1971. "Alienation, Freedom, and Economic Organization." *Journal of Political Economy* 79 (5): 1084–1094.

Dolan, Paul, Antony Elliott, Robert Metcalfe, and Ivo Vlaev. 2012. "Influencing Financial Behavior: From Changing Minds to Changing Contexts." *Journal of Behavioral Finance* 13 (2): 126–142.

Dominguez, Adrian, Joseba Saenz-de-Navarrete, Luis de-Marcos, Luis Fernandez-Sanz, Carmen Pages, and Jose Martinez-Herraiz. 2013. "Gamifying Learning Experiences: Practical Implications and Outcomes." *Computers & Education* 63: 380–392.

Douthat, Ross. 2005. "The Truth about Harvard." The Atlantic, accessed December 22, 2013, http://www.theatlantic.com/magazine/archive/2005/03/the-truth-about-harvard/303726/

Ehrenberg, Ronald G. 2012. "American Higher Education in Transition." *Journal of Economic Perspectives* 26 (1): 193–216.

Elmer-DeWitt, Philip. 2013. "Owning a Kindle Boosts Spending on Amazon by $433." CNN Money.

Emmons, William R. and Bryan J. Noeth. 2013. "Why Did Young Families Lose So Much Wealth During the Crisis? The Role of Homeownership." Federal Reserve Bank of St. Louis Review 95 (1): 1–26.

Etherington, Darrell. 2013. "Android Nears 80% Market Share in Global Smartphone Shipments, as iOS and BlackBerry Share Slides, Per IDC." Techcrunch.

Evangelho, Jason. 2012. "'League of Legends' Bigger than 'WoW,' More Daily Players Than 'Call of Duty.'" Forbes October 12, accessed January 5, 2014, http://www.forbes.com/sites/jasonevangelho/2012/10/12/league-of-legends-bigger-than-wow-more-daily-players-than-call-of-duty/

Evans, Carol. 2013. "Making Sense of Assessment Feedback in Higher Education." Review of Educational Research 83 (1): 70–120.

Feldman, David H. "Myths and Realities about Rising College Tuition." National Association of Student Financial Aid Administrators. National Association of Student Financial Aid Administrators, accessed December 1, 2013, http://www.nasfaa.org/advocacy/perspectives/articles/Myths_and _Realities_about_Rising_College_Tuition.aspx

Feller, Irwin. 2004. "Virtuous and Vicous Cycles in the Contributions of Public Research Universities to State Economic Development Objectives." Economic Development Quarterly 18 (2): 138–150.

Flowers, Stephen. 2008. "Harnessing the Hackers: The Emergence and Exploitation of Outlaw Innovation." Research Policy 37 (2): 177–193.

Frame, W. Scott and Lawrence J. White. 2005. "Fussing and Fuming Over Fannie and Freddie: How Much Smoke, How Much Fire?" Journal of Economic Perspectives 19 (2): 159–184.

Frank, Robert H. 2004. "Are Arms Races in Higher Education a Problem?" Forum for the Future of Higher Education, accessed December 1, 2013, https://net.educause.edu/ir/library/pdf/FFP0412S.pdf

——. 1999. Luxury Fever: Money and Happiness in an Era of Excess. Princeton: Princeton University Press.

Frederick, Shane and George Loewenstein. 1999. "Hedonic Adaptation." In Well-being: The Foundations of Hedonic Psychology, edited by Daniel Kahneman, Ed Diener, and Norbert Schwarz, 302–329. New York: Russel Sage Foundation.

Frederick, Shane, George Loewenstein, and Ted O'Donoghue. 2002. "Time Discounting and Time Preference: A Critical Review." Journal of Economic Literature 40 (2): 351–401.

Freeman, Tierra M., Lynley H. Anderman, and Jane M. Jensen. 2007. "Sense of Belonging in College Freshmen at the Classroom and Campus Levels." Journal of Experimental Education 75 (3): 203–220.

Friedman, Milton. 1962. Capitalism and Freedom. Chicago: University of Chicago Press.

Gallini, Nancy T. and Ralph A. Winter. 1985. "Licensing in the Theory of Innovation." The Rand Journal of Economics 16 (2): 237–252.

Gee, James Paul. 2007. What Video Games Have to Teach Us about Learning and Literacy. 2nd ed. New York: Macmillan.

Gillette, Felix. 2013. "Snapchat and the Right to be Forgotten. (Cover Story)." *Bloomberg Businessweek* (4316): 42–47.

Glimstedt, Henrik, Donald Bratt, and Magnus P. Karlsson. 2010. "The Decision to Make or Buy a Critical Technology: Semiconductors at Ericsson, 1980–2010." *Industrial and Corporate Change* 19 (2): 431–464.

Goldin, Clauda D., and Lawrence F. Katz. 2008. *The Race between Education and Technology.* Cambridge: Belknap Press.

Gonzales, Amy L. and Jeffrey T. Hancock. 2011. "Mirror, Mirror on My Facebook Wall: Effects of Exposure to Facebook on Self-Esteem." *Cyberpsychology, Behavior, and Social Networking* 14(1–2): 79–83.

Gregg, Gary S. 1991. *Self-Representation: Life Narrative Studies in Identity and Ideology.* New York: Greenwood Press.

Guthrie, Doug. 2013. "The Coming Big Data Education Revolution." US News & World Report August 15, accessed August 21, 2013, http://www .usnews.com/opinion/articles/2013/08/15/why-big-data-not-moocs-will -revolutionize-education

Hagedorn, Linda Serra. 2012. "The Meaning of Academic Life." *The Review of Higher Education* 35 (3): 485–512.

Hayek, Friedrich A. 1945. "The Use of Knowledge in Society." *American Economic Review* 35: 519–530.

Heckman, James J., Lance J. Lochner, and Petra E. Todd. 2005. "Earnings Functions, Rates of Return and Treatment Effects: The Mincer Equation and Beyond." National Bureau of Economic Research, Inc., NBER Working Papers: 11544, Cambridge.

Henderson-King, Donna and Amanda M. Mitchell. 2011. "Do Materialism, Intrinsic Aspirations, and Meaning in Life Predict Students' Meanings of Education?" *Social Psychology of Education* 14: 119–134.

Hirshleifer, David. 2001. "Investor Psychology and Asset Pricing." *Journal of Finance* 56 (4): 1533–1597.

Hirumi, Atsusi, Stephen Sivo, and Kelly Pounds. 2012. "Telling Stories to Enhance Teaching and Learning: The Systematic Design, Development and Testing of Two Online Courses." *International Journal of E-Learning* 11 (2): 125–151.

Holmes, Andrew and Paul Horvitz. 1994. "Mortgage Redlining: Race, Risk, and Demand." *Journal of Finance* 49 (1): 81–99.

Horowitz, Helen Lefkowitz. 1987. *Campus Life: Undergraduate Culture: From the End of the Eighteenth Century to the Present.* New York: Knopf.

Howe, Jeff. 2012. "The Crowdsourcing of Talent." Slate February 27, accessed September 14, 2013, http://www.slate.com/articles/technology/future_tense /2012/02/foldit_crowdsourcing_and_labor_.html

Hoxby, Caroline M. 2009. "College Admissions: The Changing Selectivity of American Colleges." *Journal of Economic Perspectives* 23 (4): 95–118.

Humphrey, David B. and Lawrence B. Pulley. 1997. "Banks' Responses to Deregulation: Profits, Technology, and Efficiency." *Journal of Money, Credit & Banking* (Ohio State University Press) 29 (1): 73–93.

Hunt, David M., Stephanie Geiger-Oneto, and Philip E. Varca. 2012. "Satisfaction in the Context of Customer Co-Production: A Behavioral Involvement Perspective." *Journal of Consumer Behavior* 11 (5): 347–356.

Hurtado, Sylvia, Kevin Eagan, John H. Pryor, Hannah Whang, and Serge Tran. *Undergraduate Teaching Faculty: The 2010–2011 HERI Faculty Survey.* Los Angeles: Higher Education Research Institute.

Johnson, Valen E. 2003. *Grade Inflation: A Crisis in College Education.* New York: Springer-Verlag.

Johnson, William R. and Sarah Turner. 2009. "Faculty without Students: Resource Allocation in Higher Education." *Journal of Economic Perspectives* 23 (2): 169–189.

Kahneman, Daniel. 2011. *Thinking, Fast and Slow.* New York: Farrar, Straus and Giroux.

Kahneman, Daniel and Amos Tversky. 1979. "Prospect Theory: An Analysis of Decisions Under Risk." *Econometrica* 47 (2): 263–291.

Kahneman, Daniel, Jack L. Knetsch, and Richard H. Thaler. 1991. "The Endowment Effect, Loss Aversion, and Status Quo Bias: Anomalies." *Journal of Economic Perspectives* 5 (1): 193–206.

Karmali, Luke. 2013. "Minecraft PC Sales at 12 Million; Franchise at 33 Million." IGN, accessed November 26, 2013, http://www.ign.com/articles/2013/09/03/minecraft-pc-sales-at-12-million-franchise-at-33-million

Keil, Thomas. 2002. "De-Facto Standardization through Alliances – Lessons from Bluetooth." *Telecommunications Policy* 26 (3–4): 205–213.

Keller, Fred S. 1968. ""Good-Bye Teacher…" *Journal of Applied Behavior Analysis* (1): 79.

Kessler, Sarah. 2013. "Exposing Yahoo's Strategy through Flickr and Startup Acquisitions." *Fast Company* (174): 40–45.

Kiley, Kevin. 2012. "Pruning the Branches." Inside Higher Ed May 31, accessed December 15, 2013, http://www.insidehighered.com/news/2012/05/31/shift-branch-campuses-reflects-changes-educational-delivery-and-demand

Kim, Changsoo, Sang-Gun Lee, and Minchoel Kang. 2012. "I Became an Attractive Person in the Virtual World: Users' Identification with Virtual Communities and Avatars." *Computers in Human Behavior* 28: 1663–1669.

Kim, Jeffrey, Elan Lee, Timothy Thomas, andCaroline Dombrowski. "Storytelling in New Media." Wikibruce., last modified June 2, 2009, http://wikibruce.com/2009/06/kim-lee-thomas-dombrowski-storytelling-in-new-media/

Kim, Jeffrey Y., Jonathan P. Allen, and Elan Lee. 2008. "Alternative Reality Gaming." *Communications of the ACM* 51 (2): 36–42.

Korn, Melissa and Jennifer Levitz. 2013. "Online Courses Look for a Business Model." *The Wall Street Journal*, January 1.

Krueger, Alan B. and Mikael Lindahl. 2001. "Education for Growth: Why and for Whom?" *Journal of Economic Literature* 39: 1101–1136.

Krueger, Dirk and Krishna B. Kumar. 2004. "Skill-Specific Rather Than General Education: A Reason for US-Europe Growth Differences?" *Journal of Economic Growth* 9: 167–207.

Kuenzi, Jeffrey J. 2008. Science, Technology, Engineering, and Mathematics (STEM) Education: Background, Federal Policy, and Legislative Action. Congressional Research Service.

Laband, David N. and Bernard F. Lentz. 2003. "New Estimates of Economies of Scale and Scope in Higher Education." *Southern Economic Journal* 70 (1): 172.

Laird, Sam. "In a Relationship: College Students and Their Smartphones." Mashable, last modified June 30, 2012, http://mashable.com/2012/06/30/smartphones-college-students-infographic/

Lang, Kevin and Russell Weinstein. 2012. "Evaluating Student Outcomes at for-Profit Colleges." National Bureau of Economic Research, Inc., NBER Working Papers: 18201.

Leibenstein, Harvey. 1950. "Bandwagon, Snob and Veblen Effects in the Theory of Consumers' Demand." *Quarterly Journal of Economics* 64: 183–207.

Levine, Arthur and Diane R. Dean. 2012. *Generation on a Tightrope: A Portrait of Today's College Student*. San Francisco: Jossey-Bass.

Levitt, Steven D. and John A. List. 2007. "What Do Laboratory Experiments Measuring Social Preferences Reveal about the Real World?" *Journal of Economic Perspectives* 21 (2): 153–174.

Lindert, Peter H. and Jeffrey G. Williamson. 1983. "English Workers Living Standard During the Industrial Revolution: A New Look." *Economic History Review* 36: 1–25.

Liu, Liqun and William S. Neilson. 2011. "High Scores But Low Skills." *Economics of Education Review* 30 (3): 507–516.

Loewenstein, George and Richard H. Thaler. 1989. "Intertemporal Choice." *Journal of Economic Perspectives* 3 (4): 181–193.

Lopez-Perez, Raul. 2009. "Followers and Leaders: Reciprocity, Social Norms and Group Behavior." *Journal of Socio-Economics* 38 (4): 137–158.

Luca, Michael and Jonathan Smith. 2013. "Salience in Quality Disclosure: Evidence from the U.S. News College Rankings." *Journal of Economics and Management Strategy* 22 (1): 58–77.

Lucas, Christopher J. 1994. *American Higher Education: A History*. New York: St. Martins.

Lumsden, Jill A. 2007. "Development and Implementation of an E-Portfolio as a University-Wide Program." *New Directions for Student Services* (119): 43–63.

Luttmer, Erzo F. P. 2005. "Neighbors as Negatives: Relative Earnings and Well-being." *Quarterly Journal of Economics* 120 (3): 963–1002.

Malkiel, Burton G. 2003. "The Efficient Market Hypothesis and Its Critics." *Journal of Economic Perspectives* 17 (1): 59–82.

Malone, Thomas W. 1981. "Toward a Theory of Intrinsically Motivating Instruction." *Cognitive Science* 4: 333–369.

Manhas, Parikshat S. 2012. "Role of Online Education in Building Brand Image of Educational Institutions." *Journal of Economics, Finance and Administrative Science* 17 (32): 75–85.

Marandi, Ebi, Ed Little, and Tim Hughes. 2010. "Innovation and the Children of the Revolution: Facebook and Value Co-Creation." *The Marketing Review* 10 (2): 169–183.

Marshall, Alfred. 1874. *Where to House the London Poor*, reprinted in Pigou, A. C., 1966, Memoirs of Alfred Marshall. New York: Kelley.

McAdams, Dan P. 1993, 1997. *The Stories We Live by: Personal Myths and the Making of the Self.* New York: Guilford Press.

McGonigal, Jane. 2011. *Reality Is Broken: Why Games Make Us Better and How They Can Change the World.* New York: Penguin.

McMillen, Daniel P., Larry D. Singell Jr., and Glen R. Waddell. 2007. "Spatial Competition and the Price of College." *Economic Inquiry* 45 (4): 817–833.

McPherson, Michael S. and Morton Owen Schapiro. 1999. "Tenure Issues in Higher Education." *Journal of Economic Perspectives* 13 (1): 85–98.

Miles, Daniel and Maximo Rossi. 2007. "Learning about One's Relative Position and Subjective Well-Being." *Applied Economics* 39 (13–15): 1711–1718.

Moisio, Risto and Mariam Beruchashvili. 2010. "Questing for Well-being at Weight Watchers: The Role of the Spiritual-Therapeutic Model in a Support Group." *Journal of Consumer Research* 36 (5): 857–875.

Monk, David H., Michael J. Dooris, and Rodney A. Erickson. 2009. "In Search of a New Equilibrium: Economic Aspects of Higher Education's Changing Faculty Composition." *Education Finance and Policy* 4 (3): 300–318.

Moretti, Enrico. 2004. "Estimating the Social Return to Higher Education: Evidence from Longitudinal and Repeated Cross-Sectional Data." *Journal of Econometrics* 121 (1–2): 175–212.

Morris, David. 2008. "Economies of Scale and Scope in e-Learning." *Studies in Higher Education* 33 (3): 331–343.

Morrow, Jennifer Ann and Margot E. Ackermann. 2012. "Intention to Persist and Retention of First-Year Students: The Importance of Motivation and Sense of Belonging." *College Student Journal* 46 (3): 483–491.

Nach, Hamid and Albert Lejeune. 2010. "Coping with Information Technology Challenges to Identity: A Theoretical Framework." *Computers in Human Behavior* 26: 618–629.

Nalley, Lanier and Andrew McKenzie. 2011. "How Much Is That Exam Grade Really Worth? An Estimation of Student Risk Aversion to Their Unknown Final College Course Grades." *Journal of Economic Education* 42 (4): 338–353.

National Survey of Student Engagement. 2012. *Promoting Student Learning and Institutional Improvement: Lessons from NSSE at 13*. Bloomington: Indiana University Center for Postsecondary Research.

Neuhauser, Peg C. 1993. *Corporate Legends and Lore: The Power of Storytelling as a Management Tool*. New York: McGraw Hill.

NG, Irene C. L. and Jeannie Forbes. 2009. "Education as Service: The Understanding of University Experience through the Service Logic." *Journal of Marketing for Higher Education* 19: 38–64.

Niman, Neil B. 2013. "The Allure of Games: Toward an Updated Theory of the Leisure Class." *Games and Culture* 8 (1): 26–42.

———. 2002. "Platform Externalities and the Antitrust Case Against Microsoft." *Antitrust Bulletin* 47 (4): 641–660.

Oliff, Phil, Vincent Palacios, Ingrid Johnson, and Michael Leachman. 2013. *Recent Deep State Higher Education Cuts May Harm Students and the Economy for Years to Come*. Washington, DC: Center on Budget and Policy Priorities.

Ordanini, Andrea. 2006. "Selection Models in the Music Industry: How a Prior Independent Experience May Affect Chart Success." *Journal of Cultural Economics* 30 (3): 183–200.

Oreopoulos, Philip and Kjell G. Salvanes. 2011. "Priceless: The Nonpecuniary Benefits of Schooling." *Journal of Economic Perspectives* 25 (1): 159–184.

Oreopoulos, Philip and Uros Petronijevic. "Making College Worth It: A Review of Research on the Returns to Higher Education." NBER Working Paper No. 19053, National Bureau of Economic Research.

Park, Andreas and Hamid Sabourian. 2011. "Herding and Contrarian Behavior in Financial Markets." *Econometrica* 79 (4): 973–1026.

Payea, Kathleen, Sandy Baum, and Charles Kurose. 2013. *How Students and Parents Pay for College*. College Board Advocacy & Policy Center.

Peicuti, Cristina. 2013. "Securitization and the Subprime Mortgage Crisis." *Journal of Post Keynesian Economics* 35 (3): 443–455.

Pentland, Alex. 2007. On the Collective Nature of Human Intelligence. *Adaptive Behavior*. 15: 189–198.

Peters, Cara, Charles D. Bodkin, and Scott Fitzgerald. 2012. "Toward an Understanding of Meaning Creation Via the Collective Co-Production Process." *Journal of Consumer Behavior* 11 (2): 124–135.

Pingle, Mark and Mark Mitchell. 2002. "What Motivates Positional Concerns for Income?" *Journal of Economic Psychology* 23 (1): 127–148.

Prahalad, Coimbatore K. and Venkat Ramaswamy. 2004. "Co-Creation Experiences: The Next Practice in Value Creation." *Journal of Interactive Marketing* 18 (3): 5–14.

Procci, Katelyn, Allysa R. Singer, Katherine R. Levy, and Clint Bowers. 2012. "Measuring the Flow Experience of Gamers: An Evaluation of the DFS-2." *Computers in Human Behavior* 28: 2306–2312.

Pryor, John H., Kevin Eagan, Laura Paluki Blake, Sylvia Hurtado, Jennifer Berdan, and Matthew H. Case. 2012. *The American Freshman: National Norms Fall 2012*. Los Angeles: Higher Education Research Institute.

Przybylski, Andrew K. and Netta Weinstein. 2013. "Can You Connect with Me Now? How the Presence of Mobile Communication Technology Influences Face-to-Face Conversation Quality." *Journal of Social and Personal Relationships* 30 (3): 237–246.

Przybylski, Andrew K., Netta Weinstein, Kou Murayama, Martin F. Lynch, and Richard M. Ryan. 2012. "The Ideal Self at Play: The Appeal of Video Games That Let You Be All You Can Be." *Psychological Science* 23 (1): 69–76.

Radford, Richard. A. 1945. "The Economic Organisation of a P.O.W. Camp." Economica, N.S. 12: 189–201.

Ray, Daniel P. and Yasmin Ghahremani. "Credit Card Statistics, Industry Facts, Debt Statistics," last modified December 26, 2013, http://www.creditcards.com/credit-card-news/credit-card-industry-facts-personal-debt-statistics-1276.php

Rieber, Lloyd P. and David Noah. 2008. "Games, Simulations, and Visual Metaphors in Education: Antagonism between Enjoyment and Learning." *Educational Media International* 45 (2): 77–92.

Roberts, Gary R. 2003. "The Case for Baseball's Special Antitrust Immunity." *Journal of Sports Economics* 4 (4): 302–317.

Robson, Arthur J. 2005. "Complex Evolutionary Systems and the Red Queen." *The Economic Journal* 115 (505): F211–F224.

Rochford, Francine. 2008. "The Contested Product of a University Education." *Journal of Higher Education Policy and Management* 30 (1): 41–52.

Sachs, Jonah. 2012. *Winning the Story Wars: Why Those Who Tell (and Live) the Best Stories Will Rule the Future*. Cambridge: Harvard Business School Press.

Salen, Katie and Eric Zimmerman. 2004. *Rules of Play: Game Design Fundamentals*. Cambridge: MIT Press.

Sander, Libby. 2013. "Ties to Home." The Chronicle of Higher Education.

Sappington, David E. M. 1991. "Incentives in Principal-Agent Relationships." *Journal of Economic Perspectives* 5 (2): 45–66.

Savitz, Edward and Jamie Tedford. 2012. "Facebook Timeline for Brands: It's about Storytelling." Forbes February 29, accessed December 14, 2013, http://www.forbes.com/sites/ciocentral/2012/02/29/facebook-timeline-for-brands-its-about-storytelling/

Schank, David. 1990. *Tell Me a Story: A New Look at Real and Artificial Memory*. New York: Charles Scribner's Sons.

Schell, Jessie. 2008. *The Art of Game Design: A Book of Lenses*. Burlington: Morgan Kaufman.

Schrader, Claudia and Theo Bastiaens. 2012. "Computer Games and Learning: The Relationship between Design, Gameplay and Outcomes." *Journal of Interactive Learning Research* 23 (3): 251–271.

Schwartz, Barry. 2009. *The Paradox of Choice: Why More Is Less*. New York: HarperCollins.

Schwarz, Fred. 2009. "20 Reasons Why Campus Learning Is Better Than Online." National Review Online September 28, accessed October 28, 2013, http://www.nationalreview.com/phi-beta-cons/40288/20-reasons-why-campus-learning-better-online

Scitovsky, Tibor. 1999. "Boredom – An Overlooked Disease?" *Challenge* 42 (5): 5–15.

————. 1992. *The Joyless Economy: The Psychology of Human Satisfaction*. Revised Edition ed. New York: Oxford University Press.

Seligman, Martin E. P. and Mihaly Csikszenthmihalyi. 2000. "Positive Psychology: An Introduction." *American Psychologist* 55 (1): 5–14.

Selingo, Jeffrey J. 2013. "A Matter of Ballast." *The New York Times*, ED8.

Shapiro, Carl and Hal R. Varian. 1999. *Information Rules: A Strategic Guide to the Network Economy*. Boston: Harvard Business School Press.

Shierholz, Heidi, Natalie Sabadish, and Nicholas Finio. 2013. "The Class of 2013: Young Graduates Still Face Dim Job Prospects." Economic Policy Institute.

Shiller, Robert J. 2003. "From Efficient Markets Theory to Behavioral Finance." *Journal of Economic Perspectives* 17 (1): 83–104.

Simon, Herbert A. 1955. "A Behavioral Model of Rational Choice." *Quarterly Journal of Economics* 69: 99–118.

Skinner, Burrhus. F. 1971. *Beyond Freedom and Dignity*. New York: Knopf.

Smith, Adam. 1976. *An Inquiry into the Nature and Causes of the Wealth of Nations*. Chicago: University of Chicago Press.

Smith, David E. and Darryl J. Mitry. 2008. "Investigation of Higher Education: The Real Costs and Quality of Online Programs." *Journal of Education for Business* 83 (3): 147–152.

Solnick, Sara J. and David Hemenway. 1998. "Is More Always Better? A Survey on Positional Concerns." *Journal of Economics Behavior and Organization* 37 (3): 373–383.

Spiegel, Uriel and Joseph Templeman. 1996. "'Bundling' in Learning." *Education Economics* 4 (1): 65–81.

Steinfield, Charles, Nicole B. Ellison, and Cliff Lampe. 2008. "Social Capital, Self-Esteem, and Use of Online Social Network Sites: A Longitudinal Analysis." *Journal of Applied Developmental Psychology* 29 (6): 434–445.

Stone, Brad. 2013. "Grading the Kindle Fire as Amazon's Tablet Turns Two." *Bloomberg Businessweek* September 27, accessed December 2, 2013, http://www.businessweek.com/articles/2013–09–27/grading-the-kindle-fire-as-amazons-tablet-turns-two

Sunstein, Cass R. 2013. "The Storrs Lectures: Behavioral Economics and Paternalism." *Yale Law Journal* 122 (7): 1826–1899.

Sweller, John and Susan Sweller. 2006. "Natural Information Processing Systems." *Evolutionary Psychology* 4: 434–458.

Szymanski, Stefan. 2003. "The Economic Design of Sporting Contests." *Journal of Economic Literature* 41 (4): 1137–1187.

Taylor, Fredrick W. 1967. *The Principles of Scientific Management.* New York: Norton.

Thaler, Richard H. and Cass R. Sunstein. 2008. *Nudge: Improving Decisions about Health, Wealth and Happiness.* New Haven: Yale University Press.

Thomas, Douglas and John Seely Brown. 2009. "Why Virtual Worlds Can Matter." *International Journal of Media and Learning* 1 (1): 37–49.

Tootell, Geoffrey M. B. 1996. "Redlining in Boston: Do Mortgage Lenders Discriminate Against Neighborhoods?" *Quarterly Journal of Economics* 111 (4): 1049–1079.

Townsend, Allie. 2012. "This is Your Life (According to Your New Timeline)." *Time.*

Turkle, Sherry. 1995. *Life on the Screen: Identity in the Age of the Internet.* New York: Touchstone.

Tuttle, Brad. 2013. "Auto Navigation Systems: Too Complicated, Too Pricey, Just Plain Unnecessary?" *Time* January 25, accessed December 10, 2013, http://business.time.com/2013/01/25/auto-navigation-systems-too-complicated-too-pricey-just-plain-unnecessary/

Vargo, Stephen L. and Robert F. Lusch. 2004. "Evolving to a New Dominant Logic for Marketing." *Journal of Marketing* 68: 1–17.

Veblen, Thorstein. 1935. *The Higher Learning in America: A Memorandum on the Conduct of Universities by Business Men.* New York: Viking Press.

———. 1899. *The Theory of the Leisure Class.* New York: Macmillan.

Vedder, Richard. 2004. "Private Vs. Social Returns to Higher Education: Some New Cross-Sectional Evidence." *Journal of Labor Research* 25 (4): 677–686.

Vedder, Richard, Christopher Denhart, and Jonathan Robe. 2013. *Why Are Recent College Graduates Underemployed?* Washington, DC: Center for College Affordability and Productivity.

Velkar, Aashish. 2009. "Transactions, Standardisation and Competition: Establishing Uniform Sizes in the British Wire Industry c. 1880." *Business History* 51 (2): 222–247.

Walstad, William and Sam Allgood. 1999. "What Do College Seniors Know about Economics?" *American Economic Review* 89 (2): 350–354.

Ward, Marc. 2013. "Why Minecraft is More Than Just Another Video Game." *BBC News* September 6, accessed November 26, 2013, http://www.bbc.co.uk/news/magazine-23572742

Warshaw, Douglas A. 2013. "Nate Silver, Data, and Storytelling." *CNN Money* July 24, accessed September 10, 2013, http://features.blogs.fortune.cnn.com/2013/07/24/nate-silver-data-and-storytelling/

Watts, Michael and Georg Schaur. 2011. "Teaching and Assessment Methods in Undergraduate Economics: A Fourth Quinquennial Survey." *Journal of Economic Education* 42 (3): 294–309.

White, Lawrence J. 2010. "Markets: The Credit Rating Agencies." *Journal of Economic Perspectives* 24 (2): 211–226.

Williamson, Oliver E. 1981. "The Modern Corporation: Origins, Evolution, Attributes." *Journal of Economic Literature* 19 (4): 1537–1568.

Wilson, Katherine A., Wendy L. Bedwell, Elizabeth H. Lazzara, Eduardo Salas, C. Shawn Burke, Jamie L. Estock, Kara L. Orvis, and Curtis Conkey. 2009. "Relationships between Game Attributes and Learning Outcomes." *Simulation & Gaming* 40 (2): 217–266.

Winn, William. 2003. "Learning in Artificial Environments: Embodiment, Embeddedness and Dynamic Adaptation." Tech., Inst., Cognition and Learning 1: 87–114.

Woolley, Anita, Chabris, Christopher, Pentland, Alex, Hasmi, Nada, and Malone, Thomas. 2010. "Evidence for a Collective Intelligence Factor in the Performance of Human Groups." *Science* 330: 686–688.

Wong, David. 2010. "5 Creepy Ways Video Games Are Trying to Get You Addicted." Cracked March 8, accessed March 19, 2013, http://www.cracked.com/article_18461_5-creepy-ways-video-games-are-trying-to-get-you-addicted.html

Worth, Sarah. 2008. "Storytelling and Narrative Knowing: An Examination of the Epistemic Benefits of Well-Told Stories." *Journal of Aesthetic Education* 42 (3): 42–56.

Yearwood, John and Andrew Stranieri. 2007. "Narrative-Based Interactive Learning Environments from Modeling Reasoning." *Educational Technology & Society* 10 (3): 192–208.

Yee, Nick. "Hours of Play Per Week," last modified February 24, 2004, http://www.nickyee.com/daedalus/archives/000758.php

Yee, Nick, Jeremy N. Bailenson, and Nicolas Ducheneaut. 2009. "The Proteus Effect." *Communication Research* 36 (2): 285–312.

Young, Jeffrey R. 2012. "Inside the Coursera Contract: How an Upstart Company might Profit from Free Courses." *The Chronicle of Higher Education*.

Zemsky, Robert. 2008. "The Rain Man Cometh – Again." *Academy of Management Perspectives* 22 (1): 5–14.

Index

Printed in the United States of America